ROCKS
OFF

50

Tracks That
Tell the Story

of the

ROLLING
STONES

ROCKS OFF

Bill Janovitz

ST. MARTIN'S PRESS
NEW YORK

www.stmartins.com

Design by Kathryn Parise

LIBRARY OF CONGRESS CATALOGING-IN-PUBLICATION DATA

Janovitz, Bill.
     Rocks off : 50 tracks that tell the story of The Rolling Stones
/ by Bill Janovitz. — First U.S. edition.
         pages cm
     ISBN 978-1-250-02631-6 (hardcover)
     ISBN 978-1-250-02632-3 (e-book)
  1. Rolling Stones.   2. Rolling Stones—History—Chronology.
3. Rolling Stones—Discography.   I. Title.
     ML421.R64J37 2013
     782.42166092'2—dc23

                                        2013009114

St. Martin's Press books may be purchased for educational,
business, or promotional use. For information on bulk
purchases, please contact Macmillan Corporate and
Premium Sales Department at 1-800-221-7945 extension
5442 or write specialmarkets@macmillan.com.

First Edition: July 2013

10   9   8   7   6   5   4   3   2   1

For Laura, Lucy, and Will

Contents

The Songs—Part 2
The Mick Taylor Years

The Songs—Part 3
The Ron Wood Years

ROCKS
OFF

It's the Singer, Not the Song

I've worked out that I'd be 50 in 1984. I'd be dead! Horrible, isn't it. Halfway to a hundred. Ugh! I can see myself coming onstage in my black, windowed, invalid carriage with a stick. Then I turn around, wiggle my bottom at the audience and say something like, Now here's an old song you might remember called "Satisfaction."

—Mick Jagger, 1966

Just as I was formulating the proposal for this book—I mean *to the day*—I finally met a real live Rolling Stone. Not just any old Rolling Stone, but the man himself, rock 'n' roll incarnate, Keith Richards. I happened to be fortunate enough to be attending the 2012 presentation of the first PEN New England Award for Song Lyrics of Literary Excellence, at the John F. Kennedy Presidential Library and Museum in Boston. It was being presented to two of the greatest song lyricists of our time, Chuck Berry and Leonard Cohen. I was even luckier to be able to be in the green room prior to the ceremony. I was there with a friend who had been tapped to give the opening remarks and invited me to come along.

In the green room was an astounding assemblage of talent, artists who were taking part in the honoring of these songwriters: Chuck and Leonard, of course, along with Elvis Costello; Paul Simon; Shawn Colvin; Peter Wolf; and authors Salman Rushdie, Bill Flanagan, Peter Guralnick, and Tom Perotta.

Oh, and Keith Richards.

After the myriad of Mount Rushmore–like group shots so amazing that they should make the Rock and Roll Hall of Fame jealous, Keith slipped out to somehow procure the only adult beverage in the JFK Library. I was just there as a fan, trying to almost literally change into a fly on the wall, as to stay clear of possibly injuring one of the legends, all the while thinking such surreal thoughts as, *I wish Paul Simon would move a little bit. He is blocking my way to Keith Richards.* When Keith came back into the room, however, he sidled up next to me and placed his drink on the console table that was between us.

Now, I am not one to be impressed with celebrity or fame on its own. Ball players, actors, and local television meteorologists are all fun to meet, sure. But as an unreligious man, these musical artists are demigods to me: those who *know,* who have tapped into my consciousness. And none of them there had a more direct line into my soul than Keith. *I have to say something,* I thought. And so I did.

"Hi, Keith. I just wanted to say hello," I said, shaking his hand as he smiled warmly. "I mean, what do I say to Keith Richards?"

His response immediately defused the tense and potentially awkward situation. "Ah, hey, thank you," he growled. And in what came across as deeply sincere humility he quickly added, "I feel the same way about Chuck Berry, man."

"Yes, well, it is so great that he is being recognized for his lyrics in particular," I noted.

"Exactly. I mean, some of the greatest songs, and some of the saddest," he explained. "Like, 'Memphis Tennessee,' one of the *saddest* of all time: 'hurry-home drops in her eye,' I mean . . ." Here, he put his hand over his heart and opened his mouth, speechless with genuine awe.

I did not tell him I had written a book about *Exile on Main Street*, or that I was planning another book about what his body of work had meant to me. I had no agenda. I just wanted to speak with him as a fan, if not a fellow guitarist/songwriter.

And so that is how I present this book, as an unabashed fan who grew up with this music; whose career path was influenced by these records; and who, as a professional recording and touring musician, hopes to add some insight to the massive Stones canon.

The point of view of this book assumes readers are familiar with much of the band's history, and many of the songs, but I hope to dig into some underappreciated album gems. It hopefully also serves as a listening guide from the perspective of a professional recording musician (albeit one slightly more obscure than, say, the Rolling Stones), songwriter, and music writer. I hope to offer new insight and spur readers into dusting off and listening to the subject tracks. The songs are not all necessarily my favorites; they were chosen, in part, to tell the story of fifty years of the band. If the book had been selected only on the basis of my favorite tracks, it would have ended around *Tattoo You* (1981).

Asked once why his impressive library contained no books on music, Keith Richards replied that music is for listening, not reading about. Okay, let's listen together.

Prologue

1961–1963:
The Run-up to Recording

It's an almost apocryphal tale, and there might be as much my-thology as sepia-toned documentation to how five pasty middle-class English kids found each other and discovered their lot in life in some obscure, scratchy American blues records. How two of these young men, Mick Jagger and Keith Richards, boyhood friends who had lost touch during adolescence, bumped into each other on a Dartford train platform at the age of nineteen. It would have been just a quick, *'ello, how've you been?* had Mick not been carry-ing an armful of hard-to-find records he had just ordered through the mail from Chess Records in Chicago. The artists Mick collected were magical names to the pair, who were venturing halfheartedly into university—Mick at the London School of Economics (LSE), and Keith at Sidcup Art College. So instead, we have an origin story.

The fact that the two had independently stumbled across this uncommercial form of music—unknown to but a small portion of fans—signified to each that the other was hip. Their boyhood friendship was rekindled on the spot. Mick had been singing and learning to play blues harp (harmonica), and had played a gig or two sitting in with bands at so-called "jazz clubs" around London with a friend and other like-minded soul, Dick Taylor, another guitar player who attended Sidcup. Keith had embraced guitar as a boy after his mother bought one for him, teaching himself Chuck Berry numbers from records. The three of them started to jam, with Taylor switching to bass, and named themselves Little Boy Blue and the Blue Boys.

Different guys would sit in on drums occasionally, but the three were not yet a complete band. They would venture down to the Ealing Jazz Club, where the godfather of the British blues and R&B scene, Alexis Korner, held court. The Ealing Jazz Club, literally under the Ealing tube stop (one could see commuters walking to the tube through the thick glass above the stage), was hosting weekly R&B club nights hosted by scene father figures Alexis Korner and Cyril Davies. "Without them there might have been nothing," Keith points out. The hunger for this music was so strong and it was so hard to come by that people traveled down to these clubs from Manchester and Scotland just to hear a live facsimile played by earnest fans. Drummer Charlie Watts and pianist Ian Stewart, who would both soon join the Rolling Stones, would occasionally sit in with Alexis Korner's Blues Incorporated.

These weekly sessions are the storied ground zero roots of the London branch of the British Invasion family tree, the blues-fed musicians who would go on to fame with groups like the Yardbirds, the Who, Cream, Led Zeppelin, and the Kinks. Mick, Keith, and Dick Taylor would frequent these jam sessions. And a young Brian Jones was a star in this setting. "He was a very good slide player," Taylor told me, "and his general musicianship was very impressive." "He was calling himself Elmo Lewis," notes Keith in his autobiography, *Life*. "He wanted to be Elmore James at the time. 'You'll have to get a tan and put on a few inches, boy.' But slide guitar was a real novelty in England, and Brian played it that night. He played 'Dust My Broom,' and it was electrifying."

Mick was one of the precious few R&B vocalists who would sit in with Korner's group at Ealing. But the few times that Keith sat in, the guitarist was already perceived as a lone wolf, playing a more aggressive rock 'n' roll style of guitar. "Korner's group were all jazz musicians," Ian Stewart explained. "They drew the line at Keith's Chuck Berry–type guitar playing. They didn't encourage Keith. They'd tolerate him but they certainly wouldn't encourage him."

"We wanted to do something more rock and roll but still with an R&B feel," Taylor recalled. "Music seemed very rigidly divided into genres at the time we started, the trad [Dixieland/Preservation Hall–style] jazz scene was really huge in the UK. . . . We were very much into urban R&B. We loved Chuck, Bo [Diddley], and Jimmy Reed. I remember buying the first available Ike and Tina record. That was what we wanted to play. Monetary success was a complete irrelevance, playing what we liked and getting 'converts' was what we were all about."

Brian wanted to form his own band. He put an ad in *Jazz News* in the spring of 1962 looking for R&B musicians to form a band. Stewart, a lantern-jawed Scotsman who played a mean boogie-woogie in the style of Albert Ammons, answered Brian's ad and started to arrange auditions. Stu (as he was known) invited Mick, who agreed on the condition that he could bring Keith, whose talents were not yet in demand. The two came down to the seedy Bricklayer's Arms pub in Soho, where Stu and Brian were holding the try-outs in an upstairs room. Keith plugged in and started jamming along with Stu, hitting it off immediately.

A core band was formed in the spring of 1962 with Brian, Mick, Keith, Stu, and Taylor on bass. They coveted a particular drummer they occasionally saw down at Ealing, Charlie Watts. Charlie, a graphic artist for an advertising agency, was a modern jazz fan who played with a bebop finesse. His image as a cool and elegant hipster was already in place. But it would take a while for the band to secure Charlie as their regular drummer. He was working the steady job and needed to be paid in order for him to lug his drums on the tube to gigs. So in the meantime, the band—still nameless—tried out a series of drummers.

Over the summer of 1962, Mick, Keith, and Brian moved into an Edith Grove flat together, which became legendary for its abject filth and the misanthropic rudeness of its three new denizens. Brian, who came from an upper-middle-class upbringing in the suburbs of Cheltenham, had no job and had already fathered three of the five children he would eventually father out of wedlock with different women. Keith joined him in the bohemian life by quitting art school, while Mick continued to go to LSE from time to time. Brian and Keith would pore over the trio's shared record collection with a monkish devotion, listening intently to forensically discern between the instruments, the tones, the dynamics, the lyrics, and the interplay between all the musicians.

Brian had by far the deepest musical knowledge and natural talent and taught Keith much of the foundation of the blues. Brian had formally learned saxophone as a boy and took up guitar at sixteen. He was known for his all-around musicianship. Keith was not interested in being a virtuoso so much as being drawn to an overall band mixture, like those heard on the old Chess Records sides, a wall of sound where the vocalist is simply part of the ensemble. These were the underpinnings for what the trio would eventually alchemize into their early sound, the two-guitar blend that Keith would refer to for decades as "the ancient form of weaving."

The band was offered their first gig at the Marquee Club in London in July 1962, filling in for Korner's band. They had been sitting in during intervals between blues and jazz bands at Ealing and a few other clubs around London, becoming more popular at each appearance. But now, with a "real" gig, they needed a name. Brian looked down at a Muddy Waters LP and saw the song title, "Rollin' Stone." And so it was.

Mick, Brian, Keith, Stu, and Dick Taylor were all certainly part of the Stones for the gig that night. The question of who played drums has been a bit of a mystery, with Keith maintaining that it was Mick Avory, later of the Kinks, who sat in. Even Taylor is uncertain, telling me, "Aargh, I really wish I could get this settled. I always thought that Tony [Chapman]—although our 'official' drummer—only managed to come to a couple of rehearsals because his work kept him away. I seem to recall Charlie coming to some of our rehearsals, and actually thought it was him who played at the Marquee. . . . When later it was said that it was Mick Avory who did the Marquee I presumed it was my memory that was at fault. I wish someone could put me out of my misery about this." The consensus is that it was Chapman.

Taylor, who remained at art college, was not thrilled with converting to the bass guitar to be a part of the band. "I was in a real quandary about whether I wanted to play guitar or bass," he explained. "I remember Brian being very complimentary about my bass playing, that really touched me as I was a great admirer of his musicianship. In the end, when I decided to leave, it was a combination of wanting to concentrate on my college work and the guitar having won over the bass." Taylor went on to form the Pretty Things, who became rock stars themselves. So dry your eyes; no Pete Best story here.

Chapman brought his mate Bill Wyman in to play bass. They had played together in previous bands. Wyman, born in 1936, had already done a stint in the Royal Air Force, was married, and had a regular job before he bought a guitar and started to learn it at age twenty-four. He was a devoted rock 'n' roller, not a blues fan. He scrounged up whatever cash he could and bought an electric guitar. He decided to switch to bass one night after seeing a band with a rock solid foundation. "The sound of their bass guitar hit me straight in the balls," he recalls. He realized what was missing in his current band. "It suited my personality. At twenty-four, I didn't see myself as an 'upfront' musician . . . I was always more attuned to the overall sound, the need for internal dynamics, and *precision*." He would go on to first acquire a Vox Phantom bass, then shortly after, a classic Vox AC30 amp.

These latter assets are what most attracted the Stones to Bill when he brought them down for the audition in December 1962. In fact, in Keith's diary entry at the time, while the Vox is mentioned by name, Bill is not. He is presumably noted in the phrase, "secured bass guitarist." Keith admits, "First off, I just wanted to separate Bill from his amplifier."

Still, even though Bill plied them with rounds of beer and smokes, which they "jumped on as if I were delivering famine relief," he felt no connection with the band personally. Only Mick had been friendly to him and there was very little overlap with their musical tastes. Bill came from the rock 'n' roll, rockabilly, and pop worlds of the 1950s, while the Stones were primarily "playing minority music with such conviction." Bill could not fathom playing slow 12-bar Jimmy Reed blues all night, so the Chuck Berry numbers were all they really gelled on.

Nevertheless, Bill's musical prospects were slim and when he got a chance for a second audition with them, he came back. This time, everyone was looser and a bit friendlier. They did not officially hire him per se, but they asked him to show up for their next gig, on December 15, 1962.

Bill had been initially shocked by Keith and Brian's "bohemian" shaggy-dog appearance. "In the pop world where I came from, smartness was automatic. I was neatly dressed, as if for work, with a Tony Curtis hairstyle," he wryly explains. Gradually, Bill got pulled in and came to understand the Stones' worldview. This older, somewhat wiser bassist could sense that they were onto something larger. They had tapped into the burgeoning youth-fueled counterculture—not so consciously, more intuitively. The long hair and off-putting behavior was a way they—consciously or not—weeded square people out. Pete Townshend said he remembers his impression of seeing the Stones in the streets before ever seeing them play. "It's amazing they didn't get killed," he said at a reading promoting his memoirs in Boston in 2012. They were distancing themselves from postwar England's striving and self-satisfied bourgeois comfort in order to get deeper into the art, into something real, not packaged for the masses—in this case, down and dirty blues. They needed to make themselves feel like "others," outsiders.

Their ongoing efforts to hire Charlie as their full-time drummer continued and their commitment and confidence convinced him to join their ranks. "I had a theory that R&B was going to be a big part of the scene and I wanted to be part of it," he recalled. He was particularly knocked out by a set they played with a great substitute drummer named Carlo Little. Charlie had been playing with another band on the bill. "The Stones were great. So I joined," he said. They fired Chapman, who tried to take Bill with him. But Bill was quite happy with his place in the band by then. Charlie played his first gig with them in January 1963 and was their official drummer the next month.

Keith educated Charlie in the chilled-out backbeat style of R&B and blues drummers, specifically Jimmy Reed's drummer, Earl Phillips, for the right feel, "That sparse, minimalized (sic) thing. And [Charlie has] always retained it," Keith points out in *Life*. It was Charlie's technical talent and finesse that had attracted him to the band, but felt they had to win him over to R&B, make him a "convert" to the style, and to get him to play with more emphasis backbeat. He soon became legendary for just this sort of straight-ahead, deceptively simple grooving.

By the time of these first Stones gigs, the Beatles were already breaking across the UK with their first single, "Love Me Do." Before the Beatles' November 1962 debut, rock 'n' roll had been seen as a 1950s teen fad that had come and gone in the UK. That's partially why the Stones considered themselves R&B, *not* rock 'n' roll. But the Beatles spearheaded a second wave of rock 'n' roll that had been bubbling under, music that stood in stark contrast to the mass-produced pop stars dominating commercial radio. Many would later describe it as sort of a youth-led awakening along the lines of a *Wizard of Oz*–like change from a buttoned-down, black-and-white culture to a color-saturated sense of freedom. Here were four musicians who wrote and performed their own songs, which was quite a rarity in the early sixties.

"When the Stones were first together we heard there was a group from Liverpool with long hair, scruffy clothes, and a record in the charts with a bluesy harmonica riff," Jagger recalled as he inducted the Beatles into the Rock and Roll Hall of Fame in 1988. "The combination of all this made me sick."

The Beatles saved rock 'n' roll, or at least made the term itself acceptable for hipsters again. The Stones took notice of the Beatles, especially Brian, who was obsessed with the idea of pop stardom. It was one of his many contradictions, though, that he played this obscure blues music, didn't write his own songs, and was not a singer. But what he did have was a great look and image, giving the Stones as a whole a leg-up in their visual presentation. In his memoirs, Bill leaves no doubt as to who he felt the leader of the band was, musically as well as in surface image. He explains the "live fast die young" Brian was one of, if not the earliest, rock 'n' roller to epitomize the sex, drugs, and rock 'n' roll ethos well before it became a catchphrase. "The group didn't really settle down until the beginning of 1963," Stewart claimed. "There were two years of pissing around. Brian would suddenly vanish for two months at a time . . . Brian would hide from his responsibilities. He had two kids by then whose mothers and mothers' mothers were always chasing him. Brian was *totally* dishonest." Via his sense of style, his rebelliousness against his stable and comfortable upbringing, and his libertine lifestyle—which was already fairly developed before his forming the Stones—Brian Jones not only gave the Stones their image before the five of them collectively had one, but by extension created an archetype for the sixties.

The band's musical energy and image had captured the eyes and ears of an enthusiastic promoter named Giorgio Gomelsky, an experimental filmmaker turned impresario, who booked the Crawdaddy Club at the Station Hotel in the well-heeled suburb of Richmond. He had seen the Stones' set once or twice, and Korner had sung their praises to him. Brian had lobbied Gomelsky relentlessly for a residency at the Crawdaddy. It was this steady gig, commencing in February 1963, that really launched the Stones' career. The crowds had been building from the sporadic gigs around town and now they started to grow bigger and more enthusiastic at the Crawdaddy. Gomelsky acted as the band's de facto manager and was their loudest champion at the time.

The Stones "played their shit. Chuck Berry, Bo Diddley, things that weren't too difficult," said Gomelsky in *Keith Richards: The Biography*. "But they were playing with guts and conviction. They were playing the blues, but they weren't an academic blues band. The Rolling Stones were more like a rebellion . . . a ritual thing. . . . In the end . . . people [at the Crawdaddy] just went berserk."

Their evangelic devotion to blues and R&B was soon gaining a cultish following from kids yearning for something other than the conformist, adult-approved pop culture dominating the mainstream outlets. Giorgio, whose talents as a promoter extended beyond his hysterically hyperbolic advertisements, openly encouraged the audience, keeping the energy level maxed up, providing one of the few no-holds-barred outlets for the pent-up, pre-Pill, sexually frustrated kids. Gomelsky would whip the club into a lather and audience members reached fevered heights, with beer-sodden, sexually charged young men and women dancing on tables in the overpacked sweltering room. "It was bigger than individual groups of people," says Bill. "I can't tell you the excitement at that place in those months. It was like, all of a sudden, you hit civilization right on the head. The energy was incredible and it gave everybody courage for years and years."

The buzz spread around London, bringing in people who would figure prominently in the Stones' future: engineer/producer, Glyn Johns; manager/PR man, Andrew Loog Oldham; and the Beatles themselves. All of them would come to bear witness to the frothy scene at the Crawdaddy. Johns, who had met various Stones members the previous year, brought them to the studio where he was working, IBC Studios, on March 11, 1963, to record some demos. He was thrilled to meet some "long-haired idiots" who were into the same music as he was, specifically, they were the only other people he knew who were aware of Jimmy Reed.

"I was afraid to introduce them to George Clewson, the guy who owned the studio," said Johns. "The effect they had on people, with their appearance, their clothes, their hair—their whole attitude— was immediate. As soon as you saw them, they showed complete opposition to society, everybody, anything."

But Clewson nevertheless signed them to a deal for free recording time with Johns in return for an exclusive six-month option to shop the resulting tapes to record companies. The tracks they covered were representative of the sets that they had been playing—all covers, of course. Clewson, however, could not drum up any interest. Though the Stones had attained a devoted cult audience around London, their hard R&B stylings were far from what was selling in the squeaky pop world of early-1960s radio. It would take a long leap of faith to find something commercially viable in that raw blues.

On April 14, 1963, Gomelsky had invited the Beatles to come see the Stones down at the Crawdaddy. At the time, the Beatles had their second single, "Please Please Me," at the top of the charts. In his book *Stone Alone*, Bill described it this way:

The room was packed and we were in good form, driven on by the Crawdaddy regulars that now formed our core audience. Soon after we began our first set, we were staggered to see the four Beatles standing and watching us. They were dressed identically in long leather overcoats. I became very nervous and said to myself: *"Shit, that's the Beatles!"*

Between sets, the two bands chatted, and the Beatles stayed for the second set and then came back to the Edith Grove flat, where the musicians sat talking about music into the wee hours. In awe, Brian received an autographed photo of the pop stars.

Journalist Peter Jones tipped off one particularly energetic and sharp nineteen-year-old PR man, Andrew Loog Oldham, to the scene at the Crawdaddy. Oldham had been working as the Beatles' London publicist. Oldham was the highly ambitious son of a single, striving mother in postwar London. He was an inveterate hustler who lived by a *fake it 'til you make it* credo, literally knocking on doors and gaining work as a jack-of-all-trades for film stars and fashion designers.

Oldham had a similar evangelical fervor, energized by the conviction that he was tapping into the slipstream of rapidly changing cultural forces. He had keen and well-developed interests in not only fashion, but in the fresh, independent, and individual expression of the French New Wave's film auteurs, the aesthetics of which he adapted for use in publicizing and art directing the fashion scene, and eventually in stylizing, grooming, and presenting the image of the Stones—the shadowy, gloomy noirish shots of the early Stones records like *Out of Our Heads,* for example.

Branching out from fashion into music, Oldham did some early work as a publicist for Phil Spector in England, and a week of handling Bob Dylan for Dylan's manager, Albert Grossman. The little bit of work he tasted in the music business pointed the way for the rest of his career. However, it was when he happened to be present, coincidentally, at the first national television appearance by the Beatles that he became spellbound. As he watched them rehearse live, with a palpable buzz in the air, he noted their fearlessness and supreme confidence, as early as this, their first television appearance.

When he finally met the Beatles' manager, Brian Epstein, Oldham could see his path forward. Oldham convinced Epstein to hire him as the Beatles' publicist in London. He started renting office space from a prematurely gray-haired, old-school showbiz agent then in his mid-thirties, Eric Easton. To Oldham, Easton was old and out of touch, but in the days when a nineteen-year-old could not yet obtain the necessary agent's license, this office rental would lead to a partnership between the two men.

While Easton literally represented the old guard, Oldham began having great success in helping take the Beatles national. He was a proselytizer for how revolutionary and genuine the group was, no comparison to the pop hits being pumped out by the "grown-ups" of postwar British showbiz. Looking again at rock 'n' roll via his fashion sensibilities, Oldham makes the analogy that the Beatles and Dylan were organic, authentic, "costly, custom-made, real, and durable," as opposed to the "cheap, off the rack, and disposable" world of the adult-approved pop acts of the 1950s and early '60s.

Oldham was looking for his first act to sign as a manager when he took Jones's tip and went down to see the Stones in May 1963. When the music started, he finally got a glimpse of what was causing the word-of-mouth hype. He saw hundreds of kids getting swept up in the Stones brand of R&B, music that "spoke of sex." To Oldham, Bill looked "gaunt, pale, almost medieval." Charlie looked to be "kinda blue, like he'd been transported for the evening from Ronnie Scott's or Birdland." Stu was "the odd man out." Keith, "ef-

fected an alchemic exchange in cool-hand heat with himself."
Brian, an "incredible blond hulking hunk . . . ugly pretty." Finally,
Jagger, was "rock 'n' roll in 3-D and Cinerama," moving like "an
adolescent Tarzan." Oldham recognized that the Stones' animalistic, loud, sweaty R&B was raw, but he knew they could be polished
enough for wider acceptance.

Oldham, though, was so overwhelmed that first night that he
had not introduced himself. A few days later, taking his partner
Easton to see the band, Oldham made his move to sign his first act.
Whether or not he actually mentioned that he had worked with
the Beatles, they knew. The word had gotten to the Stones. When
they met, Oldham impressed upon them that there was a commercial market ready for what they were doing. If the Beatles could to
it, he explained, so could the Stones.

Oldham had learned an essential lesson about the music business from his mentor, Phil Spector: stay independent. Spector had
told Oldham that if and once he discovered a band to manage or
produce, he should retain control, remain independent, and produce the act himself, rather than take advances from a label for
recordings. Oldham, heeding the advice, convinced Easton that it
was necessary to form an independent recording and management
deal, which they did, naming it Impact Sound. It was set up primarily to keep Oldham in as much control as possible, including
the record production, about which he knew next to nothing.

The Beatles had adapted to the white-lab-coat environment in
early-1960s UK recording studios, with the invaluable midwifery of
George Martin. But the visceral, unpolished live energy of the
Stones would be difficult, if not impossible, to capture in that stale
atmosphere of clinical early-1960s English record company studios, accustomed to pumping out whatever pop dreck was handed
to them that day. It would be a challenge Oldham would take on
himself, not just managing the band, but producing them as well.

He extricated them from the contract with IBC with a bit of smoke and mirrors, alienating their early supporter, Glyn Johns, who had brought them to IBC.

Notably, Johns did not engineer any more sessions for the Stones until 1966. With this transaction a pattern was forming— the band cut out anyone who got in the way of their success. This had left Chapman by the side of the road. And getting out from under the contract with Clewson meant losing Johns.

But then the band itself became a target for the Machiavellian Oldham, who felt Ian Stewart did not fit in with the image that the new manager wanted to present. Oldham also claimed that record companies and press would not get behind a band with more than five members without losing focus. Either way, it was clearly no longer just about a group of R&B musicians. Oldham's fashion sense attracted him to "the pretty, thin, long-haired boys," in the words of Cynthia Stewart, Stu's widow. Stu, with too-short hair, plain clothes, and a protruding jaw (due to a calcium deficiency in his youth) just looked too straight for Oldham, whose main focus was making Mick Jagger a star. So, graciously, Stu agreed to step out of the photo shoots and live shows, and became relegated to road manager for the band that he had formed with Brian Jones.

With IBC out of the way, the Stones signed with Impact Sound, and Oldham booked a session. On May 10, 1963, the same month that Mick started a sabbatical from the London School of Economics—where he had still not completed his degree—Oldham and the band recorded the little-known Chuck Berry song, "Come On," which was brought to Decca Records, and only Decca, for their consideration. The record company had already been tipped off to the Stones' phenomenal residency at the Crawdaddy by George Harrison. Of all the Beatles, Harrison had taken the greatest early interest in the Stones and advised Decca Records executive Dick Rowe that he should go see the band at the Crawdaddy.

Rowe was in bad need of reputation restoration, as he was the man who will be forever known as "the guy who passed on the Beatles." (The Fab Four signed to EMI instead.) Rowe signed the Stones.

"[Rowe] could not afford to make the same mistake twice," said Keith. "Decca was desperate—I'm amazed the guy still had a job. At the time, just like anything else in 'popular entertainment,' they thought, it's just a fad, it's a matter of a few haircuts and we'll tame them. But basically we only got a record deal because they could just not afford to fuck up twice. Suddenly they realized, bang, welcome to the twentieth century, and it's 1964 already."

Nineteen sixty-four, and the Rolling Stones were whipping up quite a frenzy as a cover band. But it was with their original compositions that they, along with the Beatles and Bob Dylan, would form the big three of the 1960s that revolutionized rock 'n' roll with songs that seared into the consciousness of an ascendent youth culture. From a wobbly, uncertain adolescence, right on through a wizened old age as grandparents, the music of the Stones has mirrored and provided a soundtrack for their own generation, while charting a road map and a catalog of timeless rock 'n' roll archetypes for those that followed.

The Songs

Part 1
THE BRIAN JONES YEARS

1
Tell Me

RECORDING:

January 1964, Regent Sound Studio, London

RELEASES:

UK LP: *The Rolling Stones,* May 1964

US LP: *England's Newest Hit Makers,* May 1964

US single, June 1964, charting at number 24

"We're making a record,
can you believe this shit?"
—KEITH RICHARDS,
reflecting on the band's first sessions

First, that wobbly adolescence. Though the Rolling Stones had been around for two years by this point, this single, their sixth, marks the first time that the band released a Jagger/Richards–authored original song. The first Stones singles had been covers of Chuck Berry and Lennon/McCartney numbers. They would also cover Arthur Alexander and Buddy Holly hits. But to really take off as a band, they needed to eventually release one of their own. That's where the money was—in song publishing. Famously, Oldham had taken the extraordinary step of "locking" Mick and Keith in a room with the directive to start writing original material. The duo came up with a handful of mostly forgettable compositions, including such chestnuts as "Shang a Doo Lang," "My Only Girl" (later released by Gene Pitney as "That Girl Belongs to Yesterday"), and "Will You Be My Lover Tonight?" before penning "Tell Me."

Like many of the Stones' first songwriting endeavors, "Tell Me" did not mimic the band's direct influences of hard Chicago blues and American rock 'n' roll. Rather, they produced this sort of dark, acoustic-based folk/pop. Oldham attempted to influence the band more toward the fashionable pop styles of the day, while the band did their best to keep true to their self-image as an R&B band, with Brian in particular remaining a blues purist. With "Tell Me," Oldham's influence won out.

The "Tell Me" lyric is a string of clichés, but with enough urgency and snarl behind them to give indication of the Stones' tougher stance than that of the Beatles. "But this time it's different . . . You gotta tell me you're coming back to me." Though clearly a nascent example of the Jagger/Richards songwriting, many of the essential elements of the band, the traits that made them great in the long run, were already well established. They would go on to become expert rock 'n' roll lyricists, despite the merely adequate start on their first original single. But it was the delivery and conviction that mattered more. And they got that right immediately. Even on their earliest recordings of cover songs, Mick sounded confident, to the point of cocksure swagger, like an old blues and soul singer who had seen it all. In 1963, this would have taken tremendous gumption from a skinny English college dropout. But his mates had his back, with surefooted, streetwise R&B that sounded leering and dirty somehow.

"Tell Me" nailed the sound Oldham was going for after the first single, Chuck Berry's "Come On" (June 1963), fell "somewhere in that flawed middle ground between what the Stones wanted and what I wanted," recalled Oldham in his memoirs. "Quite simply, it wasn't Willie Dixon and it wasn't the Ronettes." (The Ronettes, not coincidentally, were burning up the charts in 1963 with their "Be My Baby.") Keith says that their recording of "Come On" was "Beatle-ized." They chose it because it was commercial and they wanted nothing more than the chance to make more records. "Then we refused to play it. Andrew Oldham almost went up the wall. 'You've got a hit record and you don't want to play it?!' 'We ain't playin' that goddamned thing . . . it's awful.'"

The independently produced first single was no artistic triumph, but it served its purpose and got them signed to Decca. But by the Stones' second single, a blistering loosey-goosey take on the Beatles also-ran, "I Wanna Be Your Man," the strengths of the whole band were evident. It's a shot of adrenaline, a youthful burst of energy, perhaps influenced by the song's genesis itself. Again, the story sounds mythical. Oldham had almost literally bumped into Lennon and McCartney as they stepped out of a cab. He invited them to the studio where the Stones were rehearsing, and right then and there, the two finished off what had been a McCartney sketch of an idea, handing it to the Stones for their single. Mick and Keith observed and learned the art of songwriting at the feet of the masters, who made it look easy.

The Stones had been shoehorning in recording sessions during the daylight hours while playing live gigs almost every night. For those first few years, they had almost no days off. So by the time of the session for "Tell Me," they had logged an impressive amount of hours together as a live band. Their self-assuredness is evident on the recording.

Keith starts the rhythm of "Tell Me" on the 12-string acoustic guitar. After the rather regal arpeggio flourish of the intro, his strumming begins unmoored from the backbeat (the two and four of the beat). It is a rhythm that seemingly does not resolve itself or reveal the obvious downbeat. If you are counting "one and two and three and four and . . ." the accents of his strumming are on the upstrokes (the "ands"). The next verse is even more on the upstroke. It creates a tension. The effect is like: *come on man, you're killing me,* so that when the rhythm gets nailed down on the pre-chorus ("I know you find it hard . . ."), it comes as a welcome release and a resolution, which slams down harder on the chorus. Then Charlie drops out again and the verse teases you again.

This is one of the fundamental building blocks of the Stones' sound as a band: Keith basically strumming away, trusting his bandmates to know where he is and to join him at the right time. As the years went on, Keith developed a highly rhythmic sense, driving, bobbing, and weaving, to the point of turning the beat around—that is, changing where beat one comes, making the band catch up to him. It is an outgrowth of his utmost confidence in the foundation laid down by Charlie, who himself has pointed out that the Stones are one of those rare bands where the drummer follows the rhythm guitar player rather than the inverse. The truth is that Charlie usually plays just slightly behind Keith, instinctually predicting where Keith is heading, and they mesh as one rhythm. This produces that almost undetectable drag that defines the sound of the Stones as much as anything else.

This mutual trust and intrinsic musical communication was clear right out of the gate with the Stones, and it is audible on "Tell Me." Keith's sense of rhythm guitar was informed in large part by listening to the records of the Everly Brothers. And in 1963, the Stones toured with the Everlys, along with Little Richard, a grueling run of dates that Oldham reckons gave the Stones a level of experience approaching that which the Beatles attained in Hamburg. The master showman, Little Richard, taught them a thing or two about dazzling an audience as well as the difference between club and theater performances, while the Everlys showed off pristine two-part harmonies and deft guitar playing. Don Everly's driving acoustic guitar is a cornerstone of rock 'n' roll, heard in the strumming hands of Pete Townshend and Paul Simon, as well as Keith's.

"Tell Me" is quintessential early Stones. It has that somewhat baroque start but quickly gets into the Phil Spector-esque, street-tough-switch-blade of a chorus, a juvenile-delinquents-in-love vibe (so much so that it fits in perfectly on the soundtrack to Martin Scorcese's 1973 film, *Mean Streets*). It stays loose, with Mick not even bothering to match up his own double-tracked lead vocal on the pre-choruses and chorus. Another signature of the Stones surfaces here as well: Keith's loose harmony (sung live into the guitar mic as he strummed) paired with Mick's assertive vocals. Keith chugs in on an overdubbed electric guitar and slides his fingering up the neck during the first pre-chorus. There is an inarticulate chord-arpeggio for a solo, also from Keith. Oldham's early love of the tambourine results in the instrument front and center in the mix, struck with a drumstick. The tempo quickens markedly out of the solo, but it somehow manages to hold together.

Taking influence from those older Chess Records releases, as well as contemporary records coming out of Memphis on labels like Stax/Volt, "Tell Me" sounds crude, presented with very little polish. Like those blues and soul records, it was about the overall feeling. In classic soul music, no one was worrying if the bass player was slightly off on a particular bar. Yet the looseness of soul was a deceiving sort, generally played over a particularly tight rhythm section, with the rest of the band playing in a laid-back pocket slightly behind or around the beat. The rhythm of the music literally swings within the beat. Otis Redding's 1962 recording of "Pain In My Heart" (which the Stones went on to record) is a good example. There is a great deal of swing to the drums and bass, but drummer Al Jackson Jr. holds down the ensemble with a steady pattern on the hi-hat, allowing the horns, organ, and most important, Redding himself, to roam.

Jackson was a direct influence on Charlie Watts and Ringo Starr, who reclaimed this swinging style of drumming back from early-1960s English producers, whose "correct" and "polite" technique dictated that bass drum and bass guitar should always be locked in together (to the point that Ringo was actually jettisoned on a couple of early Beatles tracks in favor of a session drummer). Keith explains the greatness of Charlie and his essence to the foundation of the Stones sound:

> . . . I love to watch his foot . . . Even if I can't hear him, I can play to him just by watching. The other thing is Charlie's trick that he got, I think from Jim Keltner or Al Jackson. On the hi-hat, most guys would play on all four beats, but on the two and the four, which is the backbeat, which is a very important thing in rock and roll, Charlie doesn't play, he lifts up. He goes on to play and pulls back. It gives the snare drum all of the sound, instead of having some interference behind it.

Oldham, his production experience quite limited, helped buffer the Stones themselves from those "polite" English engineers who might otherwise have sucked the life out of the music in the control room. Oldham barely knew anything about making music, never mind how to engineer. His role as producer was more in line with his role model, Phil Spector, a big-picture point of view. But while Spector composed music as well as produced it, Oldham approached the position more as an in-house A&R (artists & repertoire) man, as well as liaison between the band and the engineers, than as a set of ears. Oldham, though, found a willing accomplice in Bill Farley, who was the house engineer at Regent Sound Studios. Farley is described as an ambitious, eager-to-please guy who had the ability to translate what Oldham would describe to him abstractly, getting it down on tape the way they wished to hear it. "We didn't have a George Martin," says Keith. "We had the band.

And we had Oldham." Ian Stewart said, "People like Mick and Keith didn't need a George Martin."

"When they first arrived," Farley later recalled, "no one had thought about arrangements. They just busked it until they got the feeling of the number. There was no dubbing. They just told me exactly what they wanted as soon as the number had been worked out. How it turned out so well in the end I never really knew."

Oldham describes Regent itself as "no larger than an average good-sized hotel room," with the control room the size of the hotel room's bathroom, "but for us it was magic." The sound from the instruments leaked into the microphones of the others, the drums coming through the microphone on Keith's acoustic. It gave the band their own version of Phil Spector's Wall of Sound. The Stones would go on to record all of their first album there.

Within weeks of the album's release, they went from playing clubs to being pop stars. The debut record, recorded in about ten days, sold 100,000 copies in its first week, going straight to number one and staying in the position for three months. By now, they were rarely being referred to as an R&B band. As with the increasingly successful Beatles, the Stones were no longer simply an R&B nightclub draw. They were now a "beat group," the marketing term of the day in England for post-Beatles pop acts.

When the LP in the States dropped, the cover had a screaming headline across the top: *ENGLAND'S NEWEST HIT MAKERS: THE ROLLING STONES*. It would be a lot to live up to.

2
It's All Over Now

RECORDING:
June 1964, Chess Studios, Chicago

RELEASES:
US LP: *12 x 5*, October 1964
UK single, June 1964, charting at number 1
US single, July 1964, charting at number 26

Touring and Recording in America

On the heels of the Stones' success in England, Oldham soon made it his priority to break the band into the gigantic US market, where the Beatles had been enjoying their legendarily meteoric rise and staggering record sales. Under Oldham's guidance, arrangements were made and the Stones first arrived Stateside June 1, 1964. As unabashed fans of American blues, soul, and country, the Stones were understandably thrilled to tour America, but the reception on this first tour was not quite what they would hope for and what they would indeed later receive. Precious few people knew who the Stones were at this early point. "A disaster" is how Bill Wyman would later describe it. "When we arrived, we didn't have a hit record [there] or anything going for us." Regarding the Stones' first US television appearance on *The Hollywood Palace*, with Dean Martin, in June 1964, Keith recalled:

> In America then, if you had long hair, you were a faggot as well as a freak. They would shout across the street, "Hey fairies!" Dean Martin introduced us (on his television show) as something like "these long-haired wonders from England, the Rolling Stones. . . . They're backstage picking fleas off each other."

"Keith was about to pop [Martin] one with his guitar," noted their tour manager at the time, Bob Bonis. (Bill Wyman wryly points out that the Stones got back at "old Dino" later, when Brian Jones "became friendly with one of Dean Martin's daughters.")

But that virgin tour certainly reaped some benefits, even if most of the country was, in Jagger's estimation, "more aware of the Dave Clark Five and the Swinging Blue Jeans" than the Rolling Stones. At a country fair sort of gig in Texas, the band met native Texan sax player Bobby Keys, who would later become a regular sideman with the band, playing on many Stones classics (most famously, the solo on "Brown Sugar"), as well as becoming an almost constant touring member and Keith's best friend. "I thought, who were these guys, you know, pasty-faced little skinny short cut-off rock 'n' roll upstarts," Keys told me in an interview. "Well, I didn't think about *all* that, but it was more like, how *dare* them! You're treading sacred ground here . . . They won me over because they were so good. Hell, they were better than our band. It sounded more like Texans playing than Englishmen."

Another benefit reaped from that tour was meeting legendary disc jockey Murray "the K" Kaufman, "the fifth Beatle," who told them that no white kids wanted to hear "Muddy Waters' kind of music or Bo Diddley's kind of music 'cause if they wanted that kind of music they'd want the original." After their first appearance on his radio show, on the day they arrived in New York, Murray played them a rocking little 1964 single, "It's All Over Now," recorded by the Valentinos for Sam Cooke's SAR Records. It was pop-soul confection, dusted with a bit of country, written by the group's Bobby Womack and his sister-in-law, Shirley Womack. The single had been breaking out on the "black" charts in the Midwest. The K suggested the Stones record it for a single. Ten days later, they did just that at the fabled Chess Studios in Chicago. The Valentinos' song offered something with commercial potential that could hit with white American kids much the way Sam Cooke himself had.

On June 10, the Stones made a pilgrimage to 2120 South Michigan Avenue in Chicago, the headquarters and studio of Chess Records, the label that had released a huge portion of the records in the band's collection, records from Muddy Waters, Bo Diddley, Willie Dixon, Howlin' Wolf, Little Walter, and Chuck Berry, among a long list of others. "In England at that time, nobody really knew how to record the sounds we were trying to get," said Keith about going to Chess. "The Beatles' stuff was easy—vocal harmonies, neat and precise. That wasn't too difficult, but to try and get that dirty sound we were after, it was just the most obvious place in the world to record it at Chess."

Not only was Chess Studios a high-quality recording facility, it was the very one in which their heroes recorded and a mecca for blues fans. It was the source out of which this origin story flowed, a mythical address Mick had written to and ordered that armful of precious records that reestablished the bond with Keith. The band was stunned to actually get to meet their musical idols, the specific men responsible for the building blocks of rock 'n' roll, and such direct influences on the Rolling Stones that the band took their very name from one of Muddy Waters's songs. And here they were in their midst. The band was gobsmacked as Dixon plugged one of his songs to try and get the Stones to record it, Berry himself came in to offer encouragement, and, if the legend is to be believed, Muddy Waters helped carry the band's gear in.

"Some people, Marshall Chess [son and nephew of Chess founders and later head of Rolling Stones Records] included, swear that I made this up, but Bill Wyman can back me up," claims Keith. "We walked into Chess Studios, and there is this guy in black overalls painting the ceiling. And It's Muddy Waters, and he's got whitewash streaming down his face and he's on top of a ladder . . . And also Bill Wyman told me he actually remembers Muddy Waters taking our amplifiers from the car to the studio. Whether he was being a nice guy or he wasn't selling records then, I know what the Chess brothers were bloody well like—if you want to stay on the payroll, get to work."

The band was not only thrilled to be in the "lap of their gods," as Oldham put it, but to be in the capable hands of the studio's head engineer, Ron Malo, who seemed to instinctually know how the band wanted to hear themselves even before they could articulate it. So excited and satisfied with the results they heard on the playback, they recorded four songs in four hours including "It's All Over Now" and "Time Is on My Side." By the end of two days, they had recorded thirteen tracks.

The Stones, and Oldham—pushing them out from their purist blues tendencies—continued to display impeccable taste at choosing covers to interpret. Just as they had reimagined Buddy Holly's "Not Fade Away" for their first LP—a song Oldham considers "the first Stones song," due to its breathtakingly inventive interpretation—the Stones made "It's All Over Now" their own. With Holly's song, the Stones had settled into an arrangement that was developed by Keith, who had been obsessively playing the song on his acoustic guitar around their flat. Unlike Holly's sparse recording, the Stones emphasized the Bo Diddley beat of the song and never took their foot off the pedal.

"It's All Over Now" is given a similar insistent approach. While the Valentinos' original recording features funky New Orleans–style shuffling drums, the Stones, Charlie in particular, keeps the rhythm tighter and straighter. They retained the main hook, the two-part harmony on the elongated "I used to love her but it's all over now." Even the bass guitar on the original had an almost-trombone-like sliding sound, resonating with tinges of New Orleans, and Bill kept that same vibe in the Stones version, plugging his bass into the mixing desk directly, bypassing any amps. But the country-meets-soul writing of the song also brings Memphis to mind on both versions.

"We never thought about it, we just played," explained Mick soon after the release of the single. "I suppose it is a bit hicky. We certainly haven't gone off R&B. We play the way we feel. If it comes out country-sounding, well it comes out that way."

The Stones make it sound more like rock music, not just lighter-swinging '50s style of rock 'n' roll, but in a darker, more aggressive, loud, and distorted manner that presaged the harder edges that would start showing up in the later 1960s, with such notable heavy rock guitarists as Jimi Hendrix, Pete Townshend, and Jimmy Page. The sped-up approach to the song brings to mind Chuck Berry's "Maybellene."

"It's All Over Now" opens with a "sordid amount of reverb," which Oldham said was his only notable production input. Guitars come crashing down with Charlie's cymbal splashes in the intro, and then everything tightens up for the verses, including the production itself, with the reverb drying up measurably.

For most of the track, two guitars are featured, with Keith playing the country-picked clean-sounding electric guitar and Brian playing curlicued accents on a 12-string electric (probably his Vox Teardrop). In the chorus, Brian slams down on the four-beat whole-note power chords and alternates with a chopping rhythm on eighth notes between the vocal lines. Keith's clean picking gets mixed out as a second guitar from Keith enters playing a much-discussed, thrilling rock 'n' roll solo, influenced—yes—by Chuck Berry, but also an early example of Keith's own identifiable style of rhythmic, staccato soloing, similar to the kind heard later on "Sympathy for the Devil." It has an edgy, minimalist feel to it, with plenty of space between some economically chosen stinging notes that slash right into the brain.

It's the favorite guitar solo of many notable fans, such as Bruce Springsteen. But Keith recalls that John Lennon criticized the solo. "He thought it was crap." Keith claims he slapped back, telling John the Beatles wore their guitars too high: "No wonder you don't swing, you know? No wonder you can only rock, no wonder you can't roll."

Mick takes some liberties with the lyrics, changing "hurt my nose open" with "hurt my eyes open" and "trying to play her high-class game" slurring into "playing her half-assed game"—blurry enough to sound vaguely like "high-fast game," but nevertheless resulting in getting the record banned at some stations. The tandem of Mick and Keith on the chorus harmonies is rough around the edges, strained and bluesy. The guitars and reverb come crashing down at the end, as Charlie lets loose some fills, laying into his half-opened hi-hat in an unpredictable pattern.

When the single was released in the UK just weeks after the recording, on June 26, it went straight to number one. Murray the K was right—the single was a certified smash. It was released in America on July 25, clawing as high as 26 on the Billboard charts, their highest chart position yet in the States, while selling enough to earn a gold record.

Like Elvis before them, the Stones were putting a young white face on music from black artists, and white kids were buying it all up as if it were new—which of course, it was, for them. But unlike Pat Boone, who had whitewashed and candy-coated the life (and sex) out of Little Richard's "Tutti Frutti," the Stones were actually offering authentic and—in the case of "It's All Over Now"—even rougher sounding versions of music from black artists. "In America," Keith recalls, "people like Bobby Womack used to say, 'The first time we heard you guys we thought you were black guys. Where did these motherfuckers come from?'"

As with "Not Fade Away," "It's All Over Now" is a revealing interpretation. Few people are even aware of the Valentinos original, but when that Stones recording comes on the stereo, the heart races and the hands slap the steering wheel (or whatever else is handy), and even the least confident singers among us strain out on the liberating kiss-off chorus, "Because I used to love her, but it's alllllllll over now!"

3
Time Is on My Side

RECORDING:

June 1964, Chess Studios, Chicago

RELEASES:

US LP: *12 x 5*, October 1964

US single, September 1964, charting at number 6

Filling a Need, Plugging a Hole for American Teens

While the Stones served as ambassadors of African-American blues and R&B in England, they were surprised to discover that they had to turn on American kids to the great soul and blues music being churned out regionally in their very own country. In the early '60s, African American soul, pop, and R&B was rolling along full force in certain musical circles but most American kids had no idea about their own home-grown music until it was fed back to them by shaggy young Brits. "White American music when I arrived," Keith explains, "was the Beach Boys and Bobby Vee. They were stuck in the past."

On the same first visit to America that produced "It's All Over Now," Oldham discovered an Irma Thomas record called "Time Is on My Side," and he was instantly smitten, recognizing this song as potentially a key stepping stone in the development of his repertoire-challenged young band. The author of "Time Is on My Side," Jerry Ragovoy, had written or cowritten some other classic soul burners, from "Cry, Cry Baby" to "Piece of My Heart," each of which were covered by Janis Joplin.* First composed with just the title chorus and the "you'll come running back" lyric hooks, "Time Is on My Side" was first recorded with only those chorus lyrics sung by an explosive ensemble of then-unknowns—Cissy Houston, Dionne Warwick, and Dee Dee Warwick—for trombonist Kai Winding, who plays the rest of the melody, solo, on his horn.

In early 1964, Thomas, a New Orleans soul singer, recorded a version as a B-side, an arrangement fleshed out with additional lyrics from songwriter/musician/singer Jimmy Norman. This is the version that Oldham had heard and the Stones used as a template for their own version, recorded later the same year as Thomas's recording. Though they had recorded a take of "Time Is on My Side" at Chess, the version on the *12×5* LP was captured back in London at the Regent with Bill Farley. While remaining somewhat true to the Thomas arrangement, the Stones once again added a harder-edged rock element. Thomas's version features a fairly elegant gospel call-and-response arrangement, with a polished backing chorus, and a tympani-pounded intro. The main musical difference—and it is a crucial one—is that her original record features a second grace chord on the chorus/refrain, a seventh that adds a spirit of melancholy. The Stones keep the 6/8 (double-waltz) time signature and change the key from C to F and just hang on the F for a second measure, skipping over where the passing seventh chord would go.

---

* Ragovoy uses the pseudonym Norman Meade here.

The effect is that the Stones' arrangement just plows right through, aggressively.

Stu begins with a churchy organ under Keith's reverb-drenched brittle and dynamic blues lead bends. During the second half of the intro, Keith picks the strings in double time, a heart-quickening anticipatory indication that this is not going to remain a somber gospel number. The Stones' version is tougher sounding than Thomas's. With its slightly out-of-tune guitars, its unsteady, rushed tambourine hits, and deliberate choice to forgo the seventh chord, it leaves that melancholy and doubt of the other version by the side of the road and the arrangement takes a defiant stance that is more directly in line with the spirit of the title. "Like I told you so many times before," answers Mick to the "You'll come running back" backing vocals (from Keith, likely joined by Bill and Brian), "Go ahead baby, go ahead. Go ahead and light up the town." There is a bit of the ad-libbed trash talk Mick would use consistently over the years, and a foreshadowing of attitude-laden lines like, "Go ahead, bite the Big Apple. Don't mind the maggots" in "Shattered."

Compared to crisp Beatles recordings from the same time, "Time Is on My Side" sounds like a raw, drunken demo, but it is a sexy sort of sloppy. "A Hard Day's Night" had been released only a few months prior and its pop is harnessed, focused, recorded, and mixed pristinely. It pops out of the radio and its presence is in your face, screaming "Good morning!" "Time Is on My Side," by contrast, sidles up behind you at closing time, in an open-collared shirt, breathing nicotine and booze in your ear. You don't need to clearly hear the words; you get the message: "You'll come runnin' back." Jagger slurs into almost every note, like one of Keith's guitar strings sliding into and back out of pitch. "Like I told you so many times befo'," he mumbles, mimicking blues artists.

The mix is a soupy wall of sound. The specter of Spector loomed large once again in the approach to the production. The Beatles were recording at Abbey Road Studios, a state-of-the-art facility, being overseen by an already renowned producer, George Martin. The Stones were in a demo/jingle studio, overseen by Oldham, a publicist and hustler with no previous studio experience before producing the Stones. For the most part, the Beatles records sounded crisp, precise, and present. The Stones sound dark, washy, and distant. The notes are slurry, bending into and out of pitch.

The single mixed and ready for release, the Stones made their debut on *The Ed Sullivan Show* on October 25, 1964 to introduce the song to their burgeoning American audience. The appearance on the show would be a watershed moment in their rise to stardom. Earlier that same year, in February, the television program had provided one of the most pivotal moments in American popular culture, when the Beatles made their first appearance on American television to an estimated 73 million viewers from coast to coast. The landmark Beatles appearance affected not just the hysterical teenage girls, but other artists and musicians ranging from the established—Bob Dylan, Tommy James, and even poet Allen Ginsberg—to those little kids who would immediately go out with their parents to buy guitars and drums. It was the event that launched thousands of garage bands and led to the next wave of bands in the late 1960s and 1970s.

The Stones had big shoes to fill as the next major British act to take the stage. But while the Beatles debuted with a song that they had tailor written for the American audience—packing in an almost impossible number of hooks and a gentle, socially acceptable lyric into a two-and-a-half-minute supernova of original pop genius—the Stones came out with two covers, the Chuck Berry rave-up "Around and Around" and the simmering adult-oriented soul song "Time Is on My Side," performed before screaming hordes of teenage girls practically melting as they squirmed in the seats of the theater. Charlie grins at the reaction. Bill leers through his heavy-lidded eyes. Mick, casually wearing a crew neck sweater, sings with puppy-dog eyes with a glint of impishness. Bill comes in with a cawing falsetto on the outro: "Time! Time! Time!"

After the show, the switchboards reportedly lit up with irate parents and adoring young females alike. This was just the sort of polarization that Oldham was after. Once he figured out—early— that the Stones were impossible to corral into wearing matching houndstooth outfits while smiling for the kids and parents alike—a strategy that had been working well for the Beatles—Oldham went for the opposite attack. He played up the Stones' subversive and unkempt image, exploiting the generation gap.

The Stones, according to Keith, used "the differences between us and the Beatles as soon as we could. In actual fact, they were the same kinds of blokes as us, but the way they were projected meant that we had to make a difference between ourselves and them, which wasn't that difficult. In a way, we were encouraged, especially by Andrew, to be a little more outrageous than we actually felt. Since then, it's become a well-known scam."

Amid the early hoopla over their appearance, Jagger pointed out that their longer hairstyles had already been in vogue at colleges and art schools around England. The hairstyles "were around when the Beatles were using Brylcreem," he quipped.

Paul McCartney was jealous, according to Peter Asher of Peter and Gordon. "The Stones really don't give a shit and don't wear suits," Asher recalls McCartney saying. "They don't get pushed around as much as we do."

The naturally rebellious John Lennon was also not pleased that Brian Epstein had so carefully groomed the Beatles to seem cute, but not sexually threatening. "Where the Rolling Stones dealt in sex," writes Ian MacDonald in *Revolution in the Head: The Beatles' Records and the Sixties,* "the Beatles supposedly respected propriety, knowing how far a young man should go with a young woman and hence how far a pop group could trespass without causing offense." (The Stones, of course, would go on to push the envelope further with "Let's Spend the Night Together" in 1967.)

In 1963, Oldham had fed the famous headline to a journalist at *Melody Maker*: "Would You Let Your Sister Go With a Rolling Stone?" With permutations like "Would you let your daughter marry a Rolling Stone?" catching on in other outlets, the rhetorical question became a cornerstone of their bad-boy image.

Ed Sullivan had voted a resounding "no" on behalf of all American parents. A week or two after the Stones' debut on his show, he announced in an apology to his viewers that he had not met the band until the day before the appearance and that he was "shocked" when he saw them. "I promise you they'll never be back on the show. It took me seventeen years to build this show and I'm not going to have it destroyed in a matter of weeks."

The Stones went on to play the show five more times.

4
Heart of Stone

RECORDING:

November 1964, RCA Studios, Hollywood

RELEASES:

US LP: *The Rolling Stones, Now!*, February 1965

UK LP: *Out of Our Heads*, September 1965

US single, December 1964, charting at number 19

Working as Hard as the Hardest Working Man in Show Business: The Stones Go Hollywood

The dark tone that the Stones set in their first self-penned single, "Tell Me," continued. But now the Stones were writing music that was their forte, a real Memphis/Otis Redding–style hard soul ballad that would set a template for a certain strain of their songwriting in coming decades. While "Tell Me" is a fine little ditty, the memorable "Heart of Stone" marks the beginning of classic Jagger/Richards songwriting, their second self-penned single after two more covers.

By the end of 1964, the sounds on UK radio were getting tougher, with the Animals, the Kinks, and Them, all starting to get airplay alongside the Stones. Amplified fuzzy guitar distortion was becoming more accepted with songs like "You Really Got Me," and "Baby, Please Don't Go," confrontational buzz-saw electric guitars pushed as high or higher in the mix than any other element. The Stones were one of the main links from piano- and vocal-driven rock 'n' roll and R&B to guitar-crazy heavy rock. They kicked the doors open for other bands of brooding and sarcastic British boys wearing black, with shaggy hair and sunglasses.

As Keith pointed out about the early days of the band at the Ealing Jazz Club, the categorization of their music as blues, rock 'n' roll, or R&B was "pointless." What mattered was "how much you lay the backbeat down or how flash you play it." And this was evident on "Heart of Stone." It features a loping, relaxed cadence, the sort found in the original country-soul recordings from Arthur Alexander, Percy Sledge, and James Carr.

"Heart of Stone" was recorded during their second American tour in the fall of 1964. The band had returned to Los Angeles and started recording at the famous RCA Studios in Hollywood with legendary figures like Phil Spector and his star arranger, Jack Nitzsche—a member of the band of studio session players known as the Wrecking Crew and chief arranger and architect of Spector's patented Wall of Sound—hanging around and contributing. Keith flat out states: "Jack was the Genius [sic], not Phil."

RCA was already a celebrated facility by the time the Stones arrived, having recorded Sam Cooke, Elvis Presley, and many more. As a complex, it contained three studios, with high ceilings, parquet floors, an extensive collection of top-shelf microphones, a Neve console, four-track tape recorders, and live echo chambers.

Bill Wyman explained that the young musicians were gobsmacked by the enormity of the studio:

When we came into LA we went to RCA. We walked into the studio and it was too big. . . . We were intimidated. We were used to recording in little places like Regent Sound. . . . But Andrew put us all in the corner of one room, turned all the lights down, and just tucked us all around in a little small circle. And we forgot about the rest of the room and the height of the ceiling. And we just did it in this little corner.

The studio also contained a vast array of musical instruments ready to be used at a moment's notice. Musical adventurer Brian Jones, whose omnivorous appetite to try new instruments was insatiable, was like the proverbial kid in a candy store. He jumped from marimbas, to glockenspiel, to dulcimers and keyboards. He may not have been writing the songs, but he was becoming a premier colorist, adding singular musical textures that helped the Stones songs stand out on the radio.

Contrary to their general approach to the studio, the structure of "Heart of Stone" was more or less worked out in advance. There was a demo version of the song with the same verses and chorus, recorded by Bill Farley at Regent from the previous July, with studio musicians (including Jimmy Page) and only Mick present from the Rolling Stones themselves; the idea here was to have a demo to hawk to publishers for other recording artists to cover. But otherwise, as with the sessions in London and Chicago, the band went in with little or no preparation. Mick and Keith's songwriting and arranging style was generally to come in with a basic sketch of an idea trying to steer the band in certain directions while having the individual members shape their own parts and influence the form of the song. But Keith would remain "obstinate," in the words of Bill, if he did not like the results.

The clinical environment of early-1960s recording studios and the punch-the-clock regular hours of session musicians were rapidly losing favor as maverick musicians who wrote and performed their own material wrote their own rules. Bob Dylan was going into studios with the same sort of improvisational approach, and of course, the Beatles would eventually give up live touring altogether and virtually camp out in the studio, using it as their laboratory for aural experimentation.

As for the Stones, "Jack Nitzsche said it was the first time in his life that he saw a band just come in with no thought or no preparation or anything," said Bill. "We'd just do it and it sorta blew his mind. Because we had no pre-plans and just do it in three takes. 'Let's do that one.'"

Nitzsche pointed out that there was a reciprocal influence. He taught the Stones how to achieve a fuller spectrum of arranging and producing while they encouraged in him a more artistic, less rigid approach to the studio. "They were really bright . . . the first [rock 'n' rollers] I saw say 'Fuck you' to everybody. There was no guidance at all on those records and very little need for it. This was the first time a band got together and just played. They changed my whole idea of recording." He points out that sessions usually ran down tunes in three hours, but the Stones changed all that for him. "That was the first really free feeling I had in the studio."

The rich depth of the RCA production can be heard clearly within the spaces of the "Heart of Stone" recording. The song is similar in mood to some of Bobby "Blue" Bland's minor-key ballads such as his simmering 1959 single, "I'll Take Care of You." There is an intimacy. Listening closely, you can discern a squeak from Charlie's bass drum pedal, audible on the quiet verses. Mick offers a mournful-yet-defiant tale of the lovelorn Lothario character he would continue to portray for decades. "There've been so many girls that I've known/I've made so many cry." Here he offers a tale of warning to another dude: "You'll never break her heart of stone." He offers a cool, understated ad-libbed "mmm" before the solo comes in at 1:10, a somewhat unexpected point for a solo, as it is where the second half of the verse lyric should come.

The most immediate hook is the ". . . never break, never break, never bre—ak," followed by the drop out. Keith had by this time emerged as the main backing vocalist for the band. Bill and Brian, both of whom had been sharing backing vocal duties, receded further into the background.

The recording was still very garage-y, but the arrangement was well assembled, with the two guitars and bass playing distinct parts. The piano (played by Nitzsche) was in the bass-end of the register, while Bill played the main riff on the neck of the bass, which sounds like the low strings on a guitar. The tremolo guitar from Brian clanged away and comes to the fore in the definitive mono mix. A sloppy off-beat tambourine echoes loudly. Unlike the pleasantly unsteady "Time Is on My Side," the band members are all on the same page here.

Those regular nine-to-five Hollywood studio hours were jettisoned for these lurking creatures of the night, perfect for this slithery, lugubrious ballad. Oldham stayed in the studio until 7:00 A.M. finishing the masters. Soon after the session he proclaimed to the press: "This session has produced a new Rolling Stones sound, and certainly brought out the best of Keith."

5
The Last Time

RECORDING:

January 17 and 18, 1965, RCA Studios, Los Angeles

RELEASES:

US LP: *Out of Our Heads*, July 1965

UK LP: *Out of Our Heads*, September 1965

UK single, February 1965, charting at number 1

US single, March 1965, charting at number 9

Jagger/Richards Find Their Songwriting Groove

One of the most important early songs from the band, "The Last Time" is a driving, angry record that combines a multitude of the band's primary influences: soul, blues, and pop. There is even a bit of rockabilly in there. The recording is an archetype, with an Everly Brothers–like acoustic guitar rhythm that chugs the song along, and one of the first of many unforgettable Stones guitar riffs—this one from Brian Jones, who can be seen playing it in live clips—that riff master Keith calls, "the first recognizable Stones riff or guitar figure." Oldham calls it the first "real, live single for the Rolling Stones." It was their first international hit.

The initial songwriting efforts from Mick and Keith tended toward ballads, most of which were on the fey side of Merseybeat and were handed off to other recording artists. (Initially, such songs were easier for Mick and Keith to write.) "The Last Time" was the first up-tempo rock song the pair felt confident in bringing to the band. The song is the title and chorus lyric derivative from the Staple Singers' arrangement of a traditional gospel number, "This May Be the Last Time." Keith had been trying to learn the chords of that one when he stumbled into his own version. Mick and Keith wrote it together in their flat in London, initially unhappy with the title and groping around for another before circling back to the original title.

The Stones were consciously tapping into the tradition of soul, gospel, pop, and even folk songwriting, the kind that extends back through American music's roots to Celtic traditions. Writing an upbeat pop song in and of itself might not be the hardest thing to do, but the importance of "The Last Time" was in discovering something in their own style that they could add to this river of shared musical consciousness, and a "bridge" song, a pivotal composition that was singularly Rolling Stones and could stand up to the repertoire of strong covers they had been recording.

By this time, Mick and Keith were sequestering themselves in their apartment, whenever home, but more often in hotel rooms wherever they happened to be, writing constantly. "I didn't take any notice of it," Charlie mused. "It was just Mick and Keith writing something that we were playing as the Rolling Stones. Slowly they were writing songs like 'Satisfaction.' I don't know how they got there."

"We'd stay in the hotel and write because the pressure was *that* great that you *had* to have a hit single *every* three months," Keith explains. "Once we found we could write songs it was a real turn-on."

In "The Last Time," the Stones amp up and mash up Buddy Holly–style rockabilly with a Link Wray–like raw guitar sound. That relentless taunting riff and the chugging rhythm guitar are answered with crashing drums. The kick drum is barely discernible, if at all, amid the din. The tambourine is perversely higher in the mix than the entire drum kit. Bill's bass is locked in with Charlie, leaving plenty of space. "The Last Time" is the sound that launched a million garage bands; it doesn't get much more punk rock than this.

The mix is murky, especially compared to their other tracks from RCA Studios, including what ended up as the B-side, "Play With Fire." RCA had no isolation booths, only baffles (moveable partitions) that they would use sparingly, so there is a lot of "bleeding" between instruments and amplifiers. "Recording live offers the advantage of audio sensuality, which layered-and-divided tech just cannot give you," writes Oldham. "A stab at the piano will leak over the room and connect with a certain smile of the high-hat or bass. They'll embrace and create a new harmonic, and you'll have that on tape, even though no one person played it. It's the voodoo of space and tone."

There is no element with any marked degree of presence in the mix, though the solo comes closest to the fore. But the performances are all urgent. At around 1:30, Brian stumbles a little on the lick, but the band rolls on, right into Keith's rocking Buddy Holly–like solo of alternating the high-string chords with bluesy bends and licks. In addition to his electric solo, Keith propels the song with an acoustic guitar blended with the rhythm section. Though famous for containing one of the first Stones riffs, the song is also an indication that the thrust of the Stones would be the rhythmic engine fueled by Keith. The two-guitar sound, with a riff snaking in and out of a steady rhythm, was established early as a hallmark of the band's sound.

Mick's vocal is low in the mix, along with Keith's spot-on harmonies, resulting in a more guitar-driven, rockier version. The Stones were reared on those Chess records, on which the lead vocalists were just one of the band. It was an overall soup of sound. Listeners would really have to zone in to discern specific lyrics, which was part of the fun for fans of the early Stones as well. It added to the enigmatic allure. "On those early records Mick was singing totally incomprehensible Southern Negro lyrics to white kids," said Keith. The lead vocal on "The Last Time" is uninhibited and assertive. Mick even gets so jazzed by the end that he slides up into that screech we would later hear on "Monkey Man" and "Sympathy For the Devil."

When the song was mixed, Oldham excitedly beckoned Phil Spector down to the studio to hear the results. Oldham knew it was their first bona fide American hit, he just wanted to hear it from Spector's lips. Phil predicted (correctly) that it would be a number ten on the US charts. In the UK, their sixth single hit number one on most charts (there being no unified hit singles chart at the time) during the second week and stayed there for close to a month.* The Rolling Stones had broken the all-important Top Ten in America, though, and with Mick and Keith under pressure and working furiously in their hotel rooms, the boys had their sites set on number one.

---

* The orchestral version from the Andrew Loog Oldham Orchestra was sampled by the Verve for their "Bittersweet Symphony" hit single in 1997, resulting in a lawsuit from Allen Klein's ABKO publishing company, owner of the rights to the song.

6
Play with Fire

RECORDING:

January 17 and 18, 1965, RCA Studios, Los Angeles

RELEASES:

US LP: *Out of Our Heads*, July 1965

UK LP: *Out of Our Heads*, September 1965

UK single, February 1965, B-side for "The Last Time"

US single, March 1965, B-side for "The Last Time"

Getting Their Kicks in LA,
and Tiaras by the Score

The B-side for the "The Last Time" single, "Play with Fire," was recorded late at night on the same day. The band was knackered, zipping into the Los Angeles studio while on a twenty-four-hour stopover, en route from a whirlwind tour of the UK to another run of dates in Australia, New Zealand, and Asia. On January 15, 1965, they made an appearance on the UK television show, *Ready, Steady, Go*. On the 16th, their second UK LP, *Rolling Stones No. 2,* was released (with the same sleeve cover as the American release of *12 X 5*). On the 17th and 18th, they were at RCA

Studios, and on the 21st, they were in Sydney. This was a fairly typical run for the band, who kept up a breakneck pace from 1963–1966. By the time they rolled tape on "Play with Fire," Mick and Keith were "the only Stones left standing," writes Keith.

The composition of "Play with Fire" was credited to Nanker Phelge, the pseudonym the band used in the 1960s for compositions that featured more of the group than just Mick and Keith as writers. A "nanker" was a particularly grotesque face that Brian, Keith, and Mick would make, usually involving fingers inserted in nostrils. James Phelge had been a roommate of theirs when they were at their rudest and crudest. He had been lauded by the band for his highly developed talent to out-disgust all comers.

"Play with Fire" was definitive to the Stones in a different way than "The Last Time." While the A-side was an archetype of the band—a swinging rocker that aims its anger at the subject (a girl who doesn't try "very hard to please"), "Play with Fire" featured more ambitious subject matter for the Jagger/Richards team. Mick, in particular, was already exploring the issue of class and societal ranking in his lyrics, a sort of satire he introduced here and which continued through other early Stones songs like "19th Nervous Breakdown" and "Mother's Little Helper," and later songs like "Respectable," even as the band would eventually enjoy the jet-set trappings and social acceptance themselves. Though some lines, like "Tiaras by the score," are funny, the message of "Play with Fire" mostly comes off as a brooding, ominous admonition from a singer who counsels his young heiress, "But you better watch your step, girl. . . ."

The hushed tone of the production of "Play with Fire" sounds like the song could not have been recorded at any other hour than late at night, which is indeed the case: The tape rolled as a janitor wandered in to clean up. Keith recalls the custodian, "silently sweeping in the corner of this huge studio, while the remaining group"—Phil Spector, Nitzsche, Mick, and Keith—recorded. Spector plays a detuned guitar to get a bass sound (credited as a "zoom bass"), and Nitzsche provides percussive harpsichord and tamtam drums, Moroccan tabla-like instruments, that rattle out hauntingly at the end. Keith plays acoustic guitar while Jagger sings and plays the tambourine.

While the recording itself has that 4 A.M. vibe, the mix is actually quite striking in its clarity, particularly paired with the noisy, clanging "The Last Time" on the A-side. Much of this effect has to do with the sparse instrumentation, with fewer open microphones and not many instruments fighting for space in the frequency spectrum. The sound is intimate and, as a consequence, the foreboding of the lyric sounds far more imminent than on the A-side or in any previous songs. Mick keeps the drama steady, spitting out lines and just barely reining in his simmering resentment—unlike "The Last Time," which finds him screeching out "no, no, no!" by the end. He harnesses the finger-pointing menace of the simmering blues songs they were covering, but with this single combination, A-side and B-side, we have the first true Stones record.

With the "English-ness" of the lyric characterized by specific districts like Knightsbridge, Stepney, and St. John's Wood, the band started to play inward for British audiences, writing with authority about places and subjects they knew, while also turning on American kids to British references that would show up with increasing frequency in Beatles, Ray Davies, and Pete Townshend–authored songs.

Here they were in swimming-pool-blue-sky Hollywood recording a surly, dark, distinctly English folk song featuring a harpsichord. With their first early songwriting efforts, "Mick immediately went into an early English style," says Charlie. "That music was the very, very beginning of flower power; there were a few bands, like Pentangle, who played that stuff." The juxtapositions resulting from the back-and-forth trips between the UK and American tours and sessions were jarring for the band.

Even as the Stones were starting to enjoy the newfound status that came with their early success, they presented themselves as outsiders from the lower rungs of English society, not boy-toys for the rich girls who undoubtedly joined the throngs of young women of all classes vying for their attention.

And the boys were presenting themselves as something hard to handle, "rollin' stones," rambling men not to get too attached to. Not quite misogynist (depending on who you ask), the Jagger/Richards team was commencing an anti-romantic theme in their writing that continued with "Under My Thumb," "Stupid Girl," "Some Girls," and so on. And even at their most benevolent, the Stones weren't writing love songs so much as lust songs. While the Beatles had just released *Rubber Soul,* with the malevolent "Run For Your Life" the month prior, they had mostly been recording straight-up love songs until this point, with relatively few exceptions. The Stones, on the other hand, were delineating a more consistent darkness in tone from other rock 'n' roll combos and writing more obviously about sex than any other white artists.

7
(I Can't Get No) Satisfaction

RECORDED:

May 11 and 12, 1965, RCA Studios, Los Angeles

RELEASES:

US LP: *Out of Our Heads*, July 1965

UK LP: *Out of Our Heads*, September 1965

US single, June 1965, charting at number 1

UK single, August 1965, charting at number 1

The Stones Blast into Worldwide Superstardom

This raw classic cemented the Stones as the nasty anti-Beatles. The timing couldn't have been more perfect as the band had just come through their latest bout of controversy.

The infamous pissing incident happened at a roadside garage on March 18, 1965. The band was rolling through London after a show, when they had to stop at an East London filling station, with Bill badly needing to take a leak. The longhairs were denied access to the facilities in the station, and so Mick, Brian, and Bill simply peed against a wall. Outraged, the mechanic on duty reported the

Stones, had them arrested, and the case reached the East Ham Magistrate's Court. They were found guilty of charges of "insulting behavior" and "obscene language" (in response to the order from the proprietor to "Get off my forecourt!" Brian pithily replied, "Get off my foreskin!") and ordered to pay fines. It all added to the band's image as antiheroes. It was mere child's play compared to what would come later.

The folklore of the band took hold around this time musically as well, with Keith's well-told creation myth about waking up in the middle of the night with the "Satisfaction" riff in his head, recording it, and falling back asleep with the tape still recording his snoring. In the morning, he said he "pushed rewind and there was 'Satisfaction.'" He presented it to Mick as a folk song originally. Keith had the line "I don't get no satisfaction," ingrained in his subconscious from years of listening to Chuck Berry's "30 Days," which includes the line, "If I don't get no satisfaction from the judge." Mick wrote the rest of the words around that famous double negative while lounging poolside at a Clearwater, Florida hotel. Keith says the way they wrote the song became typical for how he and Mick collaborated. "I would say on a general scale, I would come up with the song and the basic idea," Keith wrote, "and Mick would do all the hard work of filling it in and making it interesting."

Four days later, they recorded a version of the track with acoustic accompaniment at Chess, with underwhelming results. But a couple of days after that, they recorded the hit version at RCA in Hollywood. "It was unusual for a song to be allowed longer than thirty minutes to find its way, let alone be given a second chance," Oldham points out. Oldham, though, recognized the potential of the song in that embryonic state.

With this second chance, Keith's riff was given a nasty distorted guitar tone that came from a new Gibson Maestro Fuzz Tone pedal bought by Stu in LA for Keith to try out. The result was the most memorable and distinctive guitar riff in rock. Keith has always claimed this guitar part was just there as a placeholder as he was trying to map out horn parts; horns were supposed to play the riff (as was done on the later cover version from Otis Redding). "But the fuzz tone had never been heard before," says Keith, "and that's the sound that caught everybody's imagination." By taking something not unlike the lick in "The Last Time" and making it sound sinister, monolithic, and sharp, like a giant angry bee, the "Satisfaction" riff formed the bony spine of a song that became a backdrop for the increasingly turbulent mid-sixties.

Neither Mick nor Keith thought of the song as a single, but Andrew knew it was a hit the moment it was in the can. So he put it to a vote and everyone voted yes, while Keith and Mick voted no. They were outvoted. "Next thing I know, we're listening to ourselves in Minnesota somewhere on the radio, 'Hit of the Week,' and we didn't even know Andrew had put the fucking thing out! At first I was mortified. As far as I was concerned that was just the [demo]. Ten days on the road and it's number one nationally."

It may not have been as perfect as Keith wanted it, but it is such imperfections that make such recordings so endearing, whether or not we are conscious of them. The most famous riff of all time: It misfires in two of the four entry points in the song. You can actually hear the fuzz pedal click back on when the riff re-enters at 0:35 and again at 1:36, where it was late coming in, missing the first four notes of the riff. When it comes in for the final time (at 2:33), Keith actually switched it on too early, jumping the gun, as if determined not to be late like the previous one. It's funny when you realize how meticulously manicured such things are now via precision digital editing tools. Would any of that "fixing" make "Satisfaction" better? I think not.

"(I Can't Get No) Satisfaction," became the sound of the summer of 1965. Beyond containing that iconic riff, all of the elements of a great single were in place. Though the fuzz-tone lick is dominant, biting, and rigid, there is actually a sexy bobbing and weaving rhythm going on, primarily within the verses, between the tambourine, the woody bass, the acoustic guitar, and the slippery surf guitar licks that could be at home on a Beach Boys track. In fact, some of the Beach Boys records were made at RCA using the same echo chambers, and it is likely Nitzsche playing tambourine on some of those Beach Boys tracks as well.* That quieter fluid guitar part is a personal favorite element of "Satisfaction." Keith is in a groove, rarely playing the same figure twice, yet making it sound like a composed part that fits right into the track.

Bill and Charlie are the only ones steady here. Indeed, Charlie is almost metronomic, allowing everyone else to groove and slide all around his foundation. He plays a relentless 4/4 beat on the snare, like an Al Jackson Jr. drum break on a Stax record, throughout the whole song. In fact, he does not switch up the pattern at all. He stated to an interviewer in 2012 that the beat was "fashionable" at the time, citing "Uptight" by Stevie Wonder, and "Pretty Woman" by Roy Orbison as two other hit records that had the same beat.

It is questionable if Brian Jones is on the famous recording. I put this question to Andrew, to which he replied, "I think he may have played with Keith on the bed of acoustics that Mick sang to." As the Stones veered away from the straight blues that had formed their foundation, Brian played the guitar less frequently in the studio. Increasingly bitter over not having a part in the songwriting and not always on board with the material that Mick and Keith were composing, Brian would either find other instruments to occupy himself with or not contribute at all. Indeed, he started to skip sessions with increasing frequency and became less reliable as

---

* To complete the Beach Boys/Stones circle, on the *Pet Sounds Sessions* box set, it's fun to hear pianist Don Randi play the "Satisfaction" riff, goofing off between takes, as Brian Wilson is heard directing the studio musicians assembled for the monumental recording of "God Only Knows," in March 1966.

he slipped into drug abuse (both uppers and downers). And when he did show up, he was usually dour, petulant, or cutting. He was known to sarcastically play the notes of the "Popeye the Sailor Man" theme song when the Stones played "Satisfaction" live.

Keith played the electric and laid down an acoustic guitar as an overdub on "Satisfaction," with that trademark Richards sense of rhythm—an emphasis on the upstroke. In addition to the inventive tambourine, which breaks up the otherwise unvarying rhythm, Nitzsche plays piano, which can be heard playing up and down a three-chord arrangement like the rest of the instruments. Oldham rightly points out that, though it is barely audible, it serves as glue to keep the various elements together. Acoustic guitar almost always serves the same function, as it does here, sitting harmonically between the drums, hi-hat, and other guitars.

The structure, as with many Stones songs, mirrors a sexual tension, a buildup, and a release—lather, rinse, repeat. The verses are relaxed, with Mick softly singing about not getting any satisfaction, no "girl reaction" (often misheard as "girly action"). He sounds almost reasonable. But quickly, he ramps it up, along with the band, climbing up a chord progression, Mick leading the way with those " 'Cause I tried, and I tried, and I tried, and I tried," like a comic wind-up of a big sneeze, until the big *ah-CHOO!* of the shouted chorus, the famous irreverent double negative of "I can't get no . . ."

Mick nailed the vocal in one take. Two of the vocal approaches from his bag of tricks are heard here—that round croon up close to the microphone, and the soul shouting. Few vocalists in pop music would have allowed themselves to sound so libidinous at the time. Mick takes a page from Elvis and exaggerates the huffing-and-puffing Big Bad Wolf routine even more. He uses the "I tried" pre-chorus to transition from the mellifluous and breathy approach, ramping up to an Otis Redding strain of belting. He stays up there—backing off the mic and shouting—for the post-choruses, which sound more like scattershot rants about some guy on television commercials bugging him about "how white my shirts can be," and another one on the radio annoying him with "some useless information." Though such awareness and satire of the advertising profession eventually became common, few songwriters were using it as subject matter in a two- or three-minute pop song in the mid-1960s.

While the lyric of "Satisfaction" lobbed humorous barbs at advertising and uptight sexual mores, the angst was generalized enough to be interpreted as reflecting a new generation's growing discontent with a sense of rigid conformity that had carried over from the 1950s. "Most young people are dissatisfied with the generation that runs their lives," Mick said shortly after the song became a hit. Sprinkled with humor and self-deprecation, the song was nevertheless a middle finger to that status quo. It offered a rallying cry for kids who were looking for something else, something which they might not have been able to articulate. Mick's protagonist (assuming it is not Mick himself) speaks only slightly more articulately than Roger Daltrey's stuttering angry young man would later that year, in The Who's "My Generation."

But with their young long-haired frontman, leering to the camera when they performed the song on *The Ed Sullivan Show* on February 13, 1966, the Stones promised an alternative beyond the square world of Lawrence Welk, Ozzie and Harriet, and toothpaste commercials. A message was received. It may sound innocent in 2012, but it would be a challenge to name a more subversive song being played on mainstream radio and television at that point.

But for all of the social commentary, really, Mick's protagonist has to admit in the end that it's the ladies letting him down, or one in particular, a girl he's trying to "make." "The dirtiest line in 'Satisfaction' they don't understand, see?" Mick admitted in 1966. "It's about *You better come back next week 'cause you see I'm on a losing streak*. But [people] don't get that. It's just life. That's really what happens to girls. Why shouldn't people write about it?"

See, if the man can't get no satisfaction while he's out on the road, or when a particular girl is on "a losing streak," telling him to "come back, maybe next week"—meaning it is *that time of the month*—all those daily annoyances are going to well up into some serious tension that can only be released in a pounding anthem like this. That release is mirrored in the drum break, where the whole band drops out to allow Charlie and the tambourine to keep pumping. As if the song needed any more hooks, they all come back in with the "Hey, hey, hey! That's what I say!" shout, a refrain that begs for singing along.

Mick was under the influence of Bob Dylan inasmuch as his lyrics are untethered to any common pop-song themes of the day. "I Got You Babe," "I'm Henry VIII, I Am," and "Help Me Rhonda" were the sorts of songs getting the most airplay in the United States. The song that finally unseated "Satisfaction" for number one in July was the Four Tops' "I Can't Help Myself (Sugar Pie, Honey Bunch)." "Satisfaction" gives just a small indication of the influence that Dylan was having on popular music in broadening the spectrum of what rock 'n' roll lyrics could explore. While the Beatles at the time were recording timeless songs on *Help!*, they were not yet the socially conscious or edgy lyrics they would later write. And, along with some mild social satire, the Stones had still been writing mostly about sex.

Much more would change in 1965, as pop music eventually followed Dylan's lead and began reflecting the shifting cultural and political forces at large. "There was trouble in America," Keith writes. "All these young American kids, they were being drafted into Vietnam. The lyrics and the mood of the songs fitted with the kids' disenchantment with the grown-up world of America, and for a while we seemed to be the only provider, the soundtrack for the rumbling of rebellion . . ."

The Beatles released "Ticket to Ride" in April 1965, and while there is no direct social or political message to the song, there is an intangible longing and restlessness implied in the lyric and an intensity to the track that had not yet been heard on the radio. But "Ticket to Ride" speaks to a more emotional and intellectual yearning, while Mick's self-deprecating, unfocused angst, set over a pumping danceable groove, still spoke more about what was going on (or not going on) below the waist than above the neck. While Dylan was setting his groundbreaking lyrics to Chuck Berry cadences much as the Stones were, "Satisfaction" was accessible to more teenagers than the headier, longer, and more obtuse Dylan songs like "Subterranean Homesick Blues."

The purely physical appeal of "Satisfaction," and the Stones' music generally, cannot be denied. While Oldham joins Keith in crediting Nitzsche with being a primary architect of the Stones sound from a technical standpoint, Jack also knew "how to inject sex into the sound . . . a gift of understanding between you and your third ear," wrote Oldham.

The sexual swagger is here in force. On their second album, the Stones had covered Muddy Waters's 1958 song, "I Can't Be Satisfied." The difference is, with Waters, the point is that he is always hungry and satisfaction never comes. His is a borderline murderous "troubled" man. Muddy's protagonist can't settle down and be satisfied by one woman. Mick's protagonist, however, is sexually frustrated and can't get *none to begin with*. Teenage boys all across the world heard someone on the radio expressing their dire situation.

Despite the sexual connotations, getting airplay proved to be no problem. The single was released in the US on June 6, 1965 and quickly became the band's first monster worldwide smash, their first number one in the US, their fourth in the UK, and a number one across Europe and Australia. It went gold (500,000 records sold) in the US in its second month. Powered by the wooly mammoth single, *Out of Our Heads* was also the band's first LP to go to number one in the US and was the biggest seller to date, eventually going platinum (one million sold). The big money started to roll in to the Stones camp.

With this commercial acceptance, the Stones became cognizant of the influence they had on their listeners and of themselves as mirrors of their time and place. "Our songs were taking on some kind of edge in the lyrics, or at least they were beginning to sound like the image projected onto us," Keith says. "Cynical, nasty, skeptical, rude." These were not words associated with 1965-era Beatles, never mind run-of-the-mill pop. "The Beatles want to hold your hand," wrote Tom Wolfe that year, "but the Stones want to burn down your town."

8
The Under Assistant West Coast Promotion Man

RECORDED:

May 10, 1965, Chess Studios, Chicago

RELEASED:

US LP: *Out of Our Heads*, July 1965

UK LP: *Out of Our Heads*, September 1965

US single, B-side to "Satisfaction"

Making Deals with Devils

Music business shysters and sleazeballs are the targets of "The Under Assistant West Coast Promotion Man," another band original that fleshed out a remarkably deep and balanced album, *Out of Our Heads*, and the US B-side of "Satisfaction."

The song's subject is a foot-soldier wannabe. It was meant as gentle ribbing of George Sherlock, the London Records promo man in America. Sherlock was a nervous guy with a George Hamilton perma-tan and teased hair, and his relatively low-level status at the label would have allowed the Stones to slyly have fun at the expense of the hustlers in the music biz without biting the hand that feeds. Of course, they were working with just such a hustler in their midst: their manager.

By 1965, the always-fragile relationship between band managers Eric Easton and Andrew Loog Oldham had come to a head. At the time, Easton was negotiating a deal with Decca that Oldham maintains was essentially his exit and a golden parachute, a deal that did not reflect the level of success the Stones had attained. Oldham thought of himself as one of the band, specifically part of the "Unholy Trinity" along with Mick and Keith. Easton could not be bothered to get involved with the band and thought of them as a flash-in-the pan, short-term, but lucrative talent. Mick and Keith sided with Oldham, while Bill and Brian mistrusted Mick, Keith, and Andrew, believing that Easton was looking after the whole band's best interest, not merely that of Mick and Keith. True to character, Charlie remained indifferent to the business side.

In early 1965, while in New York, Oldham, Jagger, and Richards met with the highly successful, old-school music-biz accountant and artist manager, Allen Klein. The arrangement they hashed out provided Oldham with the sort of business management muscle Oldham himself lacked. Klein could sense that Oldham was out of his depth from a business perspective and lacked the ability to manage the band during the next steps on their meteoric rise. Klein helped Oldham extricate himself and the Stones from the connections with Easton, but in the process Oldham assigned Klein the role of "comanager" of the group, with a 20 percent cut on earnings resulting from agreements forged by Klein. This deal resulted in mistrust within the band and would prove to have disastrous long-lasting financial ramifications.

Keith has often told the story about how Klein brought the boys into Decca to renegotiate their contract, telling the band to just keep their mouths shut and look tough. Wyman puts it that Klein meant to show a unity of purpose, and a "show of strength." As

Keith tells it, however, they had sunglasses on and stood behind Klein like mafia muscle, walking out with a great deal. "'We're going to work on these motherfuckers,'" he quotes Klein as saying. "'We're going to come out with the best record contract ever . . .' They crumbled and we walked out of there with a deal bigger than the Beatles'."

Brian and Bill's mistrust of Klein proved to be well-placed. All admit that Klein quickly ushered the band to a new level of bookings, bringing in far more earnings than they had ever imagined. However, this was thanks in no small part to the success of "Satisfaction," which Klein clearly had nothing to do with, other than being in the right place at the right time and having the experience and knowledge of what to do with this running start.

It took the band years to catch on that Klein was legally robbing them blind. Klein had deceptively formed a company in the US that had the same Nanker Phelge name as the band's collective partnership in the UK. Naturally, this led them to believe the company was the same, just with an overseas branch. On the contrary, this version of the company was owned completely by Klein and all funds were going into the US version of Nanker Phelge, which was fully controlled by Klein. "He still owns the publishing [rights] to 'Satisfaction' too, or his heirs do; he died in 2009," said Keith. "But I don't give a shit. He was an education."

Before the Stones understood all this, however, they just thought of these slick Americans like Sherlock and Klein as colorful characters. Klein proved worse than that, but for the time being, they enjoyed poking fun at guys like Sherlock. "The Under Assistant West Coast Promotion Man" is lifted from the Buster Brown rave-up, "Fannie Mae." A swinging 12-bar blues with an unyielding riff that serves as the hook, it places Brian Jones back in his wheelhouse, wailing on the blues harp like he is jamming back at the Ealing Jazz Club or the Crawdaddy. Charlie is loose-limbed, at his jazzy finest, with a bit of giddy-up in fills every four bars or so. His kick drum is nice and full sounding, thanks to Ron Malo's engineering back at Chess Studios. And as always, Bill plays with authority, setting well-chosen notes in just the right spaces left by Charlie. Bill plays like an upright bass player in an old rock 'n' roll combo, like Bill Black on Elvis Presley's early Sun records. Stu also seems to be having a boogie-woogie blast, audible in the mix for a change, playing up in the higher octaves.

Jagger artfully spews out seemingly cumbersome lyrics like "I'm the necessary talent behind every rock 'n' roll band" and the title itself, a self-important job title pointing to a level of bureaucracy worthy of *Catch-22*–like satire. The wordy title itself seemed like it could have easily been ripped off the back of a Bob Dylan album.

Mick, as usual, is the compelling force behind an otherwise also-ran number, which was the final band composition to be credited to band pseudonym Nanker Phelge. The lyric is clever, but not hilarious. Most 12-bar blues songs like this—even revved up here with a brisk R&B tempo—are by their very nature dependent on a strong vocal and lyric to keep listeners' attention. And Mick does not disappoint, swinging his vocal in an otherwise dry first-person account of how "They laugh at my toupee, they're sure to put me down," like a music industry Eeyore.

The song was recorded in a nine-hour session on May 10 at Chess, the same that had produced the first version of "Satisfaction," along with "Mercy, Mercy," "That's How Strong My Love Is," and "Try Me." It is indicative of how solid and unified *Out of Our Heads* is as an LP, arguably the first cohesive and consistently excellent Stones LP. It sounds and feels more self-assured, solid, and purposeful than their previous albums, which are merely collections of songs. It marks the beginning of a long career of iconic Stones albums, coinciding with the peak of rock 'n' roll's cultural significance, and the apex of the LP album's importance as a medium.

The Stones were no longer just a blues band, though that music remained their first love. Their pop success allowed them to not only add a straight-up blues number to a B-side, as in this case, but they had already leveraged their popularity in the UK to release "Little Red Rooster" as a single. And in the US, they even requested to have Howlin' Wolf and Son House on the television show *Shindig!* with them in May 1965. They took their role as ambassadors for the blues seriously.

And people noticed. When he turned on *Shindig!* a young white American blues fan, Peter Guralnick—who went on to be the acclaimed author of *Sweet Soul Music: Rhythm and Blues and the Southern Dream of Freedom,* and biographies of Sam Cooke and Elvis Presley—couldn't believe he was seeing his obscure musical idols when he turned on the television: Howlin' Wolf and Son House!

I asked Guralnick what his general reaction to the Stones had been as one of the relatively few kids "in the know" about American blues, one who didn't necessarily need to have a British band evangelizing to him and his friends, the already converted. Guralnick shared with me a recollection he had just written for the *Times of London*:

I first saw the Rolling Stones in person in Worcester, Massachusetts, a mid-sized city forty-five miles outside of Boston, on April 30, 1965. It was the start of their third U.S. tour, and we were excited most of all by their unabashed love of the blues. All the marketing publicity in the world couldn't hold a candle to their embrace of a music that my friends and I felt no one else could love the way we did . . . but the Stones presented the music with incandescent belief, and for me the most indelible moment of this American visit would come three weeks later when Brian Jones and Mick Jagger introduced the Howlin' Wolf to a national television audience on *Shindig!*, and mainstream America for the first time saw the real face of the blues. It was epic.

And bluesmen like Muddy Waters appreciated it; many years later, Waters stated "When I started out, they called my music 'nigger music.' People wouldn't let that kind of music into the house. The Beatles started, but the Rolling Stones really made my kind of music acceptable. I really respect them for opening doors for black music . . . I'll tell ya, the guitar player ain't bad either."

9
I'm Free

RECORDED:

September 6, 1965, RCA Studios, Los Angeles

RELEASES:

US LP: *December's Children (And Everybody's)*,
December 1965
UK LP: *Out of Our Heads*, September 1965
B-side to US single "Get Off of My Cloud," September 1965

Freedom Comes with an Expanding Sonic Palette

The band was pumping out hooky hits with consistency by this time. *December's Children (And Everybody's)** was the US LP that had the smash hit "Get Off of My Cloud," an undeniably

---

* The America-only-released LP, *December's Children*, is widely regarded as an inconsistent album of odds and ends, compiled mainly of tracks that had been released on the UK version of *Out of Our Heads*. "*December's Children* isn't an album, it's just a collection of songs," is how Mick put it in 1968. The UK LP version of *Out of Our Heads* and the US LP *December's Children (And Everybody's)* are almost identical.

catchy number and follow-up single to "Satisfaction," that went to number one more quickly in America. While different in sound, "Get Off of My Cloud" has a similar raving sort of vocal as "Satisfaction" and an up-and-down riff like the previous hit. It captures a taste of the mod mid-sixties, the amphetamine-fueled "Swinging London" culture, as well as chronicles the go-go Stones themselves—a pleading rant from a stressed-out band to be left alone for a spell.

Though, with its frantic lyric and unimaginative "La Bamba"/"Twist and Shout" chord changes, it is a weak follow-up to one of the all-time great rock 'n' roll songs. Its B-side, "I'm Free," however, heralded a new sort of relaxed, shuffling Stones sound that would resonate forward into songs ranging from "Under My Thumb" to "You Can't Always Get What You Want" and beyond. If the Stones sounded like they had been amped up on speed and hormones early on, "I'm Free" sounds like they had discovered pot.

The most apparent influences on "I'm Free" are the Beatles, Motown, and folk rock. With their early-1960s trips to America, the Stones had wide exposure to the contemporary hits of Stax and Motown, whose soul artists were mapping out a future for pop music that had depth and integrity, unlike most of the disposable packaged pop hits in the US and UK. The Stones were avowed fans of the music produced by Motown, but they initially chose to steer clear of covering it, as it was more the turf of the Beatles. The Stones gravitated more toward the raw Southern strain of soul—Otis Redding, Aretha Franklin, Solomon Burke, and William Bell.

On "I'm Free," though, you can feel the sway of the Funk Brothers, the studio band on most of Motown's records—that swinging groove heard on numbers like "How Sweet It Is (To Be Loved By You)" and "The Way You Do the Things You Do." There are also the strains of the upbeat soul-pop of Don Covay, who was a primary influence on Mick in particular during this era and whose records featured the fluid guitar playing of a young James "Jimi" Hendrix.

Mick nudges "I'm Free" away from its sunny major-key pop vibe with his style of singing, which stemmed from his experience singing blues, as well as the more immediate influence of the contemporary soul records he had been soaking up. He could not sing a song straight if his life depended on it. His approach has always been to slide up and down into and out of notes, hitting blue notes in between. He and Keith were never as precise as the singers in the Beatles. For example, the way the Beatles approached "You Really Got a Hold On Me" was to sing it straighter than Smokey Robinson's original. The Stones, by contrast, always played up the bluesy qualities on Motown covers like "Hitch Hike." As the years went by, the Beatles seemingly learned to loosen up those early habits of landing spot onto a note. Mick arrived on record singing like the black artists he so emulated. On "I'm Free," he also backs himself up with some overdubbed funky falsetto, and it operates as another hook.

And yet, the imprint of the burgeoning sound of folk-rock on "I'm Free" is as evident as any soul or R&B influence. The Byrds, who were directly influenced by the more jangly Rickenbacker 12-string moments of the Beatles, had just released their landmark debut LP, *Mr. Tambourine Man,* over the summer of 1965. That LP had followed the April release of *Help!,* with the monumental "Ticket to Ride" and its distinctive swirling riff around the open 12-string-guitar chord.*

Some have pointed to Lennon and McCartney's first experience with LSD, or at least their acquaintance with marijuana, as inspiration leading to the newfound intensity of the sound of "Ticket to

---

* As opposed to a bar—or "barre"—chord. Open chords can both ring out and create a drone. If you move back and forth between, say, an open D and an open G chord, you can keep the open G string chiming over the changes.

Ride." The shimmering guitars offer a feeling of unmoored floating over the pounding bass and rumbling tom tom drums. While it scintillates on the top, it rumbles low and heavy on the bottom, perhaps an influence from the powerful band, The Who, who had started to become a popular live attraction around London in 1965. "Ticket to Ride" is also the first Beatles recording longer than three minutes, and as such, freed in another way.

The sound of the sixties was opening up from pop and rock 'n' roll into something psychologically and musically deeper—into late-1960s psychedelia and heavy rock. The word "hippy" and the sensibilities it signified would not take root until 1966, but the seeds of such ideas were in place in 1965. Within a year, the impact of pot and acid would be heard throughout pop music made on both sides of the Atlantic.

"I'm Free," while a catchy number, does not have anywhere near the same musical heft as "Ticket to Ride." The Stones' recording sounds as if the band did not attempt more than one take of the track. It is a rare recorded case of plain sloppy playing on Charlie's part. Though he ambles along pleasingly on the verses, he never sounds completely confident on the chorus stops, feeling his way, and stumbling badly coming out of the forgettable guitar solo from Keith, at about 1:30. Studio percussionist James Alexander tries to match up with him on the tambourine. And there is an audible clam (bum note) on the bass at 2:02.

The influence of the swirling guitars and tambourines of the Byrds—who had opened up shows for the Stones West Coast shows over the summer—indicated a widening of the Stones' sonic palette. Keith's guitar has a coruscating effect, like tremolo. Brian, who had been struggling to find his role as Mick and Keith wrote more songs—and as Mick became the obvious star of the band—had started to experiment with instruments around RCA Studios. On "I'm Free," he adds a bed of organ chording that meshes perfectly with the guitars, resulting in a bit of droning to create the wall of sound the band had been cultivating under Oldham's watchful eye.

Playing "Ticket to Ride" and "I'm Free" back-to-back, one is struck by the similarity of the musical approach. It is also obvious how weak the latter is compared to the former—which is not a fair comparison, nor is it the point. "I'm Free" sports an easygoing grooving sound also found on "Gotta Get Away," on the same album. Both of the Stones songs had the relaxed shuffle feel and a singsong verse, nailed down by a more strident chorus.

Aside from the musical similarities, there is the common theme of freedom. In "Ticket to Ride," it is the female subject that the narrator sings about in the second person who has found her freedom: "She would never be free when I was around." In "I'm Free," though, it is the freewheeling young single guy narrating the song who has left the shackles of his girl behind: "Love me, hold me . . . But I'm free."

This would become a consistent subject in the early triumphant years of the Stones, as the band members found themselves in demand musically and personally, leaving the remnants of their early love lives behind in England while young women vied for their affection everywhere they went. The guy who couldn't get "no girl reaction" just months prior now felt fancy-free and in demand. The song more or less declares how Mick lived his love life for the decades that followed, and might have served well as a prenuptial warning to his future love interests.

Additionally, the concept of freedom would become a predominant pop songwriting theme throughout the rest of the 1960s and 1970s. Sure, there was the free-love/summer of love/"love the one you're with" hippy philosophy, but freedom had obvious social and political resonance as countercultures in western countries struggled against the generally conservative status quo. And there were concrete and vital struggles for freedom seen in the Civil Rights marches in the American South and in suppression behind the Iron Curtain.

It is not that "I'm Free" in and of itself addresses these specific larger concerns directly. It's just about a dude not wanting to settle down. But it was consonant with other songs of the era about spreading one's horizons and casting off personal shackles—like "She's Leaving Home," "Ruby Tuesday," and "Me and Bobby McGee"—and ran concurrently through the Zeitgeist of the mid-to-late 1960s with more broadly sociopolitical songs, like Dylan's 1964 "Chimes of Freedom."

"I'm Free" is a simple little B-side that the Stones performed as late as 1969 but then was largely forgotten for another twenty-one years. It was covered in 1990 by the Soup Dragons, who scored a hit with their dance version of the song. The Stones themselves revisited it for their *Stripped* live LP in 1995, and again in the Martin Scorsese *Shine A Light* live documentary, probably encouraged by the use of the song in a television commercial.

" 'I'm Free,' I had forgotten about that for nearly thirty years," said Keith in 1995. "It just came out of a dinner break. I wasn't hungry, nor was Chuck Leavell, and we started playing 'Tracks of My Tears' for fun. Everybody was eating while we were playing and having fun. I looked at Chuck and said, 'Do we have one that goes like this, like '60s soul? We must have one somewhere.' Suddenly, from somewhere, it came to me: 'I'm Free.' "

10
As Tears Go By

RECORDED:

October 26, 1965, IBC Studio, London

RELEASES:

US LP: *December's Children (And Everybody's),*
December 1965
UK LP: *Out of Our Heads,* September 1965
US single, December 1965, charting at number 6
UK B-side to "19th Nervous Breakdown," February 1966

Orchestrating Commercial Success
with Marianne Faithfull

While it would be possible (though difficult) to write about the early to mid-sixties Beatles without mentioning the Stones, it would be impossible to do the inverse. By the time the Stones finally released their version of "As Tears Go By," the first song that Mick and Keith wrote, the Beatles had come out with "Yesterday," one of the most beautiful ballads and most-recorded songs of all time. Coming out with another chamber-laden lonely-boy lament was sure to elicit comparisons, and certainly the Stones did not do much to avoid the similarity. Indeed, recording it was a calculated commercial decision.

However, the song was *written* years before anyone heard "Yesterday." The accepted narrative of the Rolling Stones' early years has it that "As Tears Go By" is the first song that the Jagger/Richards songwriting team produced from their initial locked-in-the-kitchen writing session in fall of 1963, and Keith mentions the song in his recounting of that episode:

> We sat there in the kitchen and I started to pick away at these chords. . . . "It is the evening of the day." I might have written that. "I sit and watch the children play." I certainly wouldn't have come up with that. We had two lines and an interesting chord sequence, and then something else took over somewhere in the process. I don't want to say mystical, but you can't put your finger on it.

Oldham had not only directed the pair to write their own songs for once, but explicitly told them not to come out of there with any more blues, for godsakes. They found these ballads easier to write anyway. But it would take a few more original compositions under their belt before they took any of those initial numbers to the band for consideration. Instead, they wrote a lot of material that they felt was following formulas, songs in which they felt no personal investment, which they gave to Oldham to pitch to other artists to record.

Oldham tweaked the original title and refrain line from "As Time Goes By," to "As Tears Go By," distancing the song from the old standard with that title made famous in the film *Casablanca*, and ratcheting up the navel-gazing melancholy in the process. Still not enamored with the song, Jagger reluctantly and nonchalantly cut a demo at Regent Studio with some session musicians to give

Oldham something with which to shop the song to other artists. Not even Keith was present at the demo session.

Oldham received a cowriting credit for the title switch and for substantial rearrangement of the song as he prepared it for his next protégée. Oldham had been looking for a new artist for his portfolio when he discovered Marianne Faithfull, an angelic seventeen-year-old from an outcast branch of an eccentric and vaguely aristocratic family, just freed from a convent school. Oldham had met her at a launch party for another young singer. "The moment I caught sight of her, I recognized my next adventure, a true star," Oldham recalled. "In another century you'd have set sail for her; in 1964 you'd record her."

Faithfull had been kicking around coffee house–type gigs with a Joan Baez–influenced repertoire. She auditioned for Oldham accompanying herself on an acoustic guitar. In Oldham's estimation she could barely sing but, combined with her stunning beauty, had a certain Grace Kelly–like appeal to her voice.

When it came time to assemble the repertoire for a record that Oldham would produce, he came to the song, still with its original title, as an idea for a B-side. He told Mick that he thought "As Tears Go By" could make a potentially great record. Jagger demurred. Oldham then replied that he thought he had someone for whom the song might work well. "Do what you bloody well like with it," Oldham recalls Jagger replying, "it's finished as far as I'm concerned." (Looking back at the song in Martin Scorsese's 2008 *Shine a Light* concert documentary, Mick introduced it with a disclaimer: "We gave it to someone else because we were slightly, *slightly,* embarrassed by it the first time we wrote it.")

On the resulting recording, made just weeks after Mick and Oldham's demo session, Faithfull sang it like she's on the middle-of-the-road, early-1960s *Eurovision* song contest: straight-up, on the beat, with minimal vibrato, chanteuse style, sort of like an English Francoise Hardy. The arrangement was far more up-tempo, though still melancholy, compared with the Stones' own take on it a year later.

"People said 'As Tears Go By' was written especially for me," Faithfull said, "but, no, the song had been written already and it wasn't suitable for [the Stones]. . . . But I always thought it was a bit odd for me to be singing a song like that. It was really meant for a woman of about forty who is looking back on her life, not some innocent seventeen-year-old girl. It took a long time to take off— about three months before it got into the charts." It was released as a single in the UK the same day in June 1964 that the Stones' UK *Five by Five* EP was released. Faithfull's record went as high as number nine in the British charts and number twenty-two in America.

Seeing the royalty checks roll in over the course of the next year spurred on Mick and Keith to continue this lucrative endeavor of writing songs. The success of the Faithfull record, coupled with that of the strings-laden 1965 Beatles smash "Yesterday," encouraged the Stones to record their own version of "As Tears Go By" in a chamber-pop style similar to what the Beatles had done. Though the Stones had written "As Tears Go By," and Oldham's orchestrated production of Faithfull's single was released well before the Beatles released "Yesterday," the Beatles track—which featured an austere and haunting arrangement with Paul McCartney accompanying himself on guitar and only a small string section backing him—certainly influenced the similar arrangement on the Stones track. Both are heavy on the rainy-day mood. The Faithfull single is downright jaunty by comparison.

The Stones recorded their version at IBC in October 1965 with their early champion, Glyn Johns. Andrew had approached Johns to make amends for luring the Stones away from their contract with IBC and wanted to once again work with the talented engineer. It took some convincing for the jilted Johns to come back on board, but he rejoined them for this session and continued to work sporadically with them into the 1970s.

On the "As Tears Go By" recording, Mick is accompanied only by Keith on an out-of-tune 12-string guitar (with an audible flub at 2:08) and a dramatic string arrangement from Mike Leander, working with Keith. Leander was an in-house arranger with Decca and went on to become one of England's most in-demand producers/arrangers, with the orchestration of the Beatles' "She's Leaving Home" to his credit.

Mick's glum opening lines get wrapped up in a bear hug of those sympathetic strings when they enter, amplifying the sentiment. In fact, they almost overwhelm the vocals. With such syrupy production devices enveloping brooding lyrics, these two songs, "Yesterday" and "As Tears Go By," form a ground zero for the Baroque pop/chamber rock subgenre that would peak during the next few years. Though Spector's early-1960s hits were highly orchestrated with layered instrumentation, it was really the doleful first-person Romantic narratives, heart-stirring small string ensembles, and more classical (less bluesy) melodies that differentiated the Baroque pop sound, which found its way into recordings by such bands as the Beach Boys and the Zombies. The Left Banke, whose 1966 hit, "Walk Away Renée," is often up as a prime example of the genre at its zenith, seemingly formed wholly from the chamber-pop influence of "Yesterday," "As Tears Go By," and subsequent songs like "Eleanor Rigby." (Fast forward to the 1990s, Belle & Sebastian were leaders in the renaissance of the sound among the indie rock set. There will always be a new set of heartsick collegiate boys and girls staring forlornly out at rainy streets from bus windows.)

Released in 1965, first in America on the *December's Children* LP, the band played "As Tears Go By," along with "Satisfaction" and "19th Nervous Breakdown," on their third appearance on *The Ed Sullivan Show*. Due to popular demand, DJs started playing the track in the US and it was consequently released as a single, backed with "Gotta Get Away," reaching the sixth position in the top ten

(Faithfull's single had peaked at 22 on the US charts). It came out in February 1966 in the UK, as a B-side to the "19th Nervous Breakdown" single.

The success of Faithfull's version of the song skyrocketed the seventeen-year-old into stardom that overwhelmed her but also brought her access to artists she idolized, such as Bob Dylan. She spent a week in his chaotic rarefied orbit at the Savoy Hotel during the tour immortalized in the D.A. Pennebaker documentary, *Don't Look Back,* as well as in her memoirs. Dylan came on to her and was frustrated when she spurned his advances, protesting that she was pregnant and engaged. But her marriage to poet John Dunbar was doomed and a relationship between Mick and Marianne would soon be blossoming romantically as he and actress-model girlfriend Chrissie Shrimpton were having a tumultuous time of it.

Marianne, along with Anita Pallenberg, were to become the most famous of the Stones' women of the sixties. Brian had met the model and actress Pallenberg in Munich on September 14, 1965, a month prior to the "As Tears Go By" session. As with Marianne, Anita came from a European aristocratic family. The attraction between Brian and Anita was immediate, intense, and the relationship grew quite serious by the middle of 1966, with Anita flying in to join the band during runs of tour dates. They were soon rock 'n' roll royalty. In New York, they would often hang out with Brian's new friend, Dylan, who announced to a Carnegie Hall audience that he had written "Like a Rolling Stone" for Brian. Dylan's anthem sketched a subject who used to be on top of it all but was slipping out of touch and was yesterday's news. There was the band reference in the title, of course, plus Dylan's own dedication. But Brian was more worried that the "Mr. Jones" of Dylan's "Ballad of a Thin Man" was a pointed reference to him. His paranoia made him wonder if he was meant as the clueless person who didn't know what was happening around him.

This paranoia did not help the already fraying relationships within the band. The real tensions between the increasingly inse-cure Brian and the Machiavellian Jagger/Richards team had yet to come to a boil, but Brian started to let his frustrations show in public. According to Bill, in response to comments from an inter-viewer that the vocals seemed buried on some tracks, Brian shot back, exasperated, "We're the *Rolling Stones,* not Mick Jagger! He might have done 'As Tears Go By' on his own, but he usually doesn't set out to be the only one on record. Mick sings, and we play the instruments. It's *us!* It's an integrated group thing and no one's trying to drown Mick out."

For the first song they wrote together, a song they had initially considered a throwaway, Mick and Keith's "As Tears Go By" be-came a pivotal song that brought Marianne fame, a relationship with Mick, hit singles for two separate acts, and a new mood and color to the palette of this hard rock 'n' roll band.

11
Under My Thumb

RECORDED:

March 6–9, 1966, RCA Studios, Los Angeles

RELEASES:

UK LP: *Aftermath*, April 1966

The Rolling Stones and Women

With songs like "Under My Thumb," the Stones invited charges of misogyny during a time of increasing feminist consciousness. Mick's narrator (not necessarily the writer/singer himself) starts off by claiming he is pushing back on a woman who once "had [him] down" and "pushed [him] around." It's another "tables turning" song like "It's All Over Now." But whereas the latter song merely has the protagonist leaving the girl who is mistreating him, in "Under My Thumb" Mick's singer ramps up a bad situation in an already dysfunctional relationship; it's payback time. By the end of it, "she's the sweetest (mmmm) pet in the world," only talking "when spoken to."

It's no wonder the Stones had to fend off criticism. The man had also penned the lyrics to "Stupid Girl," and would later write "Bitch" and "Some Girls." The humor, the concept of a distrustful narrator, and self-caricature within such songs, was not self-evident to all listeners. In an interview given about ten years after they recorded "Under My Thumb," Mick wrote it off as "adolescent" and "about adolescent experiences." Keith also chalked up such lyrical fodder as a "product of [their] environment." Too many possessive groupies and "dumb chicks." Keith posits that true women's liberation meant that it cut both ways, and young rock 'n' rollers weren't about to let women off the hook: "The Beatles and the Stones particularly did not release chicks from the fact of 'I'm just a little chick.'" Mick's explanation was that he was writing specifically about some bad early love affairs. "Obviously I was going through a series of bad relationships at the time," he later recalled of the "Under My Thumb" era. "It's a reflection of that." Keith also supports this more contained explanation: "The songs also came from a lot of frustration from our point of view. You go out on the road for a month, you come back, and she's with somebody else. Look at that stupid girl. It's a two-way street."

It wasn't just the touring that was having an edgy effect on the lyrics. The band was filling in any extra hours with studio time. The amount of recorded output and creative growth in 1965 was staggering. The band kicked off the year with *The Rolling Stones No. 2* (UK) and *The Rolling Stones, Now!* (US) in quick succession in January and February. By the end of the year, they had released *Out of Our Heads* (with two significantly different versions in the UK and US), *December's Children,* and seven singles, including their signature, "(I Can't Get No) Satisfaction."

And even then the group didn't let their foot off the accelerator. Before *December's Children* was released—poetically, in December 1965—the Stones had already regrouped for five days at RCA Studios in Hollywood to record a good chunk of what would be their next album, *Aftermath,* plus the single, "19th Nervous Breakdown," a hook-filled rocker that displayed remarkable songwriting growth and a unique mélange of sounds and textures. Wyman calls that track one of Jagger/Richards' "acerbic counterparts to the burgeoning hippy movement" and a "condemnation of the spoiled debutantes who, cushioned by material comfort, became self-indulgent."

Despite the unrelenting work schedule and all the perceived misogyny, the Stones were actually showing signs of settling down. Charlie had married Shirley Ann Shepherd in 1964 (and they remain married to this day). Bill married his wife, Diane, in 1959, well before he joined the band (although he didn't let that get in the way of his love life on the road). Keith had begun a relationship with Linda Keith, for whom he would write "Ruby Tuesday." Anita had moved in with Brian, a pad that quickly became one of the center points for Swinging London. Anita and Brian were like mirror images of each other, blond, beautiful, young people who helped set the glamorous image of cutting-edge 1960s London. Brian continued the rebellious and flamboyant style that had been his hallmark even before the Stones were famous. Anita already had been running in circles of "aristos" and artists. Together, they melded as a (flower) power couple. "How Anita came to be with Brian is really the story of how the Stones came to be the Stones," writes Marianne Faithfull. "She almost single-handedly engineered a cultural revolution in London by bringing together the Stones with the *jeunesse dorée*" (the young and wealthy).

Marianne would often visit them, staying at their flat as she fled her troubled first marriage with John Dunbar. Faithfull recalled the scene at Brian and Anita's pad as "bohemian" and a "mess," clouded with drugs, mostly marijuana. "I think Anita loved Brian very much," Marianne later reflected, "but he was very difficult to love. There were strange things going on with him and between them. There were bruises on her arms and we knew it was Brian."

In late 1966, Marianne started living with Mick after his relationship with Shrimpton started to fall apart. "The two of them used to have terrible fights." said Marianne. "They were quite nasty, really. You can hear the venom on their songs of the time like 'Under My Thumb.'" Marianne reads "19th Nervous Breakdown" as "a pitiless recital" of an emotional collapse that Shrimpton had on her first acid trip. There were dramatic blow-out fights with Mick and Shrimpton by this time. It was reported that she attempted suicide some time soon after Mick left her for Marianne. Shrimpton was admitted to a facility for treatment, the bill for which was sent to Mick, who returned it with instructions that all such bills be sent to Shrimpton directly.

As Marianne's marriage was crumbling, Mick showered her with attention and affection. She credits Mick—who only enjoyed drugs occasionally and managed to generally remain in control of himself—for saving her from falling too deeply and quickly into drugs. Marianne did, however, eventually succumb to well-documented lows in her struggles with addiction. Still, she points out, "I hate to think if I were involved with someone else more like me at the time. I probably wouldn't be here now."

It is this frenzied and drug-enhanced rock 'n' roll tableau in which the Stones were coming of age that provides the stage for the conversational "Under My Thumb." It's like the singer is intimating to a mate of his at one of these parties that all is under control now, as they eye his well-behaved girlfriend, this "squirmy dog who's just had her day," across the room. Mick's lyric is generally read as either a simple vindictive tale about a dysfunctional relationship between lovers, or worse, a misogynous rant from a sexist Neanderthal with control issues. The restrained cool of the music and vocal delivery reflects Mick's actual personal control, one who could observe the chaos around him and know when to pull back, observe, and then report in his songs.

The Jagger/Richards songwriting team generally would divide the duties of music (Keith) and words (Mick) though there were many cases where the division was not so clear cut, with Keith writing more words. *Aftermath* was the Stones' first LP to consist of all original Jagger/Richards songs. Though he has no songwriting credits on *Aftermath,* it's considered as much a Brian Jones record as a Mick and Keith record.

With sitar on "Paint it Black"; dulcimer on "Lady Jane" and "I Am Waiting"; an unrecognizable 12-string guitar played with a slide on "Mother's Little Helper"; a Japanese koto on "Take It or Leave It"; marimbas on "Out of Time" and "Under My Thumb"; and harpsichord on numerous tracks, Brian's exotic textures were increasingly layered across the stereo soundscape of *Aftermath* and on the singles from the era. With Keith left to handle most of the rock 'n' roll guitar parts, Brian became the Stones' "colorist" (Mick's term). He brought back influences and instruments from holidays in North Africa to combine with the ample supply of goodies at RCA Studios. "His contributions can be heard on every track," Oldham (who despised Brian by this point) admitted. "Sometimes Brian pulled the whole record together."

The first thing you notice on "Under My Thumb" is the marimba, of course, played by Brian. But the song starts with Charlie just tapping out three notes of time before he slips into one of the great Stones grooves, a shuffle right out of the playbook of Bernard Purdie, another drummer raised on jazz, who had been playing with James Brown, Aretha Franklin, and other giants of the 1960s. But it is predominantly the sound of Motown that we hear on "Under My Thumb." Compare the feel and finesse from Charlie—coupled with Bill's strong, very present bass—to tracks such as Mary Wells's "My Guy." As with the drumming on that 1964 track, Charlie adds a little giddy-up to the snare drum. It's not just the backbeat that he plays; it's all the jazzy shuffling in between the beats, the snare and hi-hat finding space left by Bill.

Bill works absolute bass magic here. Varying his counterintuitive bass pattern in a push-and-pull around Charlie's steady beat, making the groove so compelling, harmonizing with the marimba. Off in the background, Mick (presumably) is snapping his fingers on the backbeats. It's a classic opening, the sort that you could listen to on its own in an endless loop. The feel of it is perfect, ripe for sampling. Yet it promises something more. It's suspenseful in a tiptoe, "Pink Panther" sort of way, the Stones at their most laid-back cool. Not coincidentally, it was the tune the band would pull out in December 1969 at Altamont to try to soothe the rattled nerves of the Hells Angels–bullied crowd.

Keith's acoustic guitar (likely an overdub) and Stu's upright piano come crashing in along with Mick's opening lines, hands clapping in the background. The piano and acoustic accents are on the downbeats, pounding almost in opposition to the swinging free-and-easy intro. Bill switches sides, joining Stu and Keith by getting up on top of the beat for the whole of the verse. He is no longer deferring, but propelling.

As the song unspools, those staccato chops from Keith on the electric guitar eventually morph into a Stones prototypical "lead" guitar—i.e., a guitar part that slips from a rhythm part—to a featured solo, to some molten licks underscoring the bottom end, and inevitably, some Chuck Berry–inspired two-stringed riffing. In other words, Keith provides just what the song needs in an extraordinary display of tasteful restraint, deferring to the composition and ensemble. When the featured solo actually comes (over an increasingly out-of-tune acoustic guitar), Keith plays it understatedly. Instead of taking the obvious tack of sliding up to the high strings to cut through the mix and perhaps add one of those "Johnny B. Goode" riffs, he plays it low down, literally down on the lower end of the neck and fretboard, with a handful of well-chosen notes. He intuitively leaves a surfeit of space to feature the bass and marimba as well in the solo section. The clip-cloppy distorted bass overdub that Bill adds on the chorus is more "rock" than anything Keith

plays. The guitar part just morphs into a solo version of one of
the variations that Keith has been playing all along. It is as if the
guitarist is caught by surprise: "Oh, it's my solo?"

It's a disciplined arrangement that simply sounds airy and cool,
as close to swinging jazz as the Stones ever got. Listeners might
have been conditioned to the widening sonic scope of each subsequent Beatles record, but if one were to have dropped the needle
on *The Rolling Stones No. 2/The Rolling Stones, Now!* and immediately follow it up with a spin of "Under My Thumb"—marking the
lapse of one year's time—the juxtaposition would be striking. By
the time of the May 1966 release of *Aftermath,* it was clear that the
band had gone even further in their aural explorations, buttressing
the growing sophistication of the songwriting. The band broke
their sonic palette wide open on the record, which was their first
recorded in true stereo. And it featured an eleven-minute jam on
"Goin' Home," the longest rock song yet recorded at that time.

It is Brian's marimba that makes "Under My Thumb" so singular. He just lays on top, a wooden xylophone neatly poised between tone and percussion. Brian could pick up any instrument
and master it. But with a fragile and naturally volatile personality,
damaged further by drugs, and increasingly triangulated out of
power in his own group, his insecurity became acute and he grew
deathly paranoid. In Bill Wyman's book, Dave Thomson, a close
friend of Brian's says:

> Brian's main worry was that they were laughing at him, not
> taking him seriously, and therefore he couldn't take himself
> seriously. Once, we were going to write a song together and he
> chopped it, saying: 'If I take it into the studio they'll just
> mock me, won't use it' . . . I saw George Harrison once put a
> sitar—an incredibly difficult instrument to play—in Brian's
> hand, and within minutes, Brian knew his way around.

Around this same time, Brian offered his own self-assessment: "I can identify myself with the group but I'm not sure about the image. This rebel thing has gone, now; life is a paradox for me. I'm so contradictory. I have this need for expression, but I'm not certain what it is I want to do. I'm not personally *insecure,* just *unsure* . . . I would like to write but I lack confidence and need encouragement."

Mick betrayed no such lack of confidence. He offers a restrained vocal to match the cool, jazzy tableau set by the marimba and the rest of the band. The breezy California atmosphere has seemingly infiltrated the session with a touch of West Coast cool. Mick adds a generous set of ad libs, almost scatting, with a lot of breathy *ah*'s whispery *oh, that's right*'s, and *take it eeeeasy babe.*

12
Paint It Black (also listed as "Paint It, Black")

RECORDED:

March 6–9, 1966, RCA Studios, Los Angeles

RELEASES:

US LP: *Aftermath*, June 1966

Single, May 1966, number 1 in US and UK

Don't Be Afraid of the Dark

The Rolling Stones' third number one single in the US and sixth number one in the UK, "Paint It Black" remains one of the gloomiest songs from a band not unfamiliar with explorations of the dark side. But the recording and the arrangement that we all know and love started as a joke. "'Paint It Black' is like *Songs for Jewish Weddings*," Mick said, looking back.

Accounts from the studio that day in March 1966 have Bill Wyman on the organ in search of a beefier bass sound. He goofed around on some hammy oom-pa parts as he poked fun at the schmaltzy showbiz past of the band's rarely present comanager, Eric Easton, who had started his career as an organist in movie

theater pit orchestras. The band had been running through variations on "Paint It Black" (sometimes printed as "Paint It, Black"
due to a mistake by Decca), a swirling mélange of influences ranging from Indian (sitar and vocal melody), Middle Eastern, and
Eastern European (rhythmically), to blues and pop (choruses and
lyrical themes).

It had apparently begun as a typical pop number, likely with a
minor-key "House of the Rising Sun" approach. "That song was going nowhere, I thought," recalled Andrew Oldham. "Another ten
minutes and it'll be time to move on, change the energy, flow, and
song, and perhaps come back to 'Black' another day." Then the
shenanigans with a "piss-take of a gypsy figure" started and it was
the *eureka!* moment. Andrew encouraged Bill to keep up the part
on the organ pedals. By all accounts, it was the inspiration of Bill's
bass part, played on his knees under the Hammond organ, that
pushed the group into the whirling dervish tempo and vaguely
Eastern pentatonic melodic direction. Keith describes his own feelings on the track: "It was a different style to everything I'd done
before. Maybe it was the Jew in me. It's more to me like 'Hava
Nagila' or some Gypsy lick. Maybe I picked it up from my grand-
dad." Or, maybe he picked it up from Bill, as accounts from both
Andrew and Bill have it.

A sitar was brought into the mix of instruments. A 1966 Jagger
quote has it that "some geezer" happened by RCA studios and had
been playing it in a "jazz group" (not many jazz groups featured
sitar in 1966). And Brian was attracted to it for its ability to play
similar scales to the western blues, as well as the pitch-bending
sound achieved as the notes are struck, a tricky thing to accom-
plish on a guitar.

Mick adapted his vocals to the feel of the track and sound of the
sitar with a more nasal approach than usual. His lyric is one of a
mournful lover at a funeral, like an old blues or folk song, but with

inspired lines with impressively poetic images, such as, "No more will my green sea go turn a deeper blue."

Charlie pummels away at the tom-toms, a galloping pack of drums that also contributes a tribal feeling to the track, though he recalls it might just as well have been the influence of some pop record they had been listening to at the time: "It could have been anything like 'Going to a Go-Go,' " he has said. But it is that low pounding in the song's frequency range that likely caused Bill to go looking for some added bass support to match the dynamic. Playing the bass pedals of a B-3 organ became a well-used studio trick to add some low end to the foundation of tracks.

At the outro of the song, around 2:20, the band settles into a tense pattern, with Keith strumming a mad bolero rhythm on an acoustic guitar off in the background. There must have been the feeling that there was some magic in the take, because soon after, Keith admitted that it was imperfect and saw almost immediately how it could be improved, yet they decided to use this take. "It's over-recorded at the end," he said. "The electric guitar doesn't sound quite right to me, the one I play. I should have used a different guitar; at least, a different sound. And I think it sounds rushed. I think it sounds as if we've said—as we actually did—'That's great. If we do anymore we'll lose the feel of it.' Because that's what we said, and that's why, I think, if we'd done a few more takes of it, to my mind it would have been a slightly better record."

The prominence of the sitar on this track is another indication of how progressive experimentation contributed to the growth of the Stones. Now they were seen as serious competitors with the Beatles, not just commercially, but artistically. It was a healthy competition that encouraged the Stones to mature beyond their beginnings as mere blues and soul fanboys, into songwriters of lasting classics and pioneers in the art and technology of recording. Until about 1968, though, the Beatles were always ahead.

"What utter rubbish," Brian replied in 1966 to accusations that the Stones were copying the Beatles in the use of sitar specifically. "You might as well say that we copy all the other groups by playing guitar. Also, everyone asks if it's going to be the new trend. Well, personally, I wouldn't like it to be. . . . Take 'Norwegian Wood.' Atmospherically, it's my favorite track by the Beatles. George made simple use of the sitar and it was very effective."

Nevertheless, John Lennon had felt threatened by the rising prominence and relevance of the Stones. In an interview with *Rolling Stone* magazine years later, he vented:

> I think Mick is a joke, with all that fag dancing. I always did . . . I'd like to just list what we did and what the Stones did two months after on every fuckin' album, on every fuckin' thing we did, Mick does exactly the same. He imitated us . . . They're not in the same class music-wise or power-wise. They never were and Mick always resented it.

But that was 1971. The Stones were still around and at their creative peak, while the Beatles had been broken up officially for a year, and had been falling apart for a few more. With "Paint it Black," they were only warming up for the more menacing and harder-textured songs to come.

13
I Am Waiting

RECORDED:

March 6–9, 1966, RCA Studios, Los Angeles

RELEASES:

UK LP: *Aftermath*, April 1966

US LP: *Aftermath*, June 1966

Folk Rock and Paranoia

By 1966, rock 'n' roll albums were becoming deep. Where LPs were once merely collections of a few singles, fleshed out with some cover songs, they were increasingly treated as cohesive long-form works in and of themselves. *Aftermath,* the first Stones album to consist of all Jagger/Richards–penned songs, was also their first record that felt like an organized and focused project. As the LP was fast becoming the medium of choice for established artists looking to make an impactful statement, it also allowed for quieter moments like the *Aftermath* deep track, "I Am Waiting." Some of the strongest Rolling Stones songs over the decades have been tracks such as this, recordings that have somehow managed to almost remain secrets as catchier and more classic hits from albums hog the spotlight on radio and on the Stones' own set lists. The twilight mood and mournful melody of "I Am Waiting" made it ripe for rediscovery in later years. And indeed it was, placed effectively in the soundtrack of Wes Anderson's 1999 movie, *Rushmore.*

"I Am Waiting" is a dark, shadowy gem in the tradition of "Play With Fire," which had been released the prior year. The Stones were largely eschewing the sunnier pop elements of the burgeoning trend of psychedelia (at least for the moment), and still hewing closer to the woeful menace of the blues and folk introspection. In addition to psychedelia, the folk revival of the early 1960s remained a lingering influence on pop music. The hushed moments of "I Am Waiting" could have fit well on Simon & Garfunkel's 1964 LP, *Wednesday Morning, 3 A.M.* or their 1966 *Sounds of Silence.* And though "Lady Jane" is the better-known song of this ilk from *Aftermath,* "I Am Waiting" is the better song. With the former, you're not sure if Mick's joking, what with the Elizabethan verbiage enunciated impeccably over precious chamber music. Really, "I pledge my troth to Lady Jane"? It's an undeniably beautiful melody, but the lyrics are worthy of *Spinal Tap* snickers. "I Am Waiting," though, offers a plainspoken colloquial lyric and counterbalances the musical tension of Appalachian and English folk influences with a smashing rock 'n' roll backbeat, which Charlie lays into to introduce the release of the hard chorus, sung with Everly Brothers–like two-part harmonies.

The track opens with a good amount of tape hiss, lending the recording a rainy-day atmosphere and an antique quality. The verses musically symbolize the "waiting" part of the lyric, without being too clever about it. The vocals—Mick and Keith in an intimate two-part harmony—weave around a 4/4 tick-tock time signature on the verses. If it were a clock, with the dulcimer, acoustic guitar, and a shaker acting as the seconds, the bass guitar acts as the minutes, and the choruses symbolically mark the hours. Mick's vocal sounds patient, banal even. There is a creeping gloom to the tone, though, until finally Mick seemingly loses patience, welcoming the chorus to vent the frustration that has been building.

The first verse has Mick tiptoeing as if in a game of hide-and-seek. But the song unfolds to reveal that it's not just a person that the singer is waiting for. The first chorus suggests a deepening perception, an opening of the mind that promises to offset the growing paranoia in the lyrics: "It happens all the time, it's censored from our minds." In the end, it's not just the sweet stuff that's blocked from our perception, but also an awareness of "escalation fears" that "will pierce your bones."

While the music is colored in tweedy earth tones and eschews the surface optimism of flower power, the lyrics of "I Am Waiting" show that the Stones were not immune to the Zeitgeist of pop music progressively tinted with Eastern thought, as well as broadening sonics and higher fidelity. Insights gleaned from marijuana and LSD use were directly influencing songwriting and record production. Mick is singing with authority about fear, paranoia, and a part of our minds closed from wider perception, which dovetails with other standout albums of the time.

Recording landmarks in 1965 included *Rubber Soul, Out of Our Heads,* and *Highway 61 Revisited.* But in addition to the Stones' own milestone *Aftermath,* 1966 brought the world Dylan's *Blonde on Blonde,* the Byrds' *Fifth Dimension,* and the pop masterpiece *Pet Sounds* from the Beach Boys. With the release of *Pet Sounds*—itself partially a response to the Beatles' *Rubber Soul*—the Beatles perceived the Beach Boys as their immediate competition in pop songwriting and studio ingenuity and set down to begin work on *Sergeant Pepper's Lonely Hearts Club Band.* At this time, these two bands were primarily turning inward, resulting in bittersweet ruminations on ebbing adolescence, a loss of innocence, and explorations of alternate levels of consciousness.

Aside from perhaps the anomaly of "As Tears Go By," one rarely got the sense that the Stones—or Dylan, for that matter—had ever had any innocence to lose. While the brooding visages of the Stones peering out from the shadows on their early album covers was a conscious projection of their image, they were generally mirrors of the music and lyrical themes contained within. "The Beatles got the white hat," says Keith in the 2012 documentary, *Crossfire Hurricane.* "What's left? The black hat."

As with Dylan, the Stones had been more attuned to the more sinister forces of human nature from the get-go, or at least attracted to writing about such stuff. Dylan had graduated from his early-1960s reputation as a "protest singer" and was laying down epic poetic ballads, songs that sounded like absinthe dreams, with amphetamine rushes of lyrics, as if from a neo-Symbolist folk troubadour fronting a Chicago blues band. Others would follow. The Beatles and Stones formed a link between the rock 'n' roll and pop of the late-1950s and the heavier "rock" of the later 1960s. Bands who mined decadence and who wrote about wickedness, violence, immorality, war, and corruption as a matter of course were looming, poised to release records that reflected the tumultuous times. Such groups as the Velvet Underground and the Doors would not release their debut albums until 1967. Buffalo Springfield, though, had released the claustrophobic "For What It's Worth" in December 1966, inspired by a standoff between police and young demonstrators on the Sunset Strip. With alarming lines like, "Paranoia strikes deep/Into your life it will creep" and "Step out of line, the man will come and take you away," the song resonated beyond its genesis in the micro-world of curfews on the Sunset Strip and took on a macro significance.

Judging from the material on *Aftermath,* the Stones' beer-and-blues days at the Crawdaddy, only three years prior, had slipped into what must have seemed a distant past. "One part of their souls resided in a bizarre revisitation of Baudelairean nineteenth-century debauch and baroque," Oldham wrote of the 1966 period of the

Stones, "the other in a Neanderthal, pretentious, psychedelically entitled, and tripped-out world."

It would be another half a year or so before The Man came knocking at the door at Redlands, Keith's country home, with the infamous drug bust of February 1967. Yet with the lyric of this somewhat obscure March 1966 album track, "I Am Waiting," Mick seems to be aware of the outside straight world creeping in on the Stones' expanding-yet-ever-more-insular one. As Oldham writes, "With leisure came drugs and their aftermath, removing the need for watchclocks or moral compasses."

"I Am Waiting" is just a whisper, but if you "stop, children, what's that sound?/Everybody look what's going down," you might hear a sagacious young Mick Jagger heralding a word of caution.

14
Let's Spend the Night Together

RECORDED:

November 3–11, 1966, RCA Studios, Los Angeles

November 8–26, 1966, Olympic Studios, Barnes,
West London

RELEASES:

US LP: *Between the Buttons*, December 1966

(left off the UK version of the LP)

Single, January 1967, charting at number 3

in the UK and number 55 in the US

The Great Ed Sullivan Compromise

Let's Spend the Night Together" is a throwback good-time number that—musically speaking—would not have sounded out of place on the radio ten years earlier alongside, say, one of the late-1950s Elvis singles such as "(Let Me be Your) Teddy Bear" or "A Big Hunk o' Love." Its doo-wop-influenced backing vocal parts betray a nostalgia for the early days of rock 'n' roll (still a young genre), providing some tonic for the ponderousness of the burgeoning psychedelic era. These young men in the Stones, who grew up on early rock 'n' roll, were now relatively wizened and worldly. Drug-colored insight and progressively tumultuous external events simultaneously heightened a perception of a loss of innocence and a yearning for ostensibly simpler times, back when music was filled with love songs and nonsense syllables. The lyrics of "Let's Spend the Night Together," however, were among the Stones' most controversial, and would lead to the Great Ed Sullivan Compromise of 1967.

The Stones started to record the song in Los Angeles at RCA, but they completed it back at Olympic Studio, in Barnes, South West London, with Glyn Johns engineering. This was the second iteration of the Olympic, just opened in 1965, and it would become the Stones' home-base studio until they left for France as tax exiles in 1971. The studio was large and state-of-the-art. Chris Kimsey, who later was the chief engineer and/or coproducer of *Some Girls, Emotional Rescue, Tattoo You, Undercover,* and *Steel Wheels,* had begun his career at Olympic. "The great thing about Olympic was that we all, all the engineers, it was really much like a family," Kimsey told me. "We would all learn from each other. It wasn't a thing of like, *I'm the engineer, you're the tape jockey, just do your job.* The engineers shared all their secrets and all their knowledge, which was very different from Abbey Road. And it created a really strong breeding ground for producers and engineers to come out of that era."

One of the most attractive aspects of the studio was also the custom mixing console. "It was all due to Keith Grant, who was the owner and had built Olympic as well," Kimsey explained. "And he got the first console which was built by him and Dick Swettenham," who had come to Olympic from Abbey Road and went on to build coveted Helios consoles. "There was a sound to that studio for sure—the room and the console together," said Kimsey. "I can't recall when Glynn first discovered Olympic, but once he did, he really didn't want to work anywhere else."

The astonishing leaps in sonic quality continued at Olympic

and such breadth can be heard on the forceful and multilayered "Let's Spend the Night Together." The fact that Keith had written the song on piano would explain that instrument's prominence as the driving thrust of the recording. Keith and Jack Nitzsche both played piano on the record. The two separate tracks can be clearly heard on the stereo mix, but the mono mix is the winner. The most prominent of the two piano parts is a clanging, twangy upright, a tight honky-tonk/boogie-woogie sound. Keith also played bass guitar on the track, which is evident in the on-top-of-the beat, 16th-note pulse of the part, foreshadowing the extra attack he lent on bass to such later tracks as "Live with Me" and "Happy." With handclaps and Charlie's pounding snare in 4/4 time, the backing track of the song is so urgent that Mick needs to vault into the upper range of his vocals to wrestle back the spotlight. It's like the band is not going to let him take a breath. The "ba-da-la-da-dap-dap-dap-da-la-da's" fill up every possible hole. And any air left over is sucked up by Brian's reedy, wheedling, and droning organ part. It truly leaves a listener breathless—one of the definitive early Stones performances (with only Bill absent).

The "Good Vibrations"–like middle-eight breakdown provides a temporary respite from the incessant pattern of verses and choruses, which run right into one another over the same three-chord progression in an otherwise unbroken loop. On the middle eight, voices cascade in a round, almost like an echo, also consisting of nonsense syllables.

With a lyric inspired by the first night Mick spent with Marianne Faithfull, at a motel in Bristol, Mick veers from passive to insistent, often within the same lines. For example, on the lines—"I'm going red and my tongue's getting tied/I'm off my head and my mouth's getting dry"—it's comical how quickly this laid-back lover boy character loses it. Mick is clearly having a laugh, imagining the same kid who couldn't "get no girl reaction" now finding himself so close to closing the deal and driven mad by his good fortune: "This doesn't happen to me every day." The effervescent joy he felt in this new relationship bubbles over in his lyrics and delivery.

But Mick must have had an even more difficult time keeping a straight face when, answering to the controversy of such a blatantly sexual lyric in 1967, he claimed, "I always say, 'Let's spend the night together' to any young lady I'm taking out. If people have warped, twisted, dirty minds, I suppose it could have sexual overtones. Actually the song isn't very rude. When you hear it you'll realize this." But then he admits, "There are a few slightly rude bits, but I've covered them up."

Well, he tried halfheartedly to cover them up with the infamous January 15, 1967 *Ed Sullivan Show* performance. After their first appearance in 1964, Sullivan had said the Stones would never appear on the show again. Of course, they were back again a few months later, in 1965. The episode with "Let's Spend the Night Together" was their fourth and final live appearance on Sullivan's program—the show later filmed them on a date of their 1969 tour and replayed it for the fifth and final appearance.

Sullivan demanded that Mick alter the lyric to "Let's spend some time together." The Stones refused but Sullivan called their bluff and said he would not allow them to perform on the show. Finally Mick capitulated, but the show's producers were in his face all day reminding him of the new lyric. Fed up, Mick launched into an obscenity-fueled tirade at the talent coordinator.

In a moment that goes down in Rolling Stones lore, and rock 'n' roll history, when it came time for the televised performance Mick famously rolled his eyes at the camera and laid into the altered line with the insolent sarcasm of a schoolboy. It was quintessentially Mick Jagger, totally in line with his personality. Mick was pissed off enough to cause trouble on the set, but when it came to show time the calculating singer was not stupid enough to burn a highly lucrative opportunity for something so trivial. *The Ed Sullivan*

Show's reach was vast and unmatched in the US, the band's biggest market by far. "Eighteen months earlier we would have told Ed to go fuck himself and walked off the show," Oldham succinctly summarizes. "But now it's show business and in this moment we're at the top, we all have something to lose."

Even though he couldn't blatantly ignore the required lyric edit, Mick was winking to his audience at home. He was sending a not-so-secret signal that told them they were all—band, fans, youth in general—above this, too hip to worry about this petty censorship. Sullivan was, after all, the same guy who also infamously explained that Elvis's "gyrations" on the show in 1956 were "controlled with camera shots," so as not to scandalize the good people of America with an unbridled exposure of a wild hillbilly's swinging hips and thrusting pelvis.

While bobby-soxers had swooned over Frank Sinatra in the 1940s, it was rock 'n' roll on television and in film in the 1950s and '60s that offered fairly common visual representations of male sexuality, with strains of androgyny beginning with Little Richard and the black eye makeup and shoeblack-dyed hair in the face of Elvis, through to Mick's skinny-wiry dance moves, pouting full lips, and long hair. By the 1960s, Sinatra's bobby-soxer girls were married mothers and in registered disapproval of this new model of male sexuality. No wonder Sinatra opined on rock 'n' roll in a 1950s magazine article: "Brutal, ugly, degenerate, vicious . . . It fosters almost totally negative and destructive reactions in young people. It smells phony and false. It is sung, played and written, for the most part, by cretinous goons. . . . This rancid-smelling aphrodisiac I deplore." It seems Frank was slightly jealous.

Mick learned quickly how to work the cameras. You can see him with a sweaty upper lip, leering into the close-up shot on "Satisfaction" and looking directly to whichever camera was taking the current shot on the earlier appearance on the *Sullivan* show. On "Let's Spend the Night Together," he is in a frilly shirt and a glittery tight jacket, dancing—prancing, really—with elbows tight to his torso. Mick famously stole many of his dance moves from James Brown, but he also unabashedly incorporated moves from women, such as Tina Turner. He provided a link between those early rock 'n' rollers and later envelope pushers like Robert Plant, Jim Morrison, and Iggy Pop, other dynamic frontmen unencumbered by guitars.

"Let's Spend the Night Together" was a controversial enough song that many American radio programmers flipped over to its other A-side (marketed by Oldham as a double A-side single), the much more romantic, less lusty, and thus more publicly palatable "Ruby Tuesday," which became a number one on the charts, while "Let's Spend the Night Together" only went as high as 55. In the UK, however, it charted at a number three. But by succumbing to Sullivan, the rebellious Stones had blinked under pressure and took a slap to their cheeky image.

15
Ruby Tuesday

RECORDED:

November 8–26, 1966, Olympic Studios, London

RELEASES:

US LP: *Between the Buttons,* December 1966

(left off the UK version of the LP)

Single, January 1967, charting at number 3

in the UK and number 1 in the US

Buddhas of the Blues

Between the Buttons is considered by its many detractors to be an odd, mostly disappointing experiment in pure pop and out of character for the band. Mick and Keith both are among those who are not fans of the album. "I hate that fucking record," Mick stated plainly to engineer Dave Jerden. And the band members have pointed out that they were simply burned out by the end of 1966, after three years of working almost every day. They barely had time to write any new material. "I really wasn't into the album," said Keith in 1971. "It was the only album I felt dragged

into making. There are still some things on it, though. We just
wanted to get home. It was the end of that tour and everybody
just wanted to zonk out."

But *Between the Buttons* has also had many other fans over the
decades who have appreciated the increasing spirit of experimentation shown by the band and the "Englishness" of the record. And
there are some truly excellent songs: "Connection"; "Miss Amanda
Jones"; and the standout, lasting classic, "Ruby Tuesday," a song
about a free spirit, more than a bit Buddhist in philosophy ("Yesterday don't matter if it's gone"; "dying all the time"). The song's
shunned narrator, though, has not learned the essential Buddhist
lesson of letting go of that which you love. Dejected, he wistfully
sings of his love's refusal to commit to him, or to become one of
his connections, obsessions, or possessions—all recurring themes
on the *Between the Buttons* album. Even during the more cynical
and satirical moments on the record, the *Buttons* songs are about
the struggle to break out of the petty, the juvenile, the commercial,
and the banal, consistent with a widening scope in other rock music of the era. The record has one foot in the past—English music
hall and sardonic early-1960s wiseguy satire—and another foot in
the burgeoning psychedelic era and the 1967 Summer of Love.
"Ruby Tuesday" is emblematic of the latter progression.

Unlike the subjects of the "anti-women" songs of *Aftermath,* Ruby
Tuesday, whoever she is, is symbolic of some as-of-yet-unattainable
salvation. She seems to know something that the narrator is not yet
hip to or at least does not want to face. The "Ruby Tuesday" character was originally inspired by Keith's recent ex, Linda Keith. Linda
left Keith for an "ersatz hip" poet. "We went off on tour," he writes,
"and when I came back, London was suddenly hippie-ville. . . . The
scene had changed totally in a matter of weeks. Linda was on acid
and I'd been jilted." The song's narrator in the song feels left behind, not just by Ruby, but by the general scene.

Keith poured his lovelorn torment into his songwriting and

"Ruby Tuesday" is one of the rare pre-1980 cases when Keith wrote the entirety of the lyrics and the music. In general, it was Mick who wrote the bulk of the lyrics, with Keith generally offering snippets, titles, and ideas, then Mick fleshing out or starting from scratch—at least until the later years when they started writing separately. "A wonderful song," Mick recalled to *Rolling Stone* in 1995 about "Ruby Tuesday." "It's just a really nice melody, really. And a really nice lyric, neither of which I wrote, but I always enjoy singing it."

The begrudging acceptance of the narrator who sings good-bye to Ruby, though, does not capture the deep pain Keith actually felt, as described in *Life*. Ruby comes across as an innocuous hippy up-date of *Breakfast at Tiffany's* Holly Golightly, not the Tuinal-hooked heartbreaker described by Keith, who subsequently left the "poet so-called" for none other than Jimi Hendrix (whose career Linda Keith helped launch).

Though Ruby was inspired by Linda Keith, she stands in for an amalgam of free-spirited women appearing in the Stones' lives. Mick left Chrissie Shrimpton and Mick's new relationship with Marianne Faithfull was symbolic of the switch from the "swinging London" era—which Chrissie embodied, in her false eyelashes and heavy makeup—to the psychedelic. Bill Wyman writes that Marianne was "a strong advocate of the hippie philosophy." The Stones had a healthy skepticism about the burgeoning hippy culture. "I'm not involved in this *love and flowers scene*," said Mick in 1967, "but it is something to bring people together for the summer—something to latch on to."

The flower-power decade of the 1960s brought the influence of Eastern thought into pop lyrics, especially those of the Beatles. But, really, it was the drugs as much as any ancient texts that opened the minds and bodies of many twenty-somethings, and the appearance of LSD formed a demarcation in pop music around this time. One can pinpoint when certain bands with hardcore R&B and blues roots, like the Pretty Things, Small Faces, and the Stones, pivoted from beer-swilling, pill-popping aspirational bluesmen to—seemingly overnight—Soul Siddharthas, Buddhas of the Blues, and Muddy Waterses of the Ganges, trading in the open-collared shirts and tight-pants of Carnaby Street for the saffron robes of the Himalayas.

Mick and Keith were using drugs—pot and acid—only recreationally at this juncture, focused as they were on their work. Bill and Charlie would only enjoy a drink now and again. But Brian and Andrew were already dealing with addictions. Andrew had battled manic depression since adolescence, undergoing electroconvulsive therapy, moving on to prescribed antidepressants, and later self-medicating with pills and eventually cocaine. Brian continued to unravel in a downward spiral of drugs (coke, Mandrax, amphetamines, acid), strain, insecurity, fatigue, ill health, and depression. He more or less discontinued playing guitar around this point, something that embittered Keith, as there was a tremendous amount of pressure to continue recording, which meant having to come up with multiple guitar parts for each song.

As the prototypical tortured and needy artist, it seems a waste that Brian was unable to write songs in order to give voice to and make art of his internal struggles. He simply was not a pop songwriter, though. "I did hear some of Brian's writing," Jack Nitzsche said, "and, Christ, it wasn't right for the Stones. The songs were about falling leaves and the park, you know?" While the band was doing inarguably well, it was Mick and Keith who were making a much larger portion of the income via songwriting royalties. Charlie was accepting of the arrangement; Bill was more resentful, but even he admits that, with "hit after hit," it was tough for anyone else in the band to argue their way—even if one were so inclined—into that songwriting juggernaut. But it tore Brian up to watch his role as band founder and—in his mind—leader diminish as Mick's and Keith's stars rose, their bank balances rising along with them.

. . .

Brian seems to have been predisposed to self-medication, whether or not he ended up in a sixties rock 'n' roll band. But his insecurity about his role in the group and easy access to drugs proved to be a lethal combination. The Stones were past the point of fighting with Brian, who could be found, more often than not, lying on the floor in a stupor. Even Oldham had been willing to put up with the one he loathed in the band because Brian's persona was so strong that his force of personality was more or less the whole basis of the band's image. But now that the rest of the five had become so famous, Brian's bratty and malignant insecurity was by far more trouble than it was worth. Rather than fight him, "the Stones would simply wait for Brian to leave," recalled engineer Dave Hassinger. "It didn't matter if it took all night. Once he'd leave they would start recording, rather than cause an argument that might freak him out." Marianne says that the band offered very little encouragement to each other, especially not to Brian, who most needed it: "Every now and again a sudden pall would settle over the sessions. If someone didn't like something the other was doing, he just wouldn't participate . . . they were very English. No one would ever say anything directly."

Brian's role as a colorist, however, was still in full bloom on "Ruby Tuesday." It is one of the few times where Brian played a wind instrument on a Stones record (if you don't count the harmonica). As with the sitar in "Paint it Black" and the marimbas on "Under My Thumb," the woody, hollow sound of Brian's recorder is essential to the track. It flutters in birdlike over the upright double bass, with Bill doing the fingering on the neck while Keith did the bowing. Along with that creaky low end, Nitzsche is once again present on piano, playing four descending chords, with each figure ending with an almost classical flourish. Marianne claims that it was actually Brian's fooling around on the recorder that inspired Keith to sit down at the piano and construct a chord progression to provide the musical bed for the plaintive sound of the wood instrument. The recorder enters on the third line, as the chords reverse their chorus and ascend as a pre-chorus, and lends a bittersweet wistfulness to the tune, not quite mournful, but with enough sorrow and regret to match the lyric.

"Ruby Tuesday" is unusual for the Stones in that it opens cold, Mick coming right in on the beginning of the track. He sings a broadly ranging melody that sweeps up and down multiple octaves. The vocals are more present, dry (almost no reverb or echo), and intimate than they have ever been on a Rolling Stones record. Mick sounds like an American crooner here, at the lowest point in his register, with a whole different vocal timbre that has only been hinted at on previous records. He sounds somewhat congested. Mick often got up close and personal to the microphone. "Mick is dancing all the time," engineer/producer Chris Kimsey explained about the singer's approach in the studio. "You never think he's going to make it up to the microphone . . . His microphone technique is amazing!"

The soupy reverb-drenched-everything days are left behind for a more present and immediate sound that heralds a new era of Stones recordings. "Andrew used to think that anything is possible if you put enough echo on it," quipped Keith. "Ruby Tuesday" ranges from a Baroque-folk opening, to one of the most rousing sing-along pop numbers of the 1960s, and finally back down to an intimate and warm folk song. As the stereo mix of "Ruby Tuesday" winds to its plaintive close, as the band drops out, at about 3:03, you can hear Keith counting the measure out to the end: " . . . *three, four* . . ." he whispers.

16
2000 Light Years from Home

RECORDED:

July–August 1967, Olympic Studios, London

RELEASES:

LP: *Their Satanic Majesties Request*, December 1967

B-side to "She's a Rainbow," December 1967

The Stones Lost in Space

Robert Greenfield: To talk about the music then [referring to *Their Satanic Majesties Request*], was Brian into acid before anyone and having been to the West Coast, was there a reluctance to play just rock 'n' roll?

Keith Richards: There was a point when it was difficult to do that. People would say, "What are you playing that old shit for?" Which really screwed me up because that's all I can play. We just sort of laid back and listened to what they were doing in Frisco whereas Brian was making

great tapes, overdubbing. He was much more
into it than we were. And we were digging what
we were hearing for what it was, but the other
thing in you is saying, "Yeah. But where's Chuck
Berry? What's he doing?" It's got to follow
through. It's got to connect.

—*Rolling Stone* **magazine, 1971**

The influence of Chuck Berry's unpretentious earthy rock 'n'
roll is nowhere to be found here. "2000 Light Years from
Home" takes us on an interstellar trip through dark inner
and outer space, to "a star with a fiery ocean." The song floats in
hauntingly. Sideman Nicky Hopkins opens the track by plucking
and strumming the piano strings, a sound echoed even more eerily
in backward tapes of the same, sounding like space debris just winging by. Keith introduces a Latin-tinged spy-movie riff on the low
strings as we are led through the cosmos by stuttering and swoosh-
ing strings via the Mellotron (a keyboard that played tape loops of
strings, voices, flutes, and other sounds) played by Brian, leaving
vapor trails on the right side as we pass by asteroids in our stereo
spaceship. Such effects as these have become rote to the point of
cliché over the course of rock history, but "2000 Light Years From
Home" still sounds fresh. The sounds are elegantly well-placed,
and used judiciously, even tastefully, not words one would often
associate with the *Their Satanic Majesties Request* album as a whole.
Marianne Faithfull writes that the album's "pervading darkness"
was reflective of the "mysterious and menacing enemy [which]
pursued" the band and their immediate circle. The events of 1967
were to change the band profoundly.

The Stones were pretty much burnt out space junk themselves
by the end of 1966. The touring that year, which included the

stopover at RCA Studios for a chunk of what became *Between the Buttons,* ended up being the Rolling Stones' last American tour dates until 1969. Until this break from touring, the Stones' schedule from 1963–1966 was almost superhuman, taking its toll most obviously on the ever-fragile Brian. But the whole band needed a break.

That break came around January 1967, as the group showed signs of settling down. Mick and Marianne were making headlines as a celebrity romance, edging out Brian and Anita as one of the most happening couples in London. Keith was a single country squire, out in his new country estate, Redlands, two hours outside of the city. He was lonely, having been dumped by Linda "Ruby Tuesday" Keith, who had moved on to newcomer Jimi Hendrix. Bill Wyman's wife had left him and he had a new Swedish girlfriend, Astrid Lundstrom, with whom he would remain for almost twenty years. Charlie was, of course, stable and married to Shirley. He and Bill had already realized that they needed to develop grounded lives outside of the whirlwind Rolling Stones in order to maintain some semblance of sanity, and Charlie was particularly adept at balancing out the rock 'n' roll circus with a solid domestic life of books and jazz records back home.

Being off the road granted some reprieve on strained relationships. By the end of 1966, Mick and Keith had been at the end of their rope with Brian. The surly blond moptop had been withdrawing ever more flamboyantly from his role in the band. There is no way that he would have lasted in the Stones had they continued touring at the same pace. This time out of the pressure cooker helped relieve some of that tension; by early 1967, Keith and Brian had rekindled their friendship, even as Brian's bitterness toward Mick intensified. He had long been jealous of the attention Mick received as a lead singer, and was further embittered about the songwriting alliance and close friendship that had formed between

Mick and Keith, the latter of whom had been his early guitar buddy at the flat on Edith Grove. Brian's strategy was to try and triangulate Mick out as he and Keith started to hang out again.

This friendship would be short-lived, though, as Keith had started to cozy up to Anita. Bill, Brian's ally in the band, had viewed this rekindled friendship between Keith and Brian as "superficial," suspecting Keith had the dastardly motive of stealing Anita. Keith, of course, viewed the situation with more nuance. "No doubt I could have got together with Anita without being particularly nice to Brian. But I was spending my time with them 'cause it seemed a good idea to cement a better relationship with Brian."

Stranded out at Redlands with no driver's license, lonesome Keith even moved in to the large flat that Brian and Anita shared in London, which had become *the* place to be, the apex of the London scene. Though Brian became less relevant musically within the band he was still an arbiter of hip, his cutting-edge sense of style enhanced via his alliance with the chic Anita. The Stones' social circle by 1967 consisted of artists, filmmakers, intellectuals, actors, models, and such socialites as Tara Browne, heir to the Guinness beer fortune, whose death in a car crash was memorialized the next year in the Beatles' "A Day in the Life."

Even as the Stones ostensibly relaxed from their touring, there remained the pressure to produce new records. But making a record no longer meant simply getting together a bunch of songs in between tour dates to take out on the road for even more touring. Brian Wilson, Bob Dylan, the Beatles, and the Stones all retreated into the studio or the country for hibernation for years. These young genius artists pushed themselves and each other to redefine what rock 'n' roll and pop music could be. Recording technology was also improving exponentially to expand to more available recording tracks, more high fidelity gear, and superior stereophonic sound, further encouraging expansive experimentation. The truncated term "rock" started to come into fashion to better describe the heaviness of the new sounds on cohesive and conceptual albums that contained grand works.

Meanwhile, a new crop of bands out on the West Coast represented the next artistic wave. The Doors, the Jefferson Airplane, the Grateful Dead, Janis Joplin, et al, along with English bands like The Pink Floyd Sound (who later trimmed down their name), Cream, The Who, and the two-thirds English Jimi Hendrix Experience were all taking music in intense new directions. By 1967, LSD's influence had thoroughly infiltrated rock music, especially that emanating from the Bay Area. Keith notes all the fear and paranoia from bad trips would not dissuade him and others like him from the next dose of acid. "It was the idea of a boundary that had to be pushed," as well as a need to feel part of "a gang thing," of those in the know who had had their minds blown.

But it was the Beatles leading the charge through the psychedelic era. With the growing intensity and deepening production of their records, as heard on *Rubber Soul* and *Revolver,* and reaching an astonishing apex with *Sergeant Pepper's Lonely Hearts Club Band* in June 1967, they were at their influential high point as pop music's standard-bearers, rivaled that year primarily by Brian Wilson and the Beach Boys for sublime pop supremacy.

While the Beatles were leading this musical conversation, the Stones seemed to lose their way artistically and stammered through *Their Satanic Majesties Request,* often thought of as a (weak) attempt to produce their own *Sergeant Pepper.* This is not to say that there were no great psychedelically tinged Stones songs. On the contrary, the band had provided some significant statements and radical new sounds in such lasting classics as the manic "Mother's Little Helper," "19th Nervous Breakdown," "Paint It Black," and "Have You Seen Your Mother, Baby, Standing in the Shadow"— wondrous songs, all released in 1966. Furthermore, prior to the release of *Their Satanic Majesties Request* in 1967, they released "We Love You" and "Dandelion," also two strong songs of the era. Seen in this context, the Stones were clearly defining their own path through the psychedelia era, not merely answering the Beatles. "I never listened any more to the Beatles than to anyone else in those days when we were working," Keith has said. "It's probably more down to the fact that we were going through the same things . . . We're only just mirrors ourselves of that whole thing."

But the album itself was not made up of that marvelous parade of singles. "There's a lot of rubbish on *Satanic Majesties,*" Mick said in 2003. "Just too much time on our hands, too many drugs, no producer to tell us, 'Enough already, thank you very much, now can we get just get on with this song?' Anyone let loose in the studio will produce stuff like that. There was simply too much hanging around. It's like believing everything you do is great and not having any editing."

Well, they *did have* a producer, technically speaking, in Oldham. They just were not listening to him anymore. Andrew had attended the early first round of *Satanic Majesties* sessions in February, but would leave the project and quit the Stones before the recordings were finished. *Between the Buttons* was the last full album the Stones would make with him and, in the words of Marianne Faithfull, "their last album as pop stars [before entering their mythic phase]." *Buttons* had been an almost perfect realization of the sort of album that most interested Oldham: impeccably produced pop with caustic put-downs of mindless bourgeois conformists, and boy-spites-girl lyrics. It was the last of the Swinging-London-era Stones before they outgrew Andrew and took a detour from their blues, rock 'n' roll, and pop, toward psychedelia and bloated self-indulgence.

Andrew's brilliance as music producer had been in simply insisting that Mick and Keith write songs, and in executing his idea to combine the raw Chicago blues and Southern soul played by a bunch of pimply English boys with the orchestrated pop sounds of Phil Spector and Jack Nitzsche. Once the Stones moved on toward

the experimental aspects on the 1967 recordings, they began to
alienate Oldham and he, in a battle with his own demons, slid into
horrendous bouts of depression and substance abuse. "The reality
was," he writes, "I was out of touch, living in my 45 rpm world."

Even the competitive pressure to try to keep pace with the Beatles was not enough to sustain the Stones' production. Any energy
that might have propelled them in the past was dissipated by
drugs. While Mick has said that drugs were so common that they
had become a bore by this time, smoking dope and dosing on acid
was something that exaggerated, by design, the already yawning
gulf between youthful musicians, artists, and hedonistic hipsters,
and nine-to-five straight society at large. As the Stones, Beatles, et al
rose in prominence, this divergence in world views between
prominent and increasingly influential musicians with too much
money, and the existing political and cultural power elite was
eventually bound to come to a head. And so it did on the weekend
of February 11 and 12, 1967.

The Stones had gotten a handful of recordings started that
month, including an early version of what would become the 1969
track "You Can't Always Get What You Want." Immediately after
one of these first recording sessions for *Satanic Majesties,* Keith had
a party at Redlands in Sussex with Mick and Marianne, George
Harrison and Pattie Boyd, and Robert Fraser, a hipster art dealer and
tastemaker. There were also a few other men, including one no one
seemed to know very well, a failed actor named David Schneiderman, called "the Acid King," who was invited because he was a
dealer of high quality LSD including the "Purple Haze" variety
celebrated in Hendrix's song of the same name.

The partiers tripped all day and had a great time out in the
countryside. Marianne felt that Mick and Keith formed an even
stronger bond that day and that more than a few future Stones
songs had their genesis in intense conversations between the two.

As the party wound down, " 'Post-acid' was the prevailing mood at Redlands on a cold February morning in 1967," as Keith describes it. George and Pattie had left late that night. Soon after came a knock at the door and there were a battalion of policemen waiting with a search warrant. (It became clear that the police had waited until one of the too-beloved-to-bust Beatles had left.) As a result of the raid, Mick and Keith were eventually (though, not immediately) arrested. Mick was charged with possession of four pep pills, amphetamines, found in his jacket. They had been given to him in Italy by Marianne to hold for her. Keith was charged with allowing his premises to be used for illegal use of cannabis based on the evidence of some resin found at the house. Fraser faced the most serious charges, in possession of heroin. Marianne had recently bathed and had come down clad in a fur rug, adding the requisite layer of sex for charges that would provide fodder for later headlines, "Naked Girl at Stones Party."

It was the sort of scandal that could only be simultaneously cooked up and covered by the British tabloids. Only a week before the raid, Mick had announced that he planned to sue the *News of the World* tabloid for libel for fabricating a story that he had been seen taking LSD at a party given by one of the Moody Blues.*

It became evident that the bust at Keith's house was a conspiracy and frame-up, the scandal sheets in cahoots with the police, payback time. The tabloid had been known for having celebrities followed by detectives, and they tipped off the police to a "drugs party" at a rock star's home. The dealer, Schneiderman, disappeared from the scene soon after the bust and was not heard from again by any of those who had been present at the house that night, almost certainly a tool in the setup.

Keith came to the realization:

---

* As Mick had more star power, it appears that the newspaper purposefully confused him with Brian, who had apparently been chatting about his drug intake at such a party.

When we got busted at Redlands, it suddenly made us realize that this was a whole different ball game and that was when the fun stopped. Up until then it had been as though London existed in a beautiful space where you could do anything you wanted. And then the hammer came down and it was back to reality. We grew up instantly. . . . [T]he powers that be actually looked upon us as important enough to make a big statement and to wield the hammer. But they also made us more important than we ever bloody were in the first place.

The tabloids reported the incident, but initially kept the identities of the pop stars anonymous until formal charges were pressed. The arraignments for Mick, Keith, and Fraser were to come in May, which is when their names were reported in stories about a drug-fueled orgy. It was decided that it would be wise for Mick and Keith to leave the country and escape the media spotlight for a while. A trip to Morocco was arranged. Included in the touring party were Marianne, Brian, Anita, and others. Brian fell ill on the way there—his frail health exacerbated by prodigious drugging—and was admitted to a hospital near Toulouse, France, for a few days. Meanwhile, the romantic connection between Anita and Keith took root in his Bentley as they rolled on through France.

As Brian got wind of it, very quickly his jealousy got the better of him and when he rejoined the touring party, amidst a haze of acid and hash, he made humiliating kinky sexual demands of Anita, involving prostitutes, that she refused. The scene turned uglier and violent. Bill writes that Anita "was beaten so severely that she said she was in fear of her life." Keith took control and left immediately with Anita in his car back to Tangier. By then, Mick and Keith had completely given up on Brian and his relationship with Anita was clearly over. The already frail Brian Jones was knocked down to the mat and almost out for the count.

Upon their return to London, Mick, Keith, and Robert Fraser

learned that they would indeed be charged. The arraignment date for Mick and Keith was set, and on the very same day, May 10, Brian got busted. Police came to his flat where they found a minuscule amount of hash. Nevertheless, he was led out in handcuffs through a swarm of waiting photographers, television cameramen, and reporters. If there was any doubt that a conspiracy was on before, now it seemed like a sure bet. Mick and Keith elected a jury trial, as did Brian when he was arraigned on June 2. Released on bail, Mick's and Keith's trials were set for late June, Brian's for October. Brian would never recover from this latest bust. Over the course of '67 and '68, he would regularly be checked in for psychiatric evaluation and treatment.

The jury trials for Mick and Keith resulted in convictions and hefty sentences of three months in prison for Mick, six for Robert Fraser, and a year for Keith. The trials produced a generation-defining note of defiance from Keith, in one of his first public glimpses of his budding outlaw image. During his trial, Keith was asked by the prosecuting attorney: "Would you agree that in the ordinary course of events you would expect a young woman [Marianne in a fur rug] to be embarrassed if she had nothing on in front of several men?" Keith spit out: "Not at all. We are not old men and we are not worried about petty morals. . . ." Shy Keith became the desperado cowboy Keith at this pivotal point. And the bad boy image of the Stones took on a whole new mythology that Svengali Andrew Oldham couldn't even have imagined. "The judge managed to turn me into some folk hero overnight," writes Keith. "I've been playing up to it ever since."

The harsh sentences occasioned a blowback from an unexpected source, an editorial in the staid Times of London. It was written by the paper's conservative editor, William Rees Mogg, and is a landmark in pop culture: an elder voice of reason making the case to his generation that they ought to ease up. It was famously titled "Who Breaks a Butterfly on a Wheel?" Mogg easily made the case that the sentences were egregiously disproportionate punishment and were more about making symbolic examples of prominent leaders in youth culture than meting out evenhanded justice.

Upon appeal, only Fraser served time. Mick and Keith spent two nights in jail and then were released on bail pending their appeals. In July, Keith won his appeal and Mick was allowed to go free on probation with a suspended sentence. The trials had hit the Stones hard, though, halting their momentum and almost derailing them completely. So one could understand the distraction of the band as they went into the studio to continue their work on *Satanic Majesties*. Drugs, arrests, and stealing a bandmate's girl might perhaps serve as grist for the songwriting mill in the long run, but rarely are such things conducive to the artistic concentration needed for the task at hand.

Now they could add "management defection" to the lists of obstacles they needed to overcome as a band. Andrew, who had been in Los Angeles at the time of the bust, remained out of the country until May, fearful that the authorities were after them all, including him. He rejoined them in the studio in June and July, but very little music was being produced. Rather than take Andrew's lead on such things, as they had in the past, Mick informed Andrew who would be the next photographer to take the cover shot for the record they were ostensibly making. "We'd recorded nothing in three weeks," he writes "and here we were discussing the fucking sleeve." With his previous business management duties now in the hands of Allen Klein, and his image-making and music-making roles now being taken over by the Stones themselves, it became clear to all that the Andrew Loog Oldham era was over. This decision was cemented by the impression that he had abandoned them during their biggest crisis.

One night in September, Andrew slipped out of the studio unnoticed, had his chauffeur drive him away in his Rolls Royce, stopped along the way, called Mick at the studio, and told him he was not coming back. Mick accepted the resignation as if he expected it. It was Mick who apparently rallied the band in the direction they were then currently taking in the *Satanic Majesties* sessions, with a direct eye toward the perceived competition. "Also, we did it to piss Andrew off," he said, "because he was such a pain in the neck. Because he didn't understand it. The more we wanted to unload him, we decided to go on this path to alienate him."

Contrary to the accepted narrative that the LP was a dud, there are more good songs than clunkers on *Satanic Majesties*: "Citadel," "2000 Man," and the sparking single, "She's a Rainbow," for example. The latter begins with Hopkins, the pianist who had first made an appearance on "Cool, Calm, Collected," from *Between the Buttons*, who would go on to play on almost every record of theirs into the late 1970s.

After Hopkins starts "2000 Light Years From Home," the song sounds as if it might float away again, as if it is merely some between-song interlude. But strap on your space helmets, we are about to hit hyperspace. Charlie lays into his toms like they are orchestral timpani (at 0:52). He leaves a slight break in the drum fill (at 0:53–0:54), just enough to hear one of Keith's audible switches on the guitar. Here he clicks his pickup selector, which sounds almost like the cocking of a gun, then, BAM! (at 0:55), Charlie comes up out of his drum fill with a crescendo and the band kicks in, Bill's bass as heavy as he has ever been. Charlie kicks a steady groove that is funked-up even more by the very present maracas. This is no fey hippy-dippy ditty; it's a heavy droning predecessor of "Gimme Shelter." It's the perfect dark B-side to the light and lilting A-side "She's a Rainbow."

"2000 Light Years from Home" was done on Olympics' four-track, but the band still tried to load up on overdubs with sound effects. "When it came to the overdubs," said engineer George Chkiantz, "all hell was let loose. We tried anything and everything." The recording achieves an epic cinematic sweep.

No song on the LP captures the sense of isolation and disorientation that the band felt more than "2000 Light Years from Home." "We found ourselves under a malign bewitchment," Marianne explained. Mick wrote the lyrics during his night in jail. When Mick was at his lowest ebb, in tears and feeling helpless from the arrests, Marianne had told him to channel those feelings into writing, telling him to "think of all those blues players you love so much, dear. You can write your own blues." As David Bowie ("A Space Oddity") and Elton "Rocketman" John would later do, Mick explores the Ray Bradbury–like theme of loneliness of space, drifting so far from home. A quintessential drug song, you could indulge in the substance of your choice, slap on your stereo headphones, stare into the far-out 3-D photo of the Stones (a few of whom were tripping themselves at the time of said photo shoot), and let Mick and crew guide you as "Freezing red deserts turn to dark."

The lyrics on *Satanic Majesties* as a whole don't really reflect the specifics of the literal trials and tribulations that the band was undergoing during its creation. "They aren't all about policemen as they could well have been . . ." joked Mick. But the lyrics of "2000 Light Years from Home," and the album generally, explore alien and changing worlds, unmoored and discordant inner and outer space, with the psychological distance of the words reflected in the thick and textured music. Mick's voice often floats in and back away like a distant radio.

The Stones were mirroring the feelings of a large segment of youth culture growing older and increasingly alarmed by the world they were inheriting. Drugs signified only a small part of the self-distancing and widening gap between generations. But, of course, it was drugs that were made illegal (LSD was legal in California until October 1966) and subsequently, the laws against them were used to bring down those with bully pulpits. The clampdown was draconian and the 1967 drug busts delineated an us/them divide.

"Up till then [pop music] had been showbiz, entertainment,

play it how you want to, teenyboppers," Keith explained. "At that point you knew they considered you to be outside—they're the ones who put you outside the law. Like Dylan says, 'To live outside the law, you must be honest.' They're the ones that decide who lives outside the law. I mean, *you* don't decide, right? You're just living."

In the end, the misplaced ire of the authorities ended up working more magic and myth than Andrew Oldham could ever conjure, an irony not lost on Andrew and the Stones themselves.

17
Jumpin' Jack Flash

RECORDED:

April 20, 1968, Olympic Studios, London

RELEASES:

Single, May 1968, charting at number 1 in the UK
and number 3 in the US

Stones Come Back Punching

There was nothing about love, peace, and
flowers in "Jumpin' Jack Flash."
—Mick Jagger

If the Stones had gotten walloped by busts, trials, and drubbings from critics in 1967, they came back swinging in 1968 with their next single, one of their greatest songs, the commanding and ballsy "Jumpin' Jack Flash." This punchy masterstroke showed that these were not some spaced-out hippies about to lay down and get squashed by authority and dismissed by critics.

. . .

The stylistic leap from the previous album, *Satanic Majesties,* to this new single cannot be overstated. When "Jumpin' Jack Flash" was finally released, the public reaction was overwhelmingly positive, which it needed to be if the band was to keep their upward trajectory as both a popular and artistically significant band. Though *Satanic Majesties* was a commercial success, it was mostly due to the momentum the band had built up and the strength of its singles that preceded it. The album as a whole was almost universally panned by critics and fans who felt the band had lost its way in offering a watered-down version of the Beatles. There was a new crop of artists with novel styles and sounds. And the Stones had already outlived the average shelf life for rock 'n' roll bands of the era— they were in danger of becoming irrelevant.

"Jumpin' Jack Flash" was not only a return to riff-based rock 'n' roll, but an even more exciting update on the sound of the Stones. This was a singular sound, distinctively their own. To a casual observer, the rediscovery of their mojo heard on "Jumpin' Jack Flash" might have seemed like the Stones had gone down to the crossroads and made a deal with the Devil. To be on the precipice of prison sentences, in danger of falling apart as a band, and to come back with this monster of a song that doubled down on their sound with a fresh, stinging clarity, was a triumphant declaration from the band: What wasn't gonna kill them was gonna make them stronger.

This muscular track, a single released to fill the gap before their next LP, *Beggars Banquet,* marks the beginning of the band's working relationship with American producer Jimmy Miller, who was at the controls for each of the band's best albums and their indisputable golden period. It was now Stones Mach II. They were never as good on record before or after the Jimmy Miller era. With "Jumpin' Jack Flash," Miller at the helm, the band navigated away from the dead-end shoals of instantly dated psychedelia and fey hippy anthems, and restored their original bluesy swagger. Miller drew out the inherent strengths of the group and over the course of at least four albums, attained a near-perfect balance of the unique blend of sounds of the Stones.

The band successfully moved their Chuck-Berry-and-Howlin'-Wolf-rooted raw essence a few notches into the future. It was no longer one way or the other—psychedelia/new rock versus old-time rock 'n' roll. Here was a true answer to the late 1960s burgeoning heavy rock. The Stones found a way to rock *and* roll, reinstating that main ingredient that had gone missing from 1967 Stones: sex. On "Jumpin' Jack Flash," the band sounds primal, intuitive, and uninhibited. What the hell is a "jumpin' jack flash," or a "crossfire hurricane"? We don't know for sure, but then, what precisely is "smokestack lighting," a "mojo filter," or "streetwalking cheetah with a heart full of napalm"? Who the hell cares?

We do know that Jumping Jack was a name Mick and Keith called the gardener at Keith's Redlands estate. Jack Dyer was a real "yokel" in Keith's words. Mick and Keith were laying about after an all-night writing session, in a half stupor at 6:30 in the morning, when they were rudely awakened by the clomping boots of Dyer in the garden. Mick, startled, asked what the hell was going on. Keith answered, "Oh, that's just Jack leaping around. Jumpin' Jack." Mick, inspired by the alliteration, announced his epiphany, "Flash!" And that's how the phrase came.

"Jumpin' Jack Flash" has much of its stream-of-consciousness lyric informed by the language of war and weaponry. In fact, "the world's forgotten boy" of Iggy Pop's 1973 song "Search and Destroy" might as well have been another version of the same guy "born in a crossfire hurricane" and "raised by a toothless bearded hag." The Stones, born during World War II and writing and recording during the height of the Vietnam War, were reborn and again reflecting their times. But this is no protest anthem or directly political song. This is not a leader of men trying to organize a peace march, nor a rabble-rouser calling, as with Jefferson Airplane, for a "counterrevolution." Rather, the protagonist of "Jumpin' Jack Flash" is highly individualistic, a lone wolf who seems to masochistically get off on the violence. It's both a kiss-off to hippiedom and a right hook thrown back at an overreaching state that thought they had backed these cocky artists into a corner. The Stones were beholden to no constituency.

In his memoirs, *Times* editor William Rees Mogg reflected on the 1967 trials and the "Butterfly on a Wheel" piece, which turned out to be one of his most resonant essays. He recalls being on a television panel with Mick soon after the trials:

> Jagger's views, in a subsequent television interview, were perhaps more important than he or we then realised; he took a libertarian view of ethical and social issues which turned out to be one of the constituents, though only one, of Thatcherism. It was not the soft-left Beatles but the libertarian Rolling Stones who best predicted the Anglo-American ideology of the 1980s. . . . Jagger used the classic John Stuart Mill On Liberty argument: that you are entitled to do anything which does not affect somebody else adversely. . . . When Jagger made these remarks in 1967, the young were beginning to revolt against the limits put on liberty by Victorian tradition and wartime necessities and by socialist paternalism.

Coming right off of his trial, Mick's language in "Jumpin' Jack Flash" is of persecution and rising above, a tough survivor for being "schooled with a strap right across [his] back . . . But it's all right now, in fact it's a gas," he sneers somewhat malevolently. In a scant three oblique verses, Mick manages to capture the essence of both the external violence churning in the world at large, and a reflection of the personal mythology that the band was already cultivating with a post-trial attitude of defiance. Or should we say, Keith's defiance, for it was he who sneered on the stand at his trial that the band was not concerned with "petty morals," while Mick admittedly cried when *his* initial sentence was handed down.

As seen in photos and film clips from this time, especially the Michael Lindsay-Hogg–directed promo clip for "Jumpin' Jack Flash," the Stones adopted a tougher look, like lost boys back from some *Lord of the Flies* world. Mick had by now morphed into the bad-boy, mouthy, leering Mick that we all loved in the 1970s. He began changing personas like masks, which was a survival strategy of sorts, a defensive bulwark. In "Jumpin' Jack Flash," through *Let It Bleed,* we are to believe he is—variously or simultaneously—a loner tough-guy, a masochistic knave prone to violence, a rock star outlaw, a street-fighting man, a prophet of gloom, and/or the Devil himself.

As for the recording itself, the first thing that strikes you is the sound and texture of "Jumpin' Jack Flash." "I remember the recording session for 'Jumpin' Jack Flash,' and not liking the way it was done very much," Mick said. "It was a bit haphazard—and although the end result was pretty good, it was not quite what I wanted. The fidelity wasn't that great; it wasn't quite as in your face as it could have been."

It's difficult to imagine it more in your face. The technology was changing. By the end of the 1960s, multitrack recorders had expanded to eight simultaneously available tracks, so the sound was cleaner. The perverse thing about this era of the Stones is, however, that as recording technology was improving exponentially, Keith became obsessed with the sounds produced by his guitars running through a low-tech portable tape recorder. Along with "Street Fighting Man," he had recorded his acoustic guitar into a Philips cassette recorder—a relatively new invention—and was inspired by the overdriven sound produced when the analog tape levels were pushed to their max, a sound unlike an acoustic guitar and not quite the same as an electric. It is that brittle, hairy, full mid-range sound that is heard on "Have You Seen Your Mother . . ." and "Street Fighting Man" as well. "Just jam the mic right in the guitar and play it back through an extension speaker," is how Keith explained his process. He recorded two acoustics amplified via the same method—one, open-tuned and with a capo, and another with "Nashville" tuning, which is essentially a six-string guitar strung with only the high strings of a 12-string guitar. Unlike an electric, you have to strum the hell out of an acoustic guitar to make it rock this heavy (just watch Pete Townshend).

"We recorded the band in a circle on the floor using Jimmy's cassette machine," said Eddie Kramer. "Then, after the track was recorded, we played it back through a little Philips speaker, and I put a mic in front of that and recorded it onto one track of the four-track. That was very revolutionary. It gave the song a raw sound, and if you listen to the intro you can hear the wow of that guitar. That machine was bloody horrible." The result is a rhythmic maelstrom and on "Jumpin' Jack Flash," Brian is shaking maracas like a Bo Diddley death rattle,* all dry, strumming and sixteenth-note shaking.

The track revs up like the high-torque engine on a race car at the starting line, with an electric guitar overdub on the other side of the stereo, peeling out with Charlie's crunchy drum sound and Keith's down-and-dirty bass playing. Then the gates open and out comes that monstrous riff. Bill claims that the lick was something he came up with while fooling around on keyboards as the rest of the band waited for Mick and Keith to arrive at the studio one day. Mick and Keith latched on to it and came back the next day with the song written completely. While it is Keith handling the bass guitar, Bill shines on the organ here. Keith also added pounding tom-toms for the recording's second half. A big shaker comes up to

---

* More precisely, it was Jerome Green rattling the maracas for Diddley.

the forefront of the mix at about 1:34, at the middle-eight, remaining in as the track goes into turbo.

It is the rhythm that grabs a hold of you. There is little melody to speak of, as the verse melody is essentially an up-tempo blues drone and Mick's vocal is buried low in the mix. On the choruses there's a nasally melody, a higher harmony, and a frog-voiced low harmony that adds to the vaguely Arabic/Georgian-chant feel of the recording. The organ rises up, with an extremely fuzzy distorted sound at the end of the recording. It sounds like bagpipes or some other reedy, droning instrument.

The groove is insistent on the track, with percussion elements helping the big bad rock riff swing sexily. Jimmy Miller brought out the percussive elements of the Stones more than any previous producer or engineer. In the process of his work with the Stones and others, Miller helped usher rock 'n' roll as a genre into a new stage of production, one that embraced authentic African American traditions and Latin/African percussion. The result is essentially the very sound of late-1960s/early-'70s rock, a combination of new-style funk with an overall return to rock 'n' roll roots and, importantly, incorporating much more of the Southern soul.*

"It's funny," Miller, who died in 1994, told an interviewer. "Through the years so many people have told me I put the Stones back where they belonged. But I had nothing to do with the fact— they'd already written 'Jumpin' Jack Flash.' They were already quite willing to go back there. I'm sure the chemistry worked." It is the records made with Miller, though, that most regard as the *peak* of the band, with an alchemy and blend of elements that formed the essence of the Stonesy sound, captured on the records made from 1968–72.

Chris Blackwell had brought Miller to the UK to produce the

---

* The leader in that brand of funky R&B, and a hero to the Stones, Otis Redding, had died in a plane crash right around the time of the release of *Satanic Majesties*.

Spencer Davis Group. Miller's hallmarks were immediately evident on Spencer Davis Group classics "I'm a Man" (cowritten by Steve Winwood and Miller) and "Gimme Some Lovin'," which he re-mixed and recorded some overdubs. It had been a complaint of many English bands that the British rhythm sections were not re-corded and/or mixed with the same oomph and hefty presence of the American counterparts. All of a sudden, booty came to En-gland. Percussion and bottom end are the driving forces on Jimmy Miller tracks, energizing the mixes. It's exactly what the Stones needed and got.

"He didn't do anything with [technically engineering] sound," Chris Kimsey, who worked with Miller on *Sticky Fingers,* explained to me. "That was all Glyn [Johns]. But definitely getting the rhythm section and percussion together and just pushing the session along in a good way. And also very good at—if he saw a problem going or an indecision outside, he would go out and sort it out, that sort of thing. Jimmy created such a great atmosphere. And he was such a good drummer himself and he really knew, if they were struggling to find a beat or a feel, Jimmy knew what to do."

Up until this point, Johns claims the Stones had not recognized him as a producer, only an engineer. "They never really under-stood what a producer did, and I don't think they really know now. I don't think they've got a fucking clue," is how Johns describes the situation to an interviewer. "Jagger came to me after *Satanic Majesties* and said, 'We're gonna get a producer.' I said, 'Okay, fine.' He says, 'We're going to get an American.' I said, 'Oh my God, that's all I need. I don't think my ego could stand having some bloody Yank in here telling me what sort of sound to get for the Rolling Stones.'" Johns, though, immediately thought of Miller, whom he greatly respected, having observed him at Olympic. "Any-thing but some strange, lunatic, drug addict from Los Angeles! . . . And the first thing Jimmy Miller did was fire me because he'd been using Eddie Kramer as an engineer. . . ."

The trajectory from 1964 to 1968 marks the sharpest growth spurt in rock 'n' roll, and the Stones, midwifed by Miller, are the second-most-important contributor to the genre after the Beatles. At this point in their respective careers, one could even say it was as close as 1(a) and 1(b), as the Stones left the pop-masterpiece stuff to the Beatles, and chose to maximize kick-ass rock 'n' roll and R&B. Miller could bring the best out of the band and helped them rediscover the elemental gutsiness at their core. While "Jumpin' Jack Flash" retains a distinct psychedelic coloring, this edgy single points the way for the Stone's unique musical path as The Greatest Rock 'n' Roll Band in the World.

18
Street Fighting Man

RECORDED:

April 1968, Olympic Studios, London

RELEASES:

LP: *Beggars Banquet,* December 1968

US single, August 1968, charting at number 48

UK single, July 1970

The Stones Go Down to the Demonstration

A driving anthem that can be heard as a cynical, sarcastic musical answer to Martha and the Vandellas' 1964 Motown smash, "Dancing in the Street," "Street Fighting Man" offers the direct counterpoint of the sixties, an archly ironic answer to a happy pop song about, literally, dancing in the streets. Much had changed in the four years since the release of the Vandellas' single. The two songs could serve as bookends to the era.

The Stones were no strangers to riots, which had been a fairly regular occurrence at performances since 1964. But, with a few exceptions, those were mostly just kids out to have a good time and getting a bit out of control. In the US, though, the streets had been burning in dozens of US cities, including Los Angeles, Chicago, Cleveland, and, yes, Detroit. Most of those riots had racial tension and injustice as their impetus and in April 1968, inner cities around the country erupted in the aftermath of the assassination of Martin Luther King Jr. In June, Robert F. Kennedy was assassinated. Later that summer, there were mass demonstrations, riots, and widespread police brutality at the National Democratic Convention.

The era was tumultuous across Europe and Asia as well. There had been a coup in Greece, student protests and nationwide strikes that almost toppled DeGaulle's government in France, and the Communist crackdown of the Prague Spring in Czechoslovakia. Back home in London, Mick had gone "down to the demonstration" in Grosvenor Square to get his "fair share of abuse," which he later made reference to in "You Can't Always Get What You Want." It was the US military response to the North Vietnamese Tet Offensive of January 1968, in particular, that unleashed the large wave of protests that year. A crowd of demonstrators had formed in Trafalgar Square and marched over to the US Embassy, where the crowd was met with riot police. Mick was present at the protests. There, he ran into a young countercultural journalist named Barry Miles.

"He was there because he felt angry and rebellious but he had no way of formulating this, of giving it any kind of structure, and in a sense he was looking for anything to rebel against," Miles recalled for *The Independent* newspaper. "I don't think he had a carefully worked-out policy against Vietnam; I mean, he had a moral outrage against the war and that was about it . . . He didn't have a political reading of it. He had a much more artistic reading. This was something that got his adrenalin going, that enabled him to create and, in fact, in the same interview, he was saying how he could never really create when he was happy or peaceful, he could write much more easily if he was up against a deadline or he was in the middle of an argument or there was some kind of really weird scene going on, then it would come pouring out of him."

At a crossroads artistically, Mick had no grand political statement; he simply fed off the energy, and his lyric reveals exactly that. "What can a poor boy do/'cept to sing for a rock 'n' roll band?/'Cause in sleepy London town there's just no place for a street fighting man." He might only have been a singer in a rock 'n' roll band, but was calling out the so-called revolutionaries in London for their games of "compromised solution."

When the "Street Fighting Man" single was released on the heels of the DNC riots, it seemed like enough of an incendiary call to violence that the radio stations in the US buried it. The BBC refused to play it and it was held back as a UK single until 1970. Just the year prior, all you needed was love, peace, flowers, and Maharishi Mahesh Yogi. Nineteen sixty-eight turned sharply and the Stones were right in tune. If the Beatles were MLK and Gandhi, the Stones were Malcolm X and Stokely Carmichael.

Of course, neither the Beatles nor the Stones were anything but musicians mirroring their times, but their messages mattered acutely in 1968. Lennon himself, not long after the Beatles broke up, admitted to Tariq Ali—one of the Grosvenor Square organizers and an inspiration for "Street Fighting Man"—that he regretted not having come to a particular 1966 march, discouraged by their manager, Brian Epstein.

Looking back, Keith said in 1971 that the Beatles had been perfect musical ambassadors, winning people over to their way of thinking with beautiful pop music and the winning image they presented of charming charisma: "They were perfect for opening doors. But somewhere along the line, they got heavy. . . . When they went to America they made it wide open for us. We could never have gone there without them. . . . If they'd kept it together and realized what they were doing, instead of doing [Lennon's song] 'Power to the People' and disintegrating like that in such a tatty way. It's a shame."

The Beatles' ambivalence about treading into their first overtly political statement (if you discount "Taxman") was evident in their first release of the song "Revolution." Notably, it was relegated to being a B-side (to the monumental "Hey Jude"). "Revolution" comes out screaming with a screechy guitar recorded directly into the mixing console, and a shrieking Lennon.* Leftists all over were likely perched beside the turntable or radio, waiting for a message that would follow through on the threat promised by the title and the musical attack. They were let down, though, by the "lamentable petty bourgeois cry of fear" (*New Left Review*).

Lennon's lyrics showed no more ambivalence than Mick's did. But even as Mick cast around in frustration, he romanticized the street demonstrators, even if he decided he could only "sing for a rock 'n' roll band." Lennon, on the other hand, took a more nuanced approach and took many of the demonstrators to task. "When you go carrying pictures of Chairman Mao/You ain't gonna make it with anyone anyhow." And he was correct, of course. This was in line with Keith's point about the Beatles, making their points with a spoonful of sugar.

Lennon, who had not given much in the way of political commentary until 1968, was suddenly on the defensive. Once a working-class hero, he was now depicted as an out-of-touch rich guy buffered by a drug haze, boatloads of money, and in the honeymoon of a Dionysian relationship with Yoko Ono concerned more with aesthetics than politics—or, perhaps more egregious to the activists on the left, believing in the former as a solution to the latter.

Meanwhile, Mick, antennae more attuned to what the Zeitgeist was at all times, was ready to click in and run with whatever was

---

* A softer version of the song was released on the self-titled LP, the so-called *White Album.*

the prevailing spirit. In 1968, the fact that Mick felt so engaged and energized by the demonstrations is evident in the fact that he sent the handwritten lyrics to "Street Fighting Man" to Tariq Ali for him to publish in Ali's radical newspaper, *Black Dwarf,* where they appeared in November of that year, a month before the album's release. Less a political renegade than a savvy opportunist, the true Mick Jagger fell somewhere in between, and by the end of the next year he quickly proved he was no revolutionary, leaving all that behind in the grandiose 1969 jet-setting tour that culminated in a tragically mishandled "free concert" at Altamont Speedway.

"Jagger was one of the most intelligent of the rock stars in that period and it's a great pity he didn't stay on side [though he was back on side during the Iraq war]," Ali explained. "I don't think he ever changed on Vietnam, just domestically. Wealth determines consciousness, alas."

The sardonic nature and ambiguous nuance of the lyrics to "Street Fighting Man" were seemingly missed by the lefty papers that printed Mick's text as some sort of manifesto. After all, he was pointing out that the Grosvenor Square demonstrations piddled out rather anticlimactically when compared to the clashes that had just happened in Paris.

Mick penned the lyrics to "Street Fighting Man" after scrapping the words to what the band was referring to as "Pay Your Dues," which itself had morphed out of a track begun at Redlands on a cassette recorder, called "Primo Grande." The group again used the cassette recording in the master track itself. Keith and Charlie tracked it live on drums and acoustic to this lo-fi recorder. Here they were in a huge room in Olympic, a state-of-the-art facility, recording primitively to a mono cassette recorder, moving around to position for optimal balance of the instruments into the single microphone of the Philips. The only electric instrument on this intensely blazing rocker was the bass guitar, overdubbed by Keith.

As the song grew from the "Primo Grande" incarnation, it was bounced up to eight-track, allowing more overdubs. The recording predated "Jumpin' Jack Flash."

Charlie played a 1930s practice drum kit, which came in a little suitcase. "Keith would be sitting on a cushion playing a guitar and the tiny kit was a way of getting close to him," Charlie explained. "The drums were really loud compared to the acoustic guitar and the pitch of them would go right through the sound. You'd always have a great backbeat broke up a lot."

When incorporated into the master track, it sounded gargantuan. The band tracked live over this basic track, which sits to one side in the stereo mix. Brian played a sitar and Dave Mason, of Traffic, brought a big bass drum that he pounded. Mason also wailed on a shehnai, a Moroccan reed instrument that comes in around 2:31, a two-note variation that takes us out of the song. Brian apparently also played tamboura, a Turkish drone instrument similar to a lute. There are multiple acoustic guitar tracks, in varying tunings and capo positions.

The sound of "Street Fighting Man" is tight, with all that exotic instrumentation swirling around the core, out of which Nicky Hopkins's piano shoots out to play those celestial figures (which Ian Stewart and Mick Jagger referred to as "diamond tiaras") at the end. Mick double-tracked his vocal for a thickening effect. There are sections where he goes off track a little. Around 2:24–2:29, he slides all around the notes and offers a couple of ad libs out of time with each other, to desirable effect.

With the single, "Jumpin' Jack Flash," the Stones had refocused on what made them great in the first place: updated bluesy riffs, compelling lyrics, propulsive rhythm, and soulful vocals. Shake-rattle-and-roll percussion became a major force within their sound. Now, on *Beggars Banquet,* the band was following through on that gambit. But with "Street Fighting Man" they did not discard the exotic instrumentation and spirit of experimentation of the psychedelic years; they incorporated those elements into their musical continuum.

Jimmy Miller summed up the energized attitude of the Stones in this period when he said, ". . . after *Sergeant Pepper* most groups thought: well, what can we do *now?* and got overcomplicated." Referring to *John Wesley Harding*, Dylan's first LP in years, he added, "It took Bob Dylan to bring simplicity back to the scene." That album, along with The Band's *Music From Big Pink*, were both manifestations of the legendary *Basement Tapes* that Dylan and the members of The Band made during his post-motorcycle-crash 1967 stay in Woodstock, New York. Both Dylan's and The Band's albums had an enormous impact on other artists, including the Beatles and the Stones, who both got to work on some of their earthiest material to date. While much of *Beggars Banquet* is acoustic-based, the propulsive "Street Fighting Man" kept them rocketing forward, in step with a back-to-roots trend that took hold of mainstream rock for another ten years or so.

19
Sympathy for the Devil

RECORDED:

June 1968, Olympic Studios, London

RELEASES:

LP: *Beggars Banquet*, December 1968

Satanic Stones Star in a Godard Film

Who knew what evil lurks in the hearts of men? Mick did. Who killed the Kennedys? "You and me," he answers in this, their most provocative song to date.

The Rolling Stones made their first concert appearance in two years at the NME (New Musical Express) Poll Winners Concert, in May 1968, debuting their new single, "Jumpin' Jack Flash," which was released that same month. Though they had been in the public eye with the trials, the images of the band from 1967 had the doe-eyed, baby-faced Mick and Keith shoulder to shoulder in scarves and ruffle-collared shirts outside the courthouse. They next appeared, a year later, in war paint, impervious behind sunglasses, cast in deep dark shadows in their "Jumpin' Jack Flash" promo clip. When *Beggars Banquet* was released the following December, songs like "Street Fighting Man" and "Sympathy for the Devil" did not depict some cowering pack of boys, but a truculent band of brothers. They emerged more defiant than ever, adopting an almost militant persona.

But it's not as if the band of brothers now meant Brian was back in everyone's good graces. The NME concert would be Brian's last live appearance with the Stones. He had expressed a desire to move into a more electronic direction, experimenting with the newly developed Moog synthesizers, for example. But the consensus in the band was that they needed to put out a great, rootsy *Rolling Stones* album. He was further deteriorating, with another arrest for drug possession and general disenchantment with the band, and the feeling was mutual. "Dead weight" is how Keith has repeatedly described Brian from this period until his actual death. Photos of him around this time show him bloated, the rings under his eyes starkly pronounced. Film clips show hands shaking, lids drooping. He was no longer the golden boy, didn't want to play on the records, and, so really, what good was he?

But since there were no tours lined up, there was no need for the band to go through the drama of replacing him. They were actually happier when he did not show up at the studio. Keith could handle the guitar parts. Nevertheless, Brian makes a few substantive contributions to *Beggars Banquet,* the last LP on which he would play a significant part. In addition to the sitar textures he wove on "Street Fighting Man," Brian played a knee-buckling slide guitar track on the sublime "No Expectations."

Meanwhile, the band was energized, off the road and recording at home. The kids out in the streets were no longer teenyboppers looking to get their rocks off; they were impassioned college-age students (for the most part) challenging the legitimacy of their governments and institutions. Young people demonstrating in the streets of the West in general were viewed as threats and the Man came down hard on them, with violent clashes with cops a common outcome. Mick fed off the energy of the streets, channeling that urgency into the Stones music.

But the whole band was able to recharge in a more civilized manner as well, enjoying the fruits of their labor, their wealth, the celebrity status, going out at night, hanging out with young artists and intellectuals, enjoying adventurous new scenes like the Living Theater and avant garde cinema. Remaining cutting edge, the Stones themselves would star in just such a film. Trailblazing film director Jean-Luc Godard approached the Stones for his newest project.

Godard had already established himself as a pillar of the French New Wave of the early 1960s with his classic first feature, *Breathless (À bout de souffle)*, in 1960. Much of his subsequent work, particularly his films from 1968 to 1980, dealt with political issues, espousing Marxist and Maoist ideals. One such film was his Stones movie, *One Plus One*, later retitled (against his will) *Sympathy For the Devil,* after the song that serves as its centerpiece.

Godard intersperses clips of the Stones at work at Olympic with depictions of Black Panthers reading from comically didactic and dated political texts, against pretentiously theatrical milieus and disruptive staged scenes. The nonmusical parts are an incoherent pastiche. Keith called it "a big intellectual wank." Even Godard was not happy with it. However, it is it's verité documentation of the evolution of this tour de force rock song that makes it valuable for fans of the music. Under the working title "The Devil is My Name," the nascent song meanders for the first few scenes, a dragging tempo that seems to only get slower. We witness Keith as he tries to steer it in the same direction as "Jigsaw Puzzle," a song they had started fooling around with, which eventually was whipped into shape for the same album.

After one of Godard's staged scenes, the film cuts back to the sessions at Olympic and it is apparently a new day at the studio. The effect is like one of Godard's early jump cuts from *Breathless*.

The band is settling into a new torrid tempo. Rocky Dijon (a.k.a. Rocky Dzidzomu), an African drummer who would go on to grace many more Stones sessions, has entered the fray on conga drums. Mick appears to be trying to find the beat on a small Moroccan drum. They are close, but as Miller is heard saying on the talk-back intercom from the control room, "If we can get a groove happening, we'll probably be all right," at which point Keith and Mick smile knowingly, Mick moans, "Oh, Jimmy. Okay, we'll try for a groove."

Soon, Keith is counting off and we hear that famous samba beat with Charlie and Dijon that begins the record. Charlie's cross-stick on the snare was later excised from the intro in exchange for a stereo spread: conga drums on one side, and an Indian tabla drum played by Charlie with sticks on the other. Shakers spread across both sides. Hopkins then launches into a propulsive piano part that clearly is going to be the backbone in the new arrangement. You can watch Nicky, often in a corner of the frame, rolling with whatever variation the band is feeling its way through, trying out different figures and sounds.

"With the Stones," Charlie explained, "we go into the studio for a month and if it hasn't worked by then we go back for another one. It's ridiculous, really, it's not how people make records now. But out of that process would come things like 'Sympathy For the Devil.' We tried everything on that before we figured out which was the best beat to do. The first time I ever heard it was Mick playing it on the doorstep at my house on a summer's night."

By the time the song has found its footing in the film, we get a sweeping crane shot that starts with a frame of a group assembled around a microphone singing the "ohh-ooh" backing part, and then swings around to the other side of the baffles to capture Mick singing the lead vocal at the same time. He is *bringing* it, his body jerking as he wrenches out the global travelogue through historic atrocities. The backing vocal group consists of Keith, Bill, Brian,

Jimmy, Charlie, and—from behind—Anita and Marianne. While Keith is swinging his arms in fluid motions to cue the group, Charlie is hilariously deadpan, arms akimbo, pallid, barely opening his mouth.

Pictured in this scene, you can see why Anita was more or less an unofficial Rolling Stone at this point, certainly an inspiration to the band. Her style merged with Brian's, heightening his own flamboyance and eventually usurping it as he faded. And her fashion sense was adopted by Keith, transforming him from a longhair greaser to a buccaneering Lord Byron for the rock set. "Anita was the epitome of what was happening at the time," said Miller. "She was very Chelsea. She'd arrive with the elite film crowd. During 'Sympathy for the Devil,' when I started going whoo, whoo in the control room, so did they. I had the engineer set up a mike so they could go out in the studio and whoo, whoo."

The first song on *Beggars Banquet,* "Sympathy For the Devil" is led by piano and percussion. There is just piano, percussion, bass guitar, and vocals for the whole song. The only guitar that survived is that lacerating solo halfway in and in the ending vamp. The track opens with the surreal muffled laughs of women, most likely Marianne and Anita at the very top of the track. The tribal drumming, whooping, and lady-laughing noises bring a ghostly voodoo ceremony feel to the track. The Stones were stepping deep into the darkness of American blues and Appalachian folk on *Beggars Banquet,* which was just that: a veritable banquet of dark, stark, hillbilly folk-evil of *Deliverance*-like spookiness, and Southern gospel and country blues. But the band was also laying down sinister city slicker vignettes like "Stray Cat Blues," "Street Fighting Man," and "Sympathy For the Devil."

Mick was also stimulated at the time by a great deal of reading: philosophy, poetry, and biography, up to his neck in literature from Rimbaud, Baudelaire, and Mikhail Bulgakov, whose allegorical and satirical novel *The Master and Margarita* he was apparently introduced to by Marianne. The book was inspired by Goethe's adaptation of the legend of *Faust,* and features Woland, a character who is Satan in disguise, and who, as a professor of the dark arts, exposes the petty emptiness of the bourgeoisie of a town.

All of this material factors into Mick's Dylan-style lyric, as does St. Petersburg, the czar, and Anastasia, all evidence of an influence by a Russian novel. But the most chilling line has always been "I shouted out who killed the Kennedys," which we see morph, astonishingly from "who killed Kennedy." The sessions took place over June 4–10. Mick changes the lyric to the plural when Robert Kennedy is assassinated on June 5. The change is presented without comment in the film.

The leaders who, at the beginning of the decade, had inspired hope and a vision for a more progressive future were now being assassinated at an alarming rate. To many in 1968, peace and love were no longer looking like viable catalysts for the change of the postwar conservative status quo in the West. Violence was being met with more violence.

Continuing the trajectory established with the single for "Jumpin' Jack Flash," the Stones had shed any remaining allegiance they had to the "All You Need Is Love" point of view of the mid-to-late 1960s, the start of a tense arc that would soon peak and burst at the time of their infamous free concert at Altamont, California. Perhaps not coincidentally, "Sympathy for the Devil" is featured in the seminal Maysles Brothers documentary, *Gimme Shelter*, though, contrary to a common misconception, this was not the song the band was playing when the Hells Angels stabbed a man to death at the concert; it was "Under My Thumb." But the mythology of the Rolling Stones is durable.

And neither would those with imbecilic minds be swayed from their belief that Mick was professing allegiance to, or even to be Satan himself. Taking on the role of Satan in 1968 was not the heavy metal cliché it came to be in the late 1970s. This might be ground zero for the evangelical fundamentalists looking to find the rise of satanism in rock 'n' roll music—that is, aside from those who thought rock 'n' roll *itself* was the Devil's music (a notion dating back to the beginnings of the music). "Before, when we were just innocent kids out for a good time," Keith recalled in 1971, "they're saying, 'they're evil, they're evil.' Oh, I'm evil, really? So that makes you start thinking about evil. What is evil? Half of it, I don't know how many people think Mick is the Devil or just a good rock performer or what? There are black magicians out there who think we are acting as agents of Lucifer, and others who think we are Lucifer. Everybody's Lucifer."

Mick was playing this role on a couple of levels: that which he intended, the Faustian character who comes and exposes that the evil is within us, not some foreign external force. And he also plays the insolent rocker tweaking the noses of the conservatives who hated the Stones and thought them to be evil incarnate. "Please allow me to introduce myself," says the newly minted rock star millionaire provocateur, Mick Jagger, knight of Satan, "I'm a man of wealth and taste."

"I never really did the subject to death," Mick has said, "but I did have to back off a little, because I could see what was happening. It's an easily exploitable image, and people really went for it in a big way."

But maybe there was something to this dangerous dance with the Devil after all. On the night of June 10, heat from Godard's film crew's lamps set the studio ceiling on fire. Jimmy and Bill rustled up all the master tapes and stored them in a vault before running out to safety. Fire crews dowsed the flames, along with all the musical equipment. Maybe Brian Jones was not the only fallen angel present at the Olympic session.

20
Stray Cat Blues

RECORDED:

June 1968, Olympic Studios, London

RELEASES:

LP: *Beggars Banquet*, December 1968

Pimps, Imps, Groupies, and Rock Stars

S tray Cat Blues" stumbles in like a drunk, and now things get truly sleazy, with lascivious rock-star wolves slobbering after underage Little Red Riding Hoods. The song sounds like it's about a rock star coming on to groupies, but it could also simply be read as a pimp's seduction of a potential runaway, like a scene from the 1976 film *Taxi Driver*. There is nothing in there specifically about the rock star milieu. But one gets the sense that the band was having some fun again at the expense of groupies while accepting yet another outlaw role handed to them by fearful parents and church elders. Mick was now living up to the image that had arisen only a couple of years prior when he wanted to "spend the night together" with a girl. It would have been interesting to hear how Ed Sullivan felt about this one.

On the *Beggars Banquet* LP, Mick expanded his role as if he were an actor in addition to a writer and singer. From the narrator of "Street Fighting Man," to the hick in a shotgun wedding in "Dear Doctor," to the Devil himself in "Sympathy for the Devil," it was as if he were changing costumes between songs. With this song, Mick doubled down on the outsized rank outsider, streetwise persona he created around "Jumpin' Jack Flash" and continued to inhabit through "Sympathy for the Devil," the unreleased "Cocksucker Blues," "Midnight Rambler," and "Memo from Turner." The lyric of "Stray Cat Blues" was catnip for those outraged about the band's collective attitude displayed toward women (or in this case, underage girls). At some point, though, listeners just stopped fretting about these topics in Stones lyrics, shrugged their collective shoulders, and said, *Oh, whatever. It's the Stones being the Stones.* They were, after all, merely continuing the rock 'n' roll and blues tradition of winking and leering at teenage girls, as in "Sweet Little Sixteen," "Sixteen Candles," "You're Sixteen, You're Beautiful, and You're Mine," and "Only Sixteen" (how many 1950s songs are *not* about teenage girls?), right on back to blues like 1937's "Good Morning Little Schoolgirl."

The street-realism influences and harder edged rock of the era's new bands like the Velvet Underground, Iggy and the Stooges, and MC5 now played a part in a circular exchange with the Stones, whose impact in turn rippled beyond music and directly influenced the early work of filmmakers like Martin Scorcese (such as *Mean Streets* in 1973) not to mention countless garage-rock bands. The first Velvet Underground LP had come out in 1967, offering a welcome shady antidote to the year's sunshiny psychedelia. "I mean, even we've been influenced by the Velvet Underground," admitted Mick to Nick Kent in *NME* in 1977. "I'll tell you exactly what we pinched from [Lou Reed] too. You know 'Stray Cat Blues'? The whole sound and the way it's paced, we pinched from the very first Velvet Underground album. You know, the sound on 'Heroin.' Honest to God, we did!"

And you can hear it. Those opening stinging guitars before Charlie flops in on the sloppy drum fill are extremely similar to the austere ringing parts with which the Velvets open "Heroin." Mick sounds like a stoned licentious pimp with a Neanderthal grunting laugh, as his partner in crime spurts out those guitar figures. When the whole band kicks in, the sound is flat and dry, Velvets style, but funkier, with a superior rhythm section, playing a chord progression that would later find its way into "Sweet Home Alabama" and countless other D-C-G songs. The choruses become a brambly knot of trebly guitars over that low rumbling funk of the bass, drums, left-hand piano, and muted rhythm guitar. It's not until the song starts to peter out of its first section (around 2:53) that you realize there is a Mellotron incongruously playing the sound of flutes (Brian), which drift off hauntingly, just as the song seems like it is going to fade out. But Charlie goes back to playing that more slick rhythm on the hi-hat he was playing in the main body of the song, keeping astride of Rocky Dijon's congas, before he lurches back into a backbeat. Out of nowhere comes an amped-up, chugging rhythm guitar part (at 3:35), jarringly high up in the mix, kicking the vamp into turbo, with some curlicue leads rounding out the other side of the stereo mix. The Mellotron wheezes back in as the recording draws to its final fade, like psychedelic rock's last gasp.

Mick sings: ". . . I bet your mama don't know you scratch like that." While the lyric pushes the envelope, the song was certainly never going to be considered for a single, and as such could remain somewhat hidden as an album track for the true fans to discover.

The Rolling Stones were not just getting back to the street on *Beggars Banquet,* they were diving into the gutter, and their first choice of an album cover was to underscore this message. They first attempted a highly stylized and overly art-directed shoot that presented the album's title in literal form, with a cast of characters at a medieval banquet table. That having failed, art director Tom Wilkes had an idea to photograph a seedy toilet at a Porsche repair shop in LA while the band was in town mixing the album (at Sunset Sound Studios). The photo was taken by his business partner and photographer, Barry Feinstein. Behind the toilet was a grimy wall featuring graffiti, which Keith, Mick, and Anita themselves embellished, by drawing and writing silly phrases, like "God Rolls His Own," "Bob Dylan's Dream" (with squiggly arrow pointing down the toilet, and the lyrics to "Parachute Woman" ("land on me tonight"), accompanied by a crude drawing of a nude woman.

Decca was not amused and found it "in dubious taste," to which Mick retorted that he found another Decca release, *Atomic Tom Jones,* with its image of an A-bomb explosion far more objectionable. "They really wouldn't budge," recalled Keith in 1971. "It stopped the album from coming out [sooner]. Eventually it got to be too much of a drag. It went on for nine months or so. It was like them saying, *We don't give a shit if your album never goes out.* After that, we knew it was impossible and started looking around to do it differently." In the end the stubborn antiauthoritarian band succumbed and put out an elegant looking plain white album cover made to look like a formal invitation, quite at odds with the music within, but, in an unfortunate coincidence, released weeks after the Beatles had released their eponymous LP in a simple white sleeve, informally referred to as the *White Album*. This predictably resulted in accusations from some that the Stones were yet again imitating the Beatles. However, *Beggars Banquet* was actually slated for release earlier than the *White Album* and it was this issue of LP cover art that held up the release of the Stones LP so that it came out after the Beatles LP. The Stones had no idea that the Beatles were planning a similar cover.

What mattered most, of course, is the music inside and not the sleeve. Consisting of country blues, biting city-slicker hard rock, gospel, and Dylan-esque folk, *Beggars Banquet* did nothing less than simultaneously chart the band's future sound while reaching back to the group's foundational roots.

"The Stones have unleashed their rawest, ludest, most arrogant, most savage record yet. And it's beautiful," wrote Carl Bernstein, later to become legendary as one of the reporters who broke the Watergate scandal. Jann Wenner wrote in *Rolling Stone*: "Their new album will mark a point in the short history of rock and roll: the formal end of all the pretentious, nonmusical, boring, insignificant, self-conscious and worthless stuff that has been tolerated during the past year in the absence of any standards set by several great figures in rock and roll." *Beggars Banquet* was the Rolling Stones' first masterpiece, five years into their career. It "was like coming out of puberty," said Keith. But it was followed by three more of equal-or-better quality that mark one of the greatest four-year runs from any artist. With this album, the band commenced a flawless five-year run that represents their peak. Only Dylan and the Beatles had matched or bettered them, but their best work was in the rearview mirror. The Stones were just getting started.

21
You Can't Always Get What You Want

RECORDED:

November 16, 1968, Olympic Studios, London

RELEASES:

LP: *Let It Bleed*, December 1969

B-side to "Honky Tonk Women" single, July 1969

The Party's Over, Bring on the Seventies

After a staid introduction sung by the London Bach Choir, Al Kooper's French horn just sort of sighs in gracefully to the wistful beginning of "You Can't Always Get What You Want," alongside Keith's tentative acoustic guitar strumming. The opaque Dylan-esque lyrics of the verses have served for decades as vessels that carry pretty much any message a listener might want to assign them. Combined with the epigrammatic sing-along chorus, "You Can't Always Get What You Want" served as the perfect song to summarize the dashed dreams of the 1960s. More than one songwriter thought, "Why didn't I think of that chorus?"

In November 1968, the Stones' regular keyboardist, Nicky Hopkins, was in the US working on another session. Al Kooper—the keyboardist, songwriter, arranger, and then-staff A&R and producer at Columbia Records—just happened to be flying to London for a little rest and shopping. He had called up his friend, record producer Denny Cordell, to see if he could pick him and his wife up from the airport, with strict instructions not to tell anyone he was in town.

Kooper had become an in-demand session player ever since he had burst on the scene with his legendary organ part on Bob Dylan's generation-defining "Like a Rolling Stone." He parlayed this session into a magical *Zelig*-like career that included playing at Dylan's first electric gigs (including Newport in 1965), founding Blood, Sweat & Tears, discovering Lynyrd Skynyrd and producing their first three albums, and years later recording with George Harrison on the night that the news broke of the shooting death of John Lennon.

Kooper might have come to London looking to escape work for a while, but when Cordell picked him up at the airport he informed Kooper that the Stones wanted him for a session. Cordell claimed he had not made mention of the fact that Kooper just happened to be in town. The timing of the call from the Stones was just coincidence, apparently. They had supposedly not known that he was in London. "The Stones called him and said 'We'd like Al Kooper to play on a session,' Kooper told me in an interview. *"Why are they calling me?"* But Kooper remained adamant that he was not going to work on this vacation.

Within the first twenty-four hours of his arrival, Kooper was in Chelsea, out shopping, when, poetically, he bumped into none other than Brian Jones. "And then that clincher of walking into Brian Jones. . . . I wasn't going to do [the session]," he remarked, still shaking his head at the coincidence. Kooper was mildly surprised that Brian had remembered him. Their only other meeting, during the Monterey Pop Festival, had been somewhat inauspicious. They were on the same Lear Jet that had been shuttling performers up from LA, "and he was *out* of it," recalled Kooper. "He was on Mars. And he sat next to me and, he wasn't there. So I thought, *this is good*. And that's when we met. But he wasn't *there*!"

In London, Brian told Kooper that the Stones were excited to have him coming to play on their session the next day. It was a *fait accomplis* at that point. Kooper decided he had to do the session. The band had wanted him for two days. He figured he could beg off the second date if the first one was no fun. But it *was* fun. And for a sideman, just as with Hopkins on "Sympathy for the Devil," Kooper has a prominent role in the final mix.

Charlie and Bill arrived soon after Kooper and they reacquainted themselves. They had met once or twice when Kooper was with Dylan. Brian arrived "and laid on his stomach reading an article on botany for the entire session," said Kooper. Mick and Keith came in later, "exploding through the door," he recalled. "Mick was wearing a gorilla coat, and Keith had on this sort of Tyrollean hat with a real long feather in it. . . . Mick and Keith were the last to arrive. When they got there, they passed out acoustic guitars [to all the musicians]. And then they just played the song over and over again until everybody could learn it." Everyone sat on the floors, passing joints. "[Percussionist] Rocky Dijon could roll joints and play congas at the same time."

" 'You Can't Always Get What You Want' was basically all Mick," said Keith. "I remember him coming into the studio and saying, 'I've got this song.' I said, 'You got any verses?' And he said, 'I have, but how is it going to sound?' Because he'd written it on guitar, it was like a folk song at the time. I had to come up with a rhythm, an idea."

They kept running through the song until everyone had gotten the concept. Then they started in on their respective instruments, running through the track for over an hour. "Just everybody learning it and staying out of each other's way," Kooper said. "I had the

Etta James 'I Got You Babe' piano part," he explained, referring to James's cover of the Sonny and Cher song, "a groove, a beat, taken from the horns on what was probably my favorite record at the time . . . It was a Muscle Shoals thing. It could have been any artist on any song. It just happened to be that lick." He hums a rhythm—imagine the push-and-pull shuffle beat of "You Can't Always Get What You Want."

"I told Keith where it was from and I played it and asked 'Is it okay if I play this?' And he said, 'That's good.'"

Brian is not on the recording. He remained in the studio, though, reading the article on botany. The basic track is Kooper on piano, Keith on guitar (the acoustic, open-tuned with a capo), Bill on bass, Mick on vocals, and Jimmy Miller on drums. "Jimmy Miller played drums on a couple of tracks on *Let It Bleed,* including 'You Can't Always Get What You Want,' which I subsequently copied," Charlie said in 2003. "That's how good Jimmy was at hearing songs. He wasn't a great drummer, but he was great at playing drums on records, which is a completely different thing. 'You Can't Always Get What You Want' is a great drum track. Jimmy actually made me stop and think again about the way I played drums in the studio and I became a much better drummer in the studio thanks to him." Charlie says that Miller instilled a certain discipline in him when it came to recording drums.

Miller had been trying to demonstrate an idea he had to Charlie. Kooper recounted that Charlie said something like, "Why don't you play it for me." And so Miller did, but he never got up from the drum set. "It's pretty amazing," Kooper said, still astonished at Miller's behavior forty-three years later. "I don't think a lot of people know that [about Jimmy staying on the drums].

"Charlie handled it with unbelievable class. I don't know that he was unhappy. But I mean, wouldn't anyone be unhappy? But you could not read that in him. He is a very classy gentleman. Which I thought Jimmy Miller was the opposite of for doing it in the first place. . . . Charlie seemed to really want to get back and play. The best thing about Miller staying on drums was that it kept him out of Mick's hair. It was Mick who really produced that session.

"It didn't *ruin* the record, so, *that's* good," Kooper added, sardonically.

Mick and Keith did not have an arrangement for the song. For example, "You Can't Always Get What You Want" had no bridge or middle-eight section. Kooper had the idea for what is there now, the tension-release breakdown (around the 4:17 mark). "I played that on piano and I sort of just brought it to everybody else."

Mick sang the guide track with the live tracking. "I always remember on the track he sang, while we were playing, when we got to the second line of the chorus, he sang 'You can't always satisfy your greed,' which I thought was a good line."

When they got to the third ("Mr. Jimmy") verse, Kooper started to riff on the organ overdub, a call-and-response with Mick's vocal lines. Keith was overdubbing the electric at the same time, so about halfway through that verse, Kooper gestured for Keith to take over, which he does on the second half of that verse. He explained, "It was common in those days," to overdub multiple instruments simultaneously. "Now each person would do their own overdub. But that's the way we would do it in those days."

The organ builds in a crescendo, the Leslie speaker starting to accelerate its rotation at just the right time. As we discussed his piano triplets—trills he plays as the song reaches its climax and beyond, before Miller and the band shift into gospel double time—Kooper said, "Mick also liked those."

When it was time to take a break during the session, Kooper was astounded at the first-class-rock-star level service. "At around ten or eleven o'clock, two vans pull up with an unbelievable array of food. Beyond catering. From soup to nuts. It was *fabulous*. I was like 'I can live like this.'" When they got back to work, Kooper was in a bit of a food coma, almost forgetting his organ part. But when they were finished and listening to the playback, Kooper turned to Mick with an idea.

"I had a whole Stax/Volt horn arrangement," Kooper explains "At the first session I said to Mick, 'If you ever want to put horns on this, I know exactly what to do.' And then he called me a year later . . . And I was working at Columbia Records. It was pretty funny, my secretary came in and said, "Some guy says he's Mick Jagger is on the phone.' I love that! [laughs] You should have seen the look on her face when I finished the call and said, 'It *was* Mick Jagger!'"

Mick remembered Kooper's idea for horns, so he told Kooper he was going to send him the tapes to overdub horns onto the song. "I was flattered for two reasons. One was that they remembered [his idea], and the second was that he didn't come *with* the tapes." Mick trusted Kooper to just chart the horns and produce the overdub session himself. So Kooper booked a session and hired some New York horn players.

"But . . . the horn players *stunk!* I hired guys that played like shit, so I couldn't use it . . . I was trying to emulate the Memphis Horns. They wouldn't, *couldn't* do it. And so it didn't sound good. And I had written a French horn part into it so that I could play on it. 'Cause I wanted to play on it. I played French horn in college. And so when they left, I said, I am going to send him this. And I know he's not gonna use it. So why don't I do something he can use. I'll replace the organ part with the French horn. And that's what I did and of course that's all he kept." Kooper erased the organ that had been there (it was a copy tape, of course). The horns played the same part he was playing on piano, more or less.

I asked if he kept a mix of the horns version. "IT WAS TERRI-BLE!" he shouts. "I never want to hear it again!"

But that melancholy French horn that survived is so fitting.

Kooper also lends the track an American gospel feel with his

organ parts during the ending. The song's gospel tone was a har-
binger of things to come for the band, especially on *Exile on Main
Street*. Similar to "Salt of the Earth," from *Beggars Banquet,* "You
Can't Always Get What You Want" is as much of a folk song as a
gospel song. But the latter features more numerous genuine
church-style elements than the former, which introduces an actual
American gospel choir, the Watts Street choir from Los Angeles, to
sing along to the chorus at the end.

"You Can't Always Get What You Want" starts off with the
decidedly non-gospel London Bach Choir, who come in as a reprise
at the vamp at the end of the song with a two-chord echo of Kooper's
organ part. Jack Nitzsche was flown over to London to arrange the
choral parts at a session on March 15. Joining the male musicians
are the female backing singers, Doris Troy—who had a solo hit in
the early 1960s with "Just One Look"—and her two backing singers, Nanette Workman (listed incorrectly as "Nanette Newman")
and Madeline Bell. The backing singers, plus Miller on drums and
Kooper on organ, lend the track the feeling of more authentic gospel than "Salt of the Earth." But the band still felt the need to un-
dercut it with irony. "I'd . . . had this idea of having a choir,
probably a gospel choir, on the track," said Mick, "but there wasn't
one around at that point. Jack Nitzsche, or somebody, said that we
could get the London Bach Choir and we said, *That will be a laugh*."

Keith explains the use of the choir: "Let's put on a straight chorus. In other words, let's try to reach the people up there as well. It
was a dare, kind of . . . what if we got one of the best choirs in England, all these white, lovely singers, and do it that way? . . . It was
a beautiful juxtaposition."

With the epic "You Can't Always Get What You Want" clocking
in at 7:30 on the LP version (a 5:00 edit appears as the B-side to
"Honky Tonk Women"), the band turned in their longest song
since "Going Home" from *Aftermath*. While Dylan had for years
been making long-form recordings that showed little regard for the

pop-music convention of having songs stay under three minutes, the practice of letting songs roll on was not yet common. The Stones were encouraged by the Beatles breaking the rules a little with "Hey Jude" in 1968, at 7:11.

As the last song on the last Stones album in the sixties, from one of the decade's most prominent bands, "You Can't Always Get What You Want" summarized how they and their fans felt about the wreckage of their optimism and ideals, as well as their own personal loss of innocence as the decade flamed to a close. Though the Stones themselves were still only in their mid-twenties, the generation who had been growing up with the band was now experienced enough to feel nostalgia for past relationships, good times gone by, and friends and siblings dead in Vietnam. There was a resonance to open-ended lyrics about seeing damaged old buddies now waiting in line for their government-issued dose of junk, and ex-lovers "practiced in the art of deception," moving on to their next victims. "Mr. Jimmy" referred to Jimmy Miller, and Mick might have partially been singing to Marianne, who had just undergone a devastating miscarriage and was slipping into deeper drug abuse partially to numb the pain. Things also looked to be fraying around the edges a bit for Keith and Anita, who started to dabble with heroin around this time. But the lyrics are wide open to interpretation. Mick was looking around and reporting on those he could see losing their grasp. Brian would play no significant part in *Let It Bleed,* and by June 1969 would be formally out of the band. Weeks later, he would be discovered drowned in his swimming pool, at the house previously owned by *Winnie-the-Pooh* author, A. A. Milne.

The Songs

Part 2
THE MICK TAYLOR YEARS

22
Honky Tonk Women

RECORDED:

June 1969, Olympic Studios, London

RELEASES:

Single, July 1969, charting at number 1 in US and UK

The End of the Brian Jones Era

An upbeat evergreen oldies radio staple, and a Jimmy Miller–kissed quintessential Stones track, "Honky Tonk Women" is that perfect blend of country, blues, and R&B that represented the unique mélange that the Stones stewed up during their 1968–1973 apex.

The band sounded like they were clicking on all cylinders, but the relationship between Mick and Keith before they entered into the 1968–69 sessions for the *Let It Bleed* LP was actually tense and possibly irrevocably scarred. Mick and Anita had engaged in a brief affair on the set of *Performance,* the 1968 film in which they both starred. But Keith had stolen Anita from Brian, after all. And while Anita and Mick were shooting one night, Keith and Marianne had their own short payback affair. By 1969, Anita and Marianne had each slept with Brian, Mick, and Keith. Keith wasn't about to let this sort of incestuous pettiness get in the way of making great recordings, though. He refused to acknowledge the infidelity to either of the principals, choosing instead to once again channel the emotions into the music.

Obviously, getting past all of this presented a challenge. The band was now right in the middle of its most productive period. So they swept it under the rug. If the two couples had hurt each other significantly, such damage was put aside for a cruise that Mick, Marianne, Keith, and Anita took in December from Lisbon to South America, to spend the holidays. While on the ship, the traveling party was peppered with questions about *just who the hell were they?* by an "upper-class . . . pre-war" set of Noel Coward castoffs. One woman begged, "Oh, do give us a hint, just a glimmer," to which Mick replied, "We're the Glimmer Twins." As any good liner-notes-reading Stones fan knows, this is the moniker later adopted by Mick and Keith for the producers' credit on their albums.

While staying on a ranch in Brazil during this holiday, the Glimmer Twins came up with the genesis of "Country Honk," the Jimmie Rodgers–hick version of "Honky Tonk Women." The former was included on *Let It Bleed* and the latter was released prior to the album as a single. But while Mick and Keith were working their way through their personal tensions, they had finally reached the end of their rope with Brian. Brian had not been stable enough to withstand the rigors of touring, and this had been tolerated as long as the band was not going out on the road. But now the band was ready to tour. "We felt like we had a wooden leg," said Mick. "We wanted to go out and play but Brian couldn't. I don't think that he really wanted to and it was this that really pissed me off. He didn't have any desire to go onstage and play." Even if he had wanted to tour, Brian could not get a visa due to a number of drug arrests.

But Brian had not even made consistent contributions to any

recording sessions since 1967. On *Let It Bleed,* his only lasting tracks are an autoharp on "You Got the Silver," and percussion on "Midnight Rambler," which Keith calls "a last flare from a shipwreck." The chronology of 1969 shows an ever-rapidly sinking Brian: more arrests; new girlfriend; psychiatric care; another new girlfriend; motorcycle crash; and finally, the inevitable sacking from the band he formed.

Before the Stones fired Brian, though, they wanted to secure a new guitarist who could record and tour with them. "The band . . . could have had anybody they wanted, including God himself," said Ian Stewart, alluding to the "Clapton is God" graffiti that had appeared in England in the mid-1960s. "Clapton came to a recording session. Mick Taylor was very quiet and shy, but they got him playing. He was right. He could play."

Shy, bluesy, and angelic as Brian had once been, Mick Taylor had been all of seventeen in 1966 when he joined John Mayall's Bluesbreakers, replacing Clapton, becoming Mayall's latest discovery in this band legendary for turning out the country's greatest blues musicians. The Bluesbreakers were like the Count Basie Band, a training ground and springboard for future stars.

Taylor had remained under Mayall's tutelage for close to three years at which point he began to grow restless.* And in 1969, Taylor amicably parted ways with Mayall. When Mick Jagger asked Mayall if he had any ideas as a replacement for Brian, Mayall issued his stamp of approval for Taylor, whom Ian Stewart had also recommended to Mick and Keith. Taylor had not even known that he was being auditioned when he was called in as a session guitarist on May 24 to add some overdubs on "Honky Tonk Women." In fact, Taylor has said the sessions were so loose that he got bored, telling the Stones, "Well, if you're not going to play, I'm going

---

* During that time, the young guitarist purchased a Gibson Les Paul guitar, a rare commodity, from none other than Keith Richards, during the *Satanic Majesties* sessions.

home." Then they told him that, unbeknownst to him, the session had been an audition and he was offered the gig, which he accepted.

Brian Jones was officially sacked from the Stones on June 8, 1969. At a session in May, he had surprised no one with his announcement that he was thinking of leaving the band in order to work on his own projects. Finishing up the mix for "Honky Tonk Women," Mick and Keith shrewdly took Charlie, in a peacemaker's role, out to Brian's house to speak with him in person. "I think Charlie believed in what we did," said Mick. "We had to. It was either stand up or fall over. I elected to stand up."

"Brian Jones had a death wish at a young age," Charlie later told Jann Wenner. "Brian's talent wasn't up to it. He wasn't up to leading a band. He was not a pleasant person to be around. And he was never there to help people to write a song. That's when Mick lost his patience. We carried Brian Jones." But it was easy on no one, least of all Charlie, who said in 1979, "It was the worst thing so far that I've ever had to do."

On June 18, within days of the June 1969 session for "Honky Tonk Women," and ten days after they had fired Brian, Taylor was formally announced as the Stones' new guitarist. The non-album "Honky Tonk Women" single (which was backed with "You Can't Always Get What You Want") was the first time that the public had heard Taylor on a Stones recording. Most of the *Let It Bleed* tracks had been finished when Jagger called Taylor to come down to the studio to contribute to the sessions. When *Let It Bleed* was released later that year, he could also be heard playing on "Live with Me," on which he traded licks with Keith live at Olympic during the actual tracking with the band. Taylor said that he and Keith clicked immediately on the session for "Live With Me." "And that was kind of the start of that particular era for the Stones, where Keith and I traded licks. He'd sometimes play rhythm, I'd sometimes play rhythm, but on stage there'd always be quite a lot of lead guitar playing, which I'd do most of."

The first thing we hear on the record is neither guitarist, though. Producer Jimmy Miller starts the recording by tapping the beat on the cowbell after which Charlie joins with the simple fill into the spartan drumbeat. Keith joins in with that slow-hand twang riff, followed by Mick's opening lines. The sparse funky drumbeat and off-beat cowbell coupled with the debut of Keith's newly discovered chunky five-string open tuning—treated with just a touch of slap-back echo—offers the closest thing to the horn-kissed country-soul that had been emanating from Stax Studios in the mid-to-late 1960s. While "Jumpin' Jack Flash" offered one template that the Stones would follow for decades, "Honky Tonk Women" provided another, the lazy big-booty beat, the heavy percussion, a memorable riff with a tone balanced between raunch and clarity, and Mick drawling out a simple few verses and catchy chorus with full conviction and humor. It's country funk.

"We've never played an intro to 'Honky Tonk Women' live the way it is on the record," said Charlie. "Either [Miller] comes in wrong or I come in wrong—but Keith comes in right, which makes the whole thing right. It's one of those things that musicologists could sit around analyzing for years. It's actually a mistake, but from my point of view, it works." The cowbell apparently had emanated from another effort by Miller to steer Charlie in a certain direction. Keith added, "I remember the looks in the studio as we were cutting the track—*Don't fuck it up now, boy, this is it.* [Laughs] You know, I mean, the track was rocking."

The tempo takes off audibly during the first chorus, and it does not come back to its slower opening. In fact, it speeds up at various points as the song progresses, only adding to that lurching excitement that Keith mentioned. "Charlie is unbelievable on that track," he says. "It was a groove, no doubt about it, and it's one of those tracks that you knew was a number one before you'd finished the motherfucker."

It's a stellar showcase of Keith's fluid rhythm guitar and riffing, a seamless style that he perfected. He tracks the rhythm guitar that weaves around the drumbeat, and Taylor enters with his wiry anticipatory licks that lead into the choruses, which is when the bass enters, along with Stu's boogie piano and backing singers. Keith had picked up the open G tuning from Ry Cooder. "I tip my hat to Ry Cooder," Keith acknowledged. "He showed me the open G tuning. But he was using it strictly for slide playing." Cooder is widely acknowledged as influencing a significant part of the Stones sound with this simple device.

It was a new Stones sound, with girlie backup parts from Reparata and the Delrons (a US singing group with some minor UK successes), plus Nanette Workman, Doris Troy, and blaring horns (from Steve Gregory and Bud Beadle) that punch the song home. It heralded a new direction for the band, one that would emphasize a modernized R&B style that could also be heard in groups like Delaney and Bonnie & Friends and Joe Cocker's Mad Dogs and Englishmen (which consisted of many of the same band member as Delaney and Bonnie & Friends), and led to the sound of early-1970s funky, gospel/R&B-rooted rock 'n' roll.

While the Stones were newly energized with their new songs, new sounds, and a new guitarist, they were about to be slammed with shocking news about their old "wooden leg." On July 3, the band got the call that Brian had drowned in his swimming pool. He was twenty-seven. "We were in the studio when we got the phone call . . . cutting with Mick Taylor," writes Keith. "There exists one minute and thirty seconds of us recording 'I Don't Know Why,' a Stevie Wonder song, interrupted by the phone call telling us of Brian's death." Mick, Keith, and Charlie sat in the studio for hours, stunned. Charlie called Bill, who had left the studio. He sat up all night crying with Astrid at the Londonderry House Hotel.

San Diego Public Library
DATE DUE SLIP
****

Date due: 8/6/2014,23:59
Title: Rocks off : 50 tracks that
tell the story of The
Call number: 782.42166
/JANOVITZ
Item ID: 31336092567982
Date charged: 7/16/2014,18:45

Total checkouts for session:1
Total checkouts:1

<><><><><><><><><><><><>
Renew at
www.sandiegolibrary.org
OR Call 619-236-5800 or
858-484-4440 and press 1
then 2 to RENEW. Your
library card is needed to
renew borrowed items.

On July 5, the Hyde Park concert that had been planned as the debut of their new guitarist, and the band's first public concert in years, opened with a tribute to Brian. Mick, in a white dresslike shirt, chastised the crowd to "cool it," and read two verses from "Adonais," Shelley's elegy to Keats, which begins:

> *Peace, peace! he is not dead, he doth not sleep*
> *He hath awakened from the dream of life*
> *'Tis we, who lost in stormy visions. . . .*

As Mick finished, thousands of white butterflies were released over the crowd of between 250,000 and 300,000. "Obviously a statement had to be made one way or another," Keith writes, "so we turned it into a memorial for Brian. We wanted to send him off in grand style. The ups and downs with the guy are one thing, but when his time's over, release the doves, or in this case the sackfuls of white butterflies."

"It was very moving," said Steve Morse, who went on to be the music critic for the *Boston Globe*. Morse was a young student who happened to be in England at the time. "Releasing the butterflies was a stunning touch and it captured everyone's attention. It was hard to hear Mick reciting the Shelley elegy, but the moment was heartfelt. The Stones debuted 'Honky Tonk Women' and did an incredibly powerful version of 'Sympathy For the Devil.' I was thirty feet away and it was exhilarating."

It was more of an exuberant celebration than a mournful wake. The Stones were still just a bunch of twenty-somethings and had just had a founding member die weeks after they had fired him. Charlie and Bill attended the funeral in Brian's hometown. "He was incredibly young when he died, when I look back on it," Charlie recollected. "I look at pictures of my wife and myself at the funeral and I just think, 'Bloody hell.' We were so young."

"Honky Tonk Women" was released as a single in the UK on

July 4, 1969, the day between Brian's death and the Hyde Park show.* It went to number one in both markets, amazingly, the final Stones single to ever hit the topmost spot of the UK charts (the band would have a few more chart-toppers in the States). The Stones had constructed a true classic barroom sing-along that has withstood the test of time, despite continuous mauling by bar bands across the world. The Stones themselves were now a different band. They had lost their founding member, added a new one, and as they stepped out of the 1960s, they entered their first phase as "survivors."

---

* It was released a week later in the US.

23
Gimme Shelter

RECORDED:

March 1969, Olympic Studios, London

October 1969, Elektra Studios, LA

RELEASES:

LP: *Let It Bleed*, December 1969

The End of the Sixties . . . Just a Shot Away

One of the greatest rock songs from any artist, "Gimme Shelter" is a glowering, snarling beast of a recording. It tiptoes in on one of music's most recognizable chord-based riffs, ghostly "oooh's," and percussion ratcheting up the tension. When the full band enters—sinister low piano notes, fuzzy harmonica, organ chimes—it grabs you by the lapels and shakes you, begging you for shelter from an ominous storm.

Keith wrote the song at Robert Fraser's apartment in September or October 1968, as Anita and Mick were off shooting *Performance*. There was a real rainstorm at the time. And there was a metaphoric storm brewing in the world, with ultraviolence televised nightly into living rooms. But the germ of the song started with the personal tempest swirling within Keith, emotional turmoil mixed in with heroin as he slid gradually into junkiedom. "I would probably have written 'Gimme Shelter' whether I was on or off the stuff," he writes. "It doesn't affect your judgement, but in certain cases it helps you be more tenacious about something and follow it further than you would have."

That tenacity is consistent with Jimmy Miller's assessment of Keith during this period. In fact, Miller was fearful that Keith would overdo it, not the drugs so much as loading on too many guitar parts as overdubs. "At times like that I'd think, 'What could Keith possibly do to help this track better itself?' . . . Then he'd just suddenly play something that knocked me out." But Keith cautions that heroin is, of course, "certainly not the road to musical genius or anything else." That's about as close as it gets to Keith saying, "just say no."

Since 1967, Keith has presented himself as a guy who could take it all. He has often been cavalier in remarks about the firing and subsequent death of Brian. But of course he had been wounded. The band was a family and all that shared experience was certain to come bubbling emotionally to the surface. And Keith had at least been winged by the breach of his trust by Mick and Anita with their on-set fling. If Mick's defense mechanism was to keep his various personalities fluid, treating every public interaction as a theater piece, Keith's was to allow an outer shell to harden. His drug use increased, and he concentrated his remaining emotional and physical energy into the creation of *Let It Bleed*. "The important thing about *Let It Bleed* is the amount of work Keith did," said Miller. "He was at a great cycle during that period, at a great point in his playing. When Brian died, that was accepted. Keith took over the musical leadership of the Stones and he did it brilliantly."

"There was this incredible storm over London, so I got into that mode, just looking out of Robert's window and looking at all these people with their umbrellas being blown out of their grasp and running like hell," Keith recalled. "And the idea came to me. You get lucky sometimes." He was writing about "storms on other people's minds," not his, he claims, in the same paragraph of his book in which he mentions Mick and Anita in a bathtub together. As a good student of the blues, Keith channelled his fury into the language of the blues—*trouble is brewing, the killing floor, I asked her for water, she gave me gasoline,* and so on back through the canon. But with all that was going on in the world, here at the end of a troubling decade, the earth, wind, and fire of the song were bound to take on metaphorical significance.

We all know everything about the sixties by now. It is perhaps the most-documented decade ever. It started so promisingly. Then bad shit started to happen. As with Dylan, the Stones had smelled it turning: the malevolence, the distrust, the inevitable human frailty and heart of darkness of it all. The Stones had already positioned themselves as the harbingers of bad news; the counterculture's cynical counterpoint; the dark to the Beatles' light. *Beggars Banquet* (1968) was just that, a cornucopia of starkly presented sleaze, ignorance, violence, and general human weakness in the face of uncompromising evil.

"Without a doubt it was a strange generation," says Keith. "The weird thing is that I grew up with it, but suddenly I'm an observer instead of a participant. I watched all these guys grow up; I watched a lot of them die. When I first got to the States, I met a lot of great guys, and I got their phone numbers, and then when I got back two or three years later, I'd call them up, and he's in a body bag from Nam. . . . Politics came for us whether we liked it or not."

"Gimme Shelter," the opening salvo from *Let It Bleed* (1969) is the most menacing of the whole slew of their 1968–72 songs with troubling subject matter. But here was fey, skinny-assed Mick Jagger reaching deep into his diaphragm and his psyche to belt out a bellowing, urgent alarm. He had never before nor since sounded so titanic. "A storm is threatening." The Stones were no longer tweaking the noses of flower children as they were on "Street Fighting Man" or "Sympathy For the Devil." There was no layer of sarcasm, humor, or irony. They were instead combining a musically and lyrically consistent horrific message about war, rape, and murder. Now it felt like the walls were really closing in. Indeed, rarely has the band been so direct and so earnest in sociopolitical commentary. Though Keith started out writing "Gimme Shelter" from a personal standpoint, the finished recorded performance has no other level to the message. There is a directness of purpose heard in these grooves.

But the Stones were also aware that the song simply works in a *musically* groovy, funky, and sexual way. It's as if it's a challenge: Just try to get off on this nihilistic death-wish trip. "That's a kind of end-of-the-world song, really," said Mick. "It's apocalypse; the whole record's like that."

Every minute of this song offers something new. The guitar riff that starts the song is a paradigm in and of itself, from the master of riffs. It is a clean but dark and reverby guitar with a deep tremolo dynamic. Opening the song, already it disorients us. Miller and Johns have a little slap-back echo off to the other side. The riff is like a stick of butter sliding around in a pan, melting, turning brown, bubbling, and burning. George Chkiantz, who engineered the sessions for *Let It Bleed* with Glyn Johns, described the amplifiers that Keith used to author Sean Egan: "The Triumph amplifiers were the key to 'Gimme Shelter.'" Keith had managed to find a "sweet spot" with these transistor amps after overheating them, letting them cool down, and then getting them fired back up again to just the right level before they conked out completely. The amps "would produce this amazing crunch once they'd just got to a certain stage of overheating . . . They're terrible amplifiers otherwise." Stu had worked out a trial deal for these models, which were used alongside Vox AC30s, some Fenders, and 15-watt Watkins amps.

The secret ingredient that sets this recording, like so many of the Miller era, over the top is the muscular percussion. On "Gimme Shelter," Miller has maracas, a shekere (a big gourd with beads on the outside), and a güiro (another gourd that you scratch with a stick to get that almost drunken cicada sound), the rhythmic ratchet that drives this arrangement. It makes the song. This is the click-clacking, bone-machine skeleton of the recording.

Mick enters without a mask, in a rarely featured low and guttural register of his voice. The vocals were overdubbed in Los Angeles. He is singing about storms threatening and fires sweeping. This is no mere "Hard Rain" that's "A-Gonna Fall." This is something happening right now, burning "like a red coal carpet, mad bull lost its way." In 1969, the Vietnam War could be the only subject here.

At about 2:04 of "Gimme Shelter," Miller's big-ass shaker comes up front; Mick's blues harp howls; Nicky Hopkins's piano clangs; a throbbing drone on this single chugging/churning chord that forms the verse section of the arrangement, until Keith's unhurried overdubbed lead finally breaks the impossible tension and the band rocks into the chorus progression. The drone is something that Keith attributes as "Jimmy Reed inspired—the same haunting trick, sliding up the fret board against the drone of the E note. . . . It's a very unlikely guitar key . . ." The music is all tension and release. The piano sounds like an upright. It is in the background, playing off of Keith's parts.

Merry Clayton sings harmonies on many of the lines, joining Keith and Mick in three-part harmony on the choruses. Clayton had started out as a member of Ray Charles' backing singers, the Raelettes, along with two singers who would later appear on *Exile on Main Street,* Venetta Fields and Clydie King. They were all in-demand session vocalists in LA during the seventies, and Clayton went on to have a solo record deal with A&M. Jack Nitzsche had worked with Clayton before when the Stones called her late at night and she came down to sing on the session while they were working on the overdubs and mixing in LA.

As the intensity is taken to a new level, with Mick ad-libbing "Hey-yay-yay," as if he is trying to get the attention of the band, it is Clayton who takes the solo vocal, the first female solo voice on a Stones record. And it's an absolute classic performance, with an otherworldly timbre even before her voice cracks (at 3:01). Everyone knows that voice crack. It sends shivers down your spine every time you hear it. But there is another little compromise in the voice on the line that precedes it (at 2:58). You get the feeling that Clayton felt it buckle a little on that first one, and it surprised her, and she made a split-second instinctual decision to push the next line even harder, rather than retreat when she felt that crack. She consciously knew that by taking the chance to push it even more it would result in something that would convey her emotion even more effectively. It's called soul.

I asked Clayton, "Did you hear that little catch in your voice, and purposefully push it harder?"

"Of course I did!" she said with a laugh. "You have captured precisely what was going on during that recording."

After her shiver-inducer, you can hear Mick off mike exclaim, "WOOH!" a real-time reaction to Clayton's legendary shriek. And she does it again to lead out of this section at about 3:06. "There was a lot of hooting and hollering going on when certain notes were hit, from Mick and the producer," said Clayton. "We were all [Mick, Keith, and Merry] singing in the room together." Clayton and Keith sang their parts on the chorus live while Mick was singing his lead vocal, resulting in three-part harmony on those parts.

The Stones had left the solo spot specifically for a female vocalist to sing. "When I sang the 'rape, murder' part, [Mick] was in the booth, I did that by myself. He came out with encouragement, in my face kind of thing, you know, doing, 'It's just a shot away, it's just a shot away.'"

If you dig hard enough, you should be able to find an amazing gift to humanity: There is a clip of just the vocal tracks, isolated from the rest of the music. This vocals-only mix just makes you appreciate the unbridled power of Clayton's masterful performance even more. On the isolated tracks you hear another "whoa!" at 3:15, the end of her last line of that solo, one that is not as audible in the full mix (blown out by the harmonica). It is as if Mick still could not believe what he just heard. It's real church.

The drama of it all sounds exhausting. Don Snowden interviewed Merry for the *Los Angeles Times* in 1986, writing, "The physical exertion of singing the part was so intense that the pregnant Clayton suffered a miscarriage after returning home from the session." Clayton told him, "That was a dark, dark period for me but God gave me the strength to overcome it."*

Everyone in the band sounds committed to the terrific gloom of the track. Charlie's drum sounds like a monster on this whole song—really, like a snarling, sweaty, limping monster. He is laying into that low-tuned kick and snare beat like he is coming after you through the fog. You know he is going to outlast you, driving with such consistency. I was only three years of age when this record came out, so I cannot imagine what it would have been like to put the needle down on side one of *Let It Bleed* and hear these four minutes and thirty seconds. I think I would be scared. And then I would have replayed it.

In 2001, writer Stephen Davis said of *Let It Bleed:* "No rock record, before or since, has ever so completely captured the sense of palpable dread that hung over its era." I would go even further and say that no one rock *song,* before or since, has so completely captured that sense of dread as "Gimme Shelter."

This sense of dread captured in the record became a self-fulfilling prophecy, as witnessed at the free Stones concert at Al-

---

* Clayton, who is working on a book of her own, declined comment on this aspect.

tamont Speedway in California, captured in the Maysles Brothers' film named after the song. From Monterey in '67, to the Hyde Park shows from the Stones and others in June of '69, to Woodstock in August '69, big rock festivals were coming into fashion as sound systems improved and rock shows matured. The vibes of those other events, however, had been about as good as vibes get when there are hundreds of thousands of people attending. But the haphazard way they were organized in general was bound to result in problems. And the problems came sooner rather than later. The Stones, facing criticism that their ticket prices—which climbed as high as the exorbitant figure of $8.00—decided that a free show after their 1969 US tour had ended was a way to give back to their fans.

The challenges of putting on this show are shown in the film. Egos mixed with immaturity. At a press conference announcing the event, Mick cocksurely stated that the planned concert would be "creating a sort of microcosmic society which should be an example to America as to how to behave in large gatherings." Naiveté and idealism obscured reasoning. The Stones took the advice of the Grateful Dead and hired the Hells Angels as security, something that in this more innocent time could still be considered as a reasonable action. The police, after all, didn't have the best image with twenty-somethings at the time. It had only been a year out from the DNC clashes in Chicago, and police had been "the pigs," busting heads at demonstrations around the country. Additionally, the Stones had actually had good luck hiring a permutation of the Angels for the same purposes in Hyde Park. However, there proved to be major differences between the English Hells Angels and the Oakland Hells Angels. The Brits were Hells Angels lite, more like Hecks Angels. The Oakland chapter was already infamous for their Visigothic outlaw lifestyle, having been profiled by Hunter S. Thompson in his mid-'60s book about the bikers.

Arriving by helicopter from San Francisco into Altamont Speedway at the end of the 1969 tour, their first in the states in three years, Charlie said it first looked like Woodstock: ". . . it was the fashion of the moment, but it was the end of the fashion. If Woodstock had started it, we stopped it." Nothing about the day boded well. The stage was fully exposed, not much bigger than a flatbed truck, and in the middle of a range of barren hills. It was a cold December night. People, including the Angels, were taking bad acid and drinking jugs of cheap skid row wine en masse. In the film, the Jefferson Airplane's singer, Marty Balin, gets decked by a Hells Angel, and Grace Slick trots out hollow hippie platitudes that are already outdated and pointless by the time they pass her lips, echoed in later ineffective peace-and-love rhetoric from Mick as he tries to calm the churning mass of hostile bodies surrounding him. Before the show, erstwhile security advisors, the Dead's Jerry Garcia and baby-faced Bobby Weir make one of the greatest exits in the history of the movies, like the proverbial last copter out of Saigon. In the end, the Angels stabbed to death eighteen-year-old Meredith Hunter, who had drawn a gun close to the stage, as seen captured in shadowy, grainy footage. The Stones were lucky to escape with their lives.

Altamont is something you could not make up. It had a distinct fin de siècle character that is expertly captured via the Maysles truth-is-more-compelling-than-fiction cinema verité. It is too easy to generalize about the "end of the sixties" and Altamont has become a cliché that way. But in hindsight, it is difficult *not* to come to such conclusions and view it as emblematic for the dark underbelly, something that came with being the black-hatted Stones. The very name, Altamont, has become shorthand for any fucked-up, poorly planned, horribly executed situation.

And the band itself became widely viewed as dangerous. If the Stones had hardened and gained more of an edge after the 1967 busts, Altamont would turn them into razorbacks. Ian Stewart can be seen on the helicopter tarmac before Mick is taken to the site of the concert, explaining to the excited singer that there were already problems at 2:00 in the afternoon. His take on the event:

> It was a disaster right from the fucking start . . . Altamont has to be one of the few things the Stones did where they had no say. . . . But the band didn't blame themselves. Although a lot of people would blame them, you really couldn't. That would be unfair because they made a genuine attempt to have a free concert.

To see Mick, visibly frightened, carting out flower power clichés like, "Brothers and sisters, why are we fighting," while Keith forcibly grabs a mike and points fingers at Angels, calling out specific troublemakers, is a study in contrasts of their personalities and neatly summarizes two contradictory forces of the late 1960s.

Mick Jagger and Charlie Watts are seen at the end, in the film within the film, as they are shown the footage of the last minutes leading up to the stabbing, as well as the isolated frames of the stabbing itself. Charlie fumbles for words. Mick, numbed, looks pale and ill, like he is about to get sick. In the last scene, the filmmakers freeze a shot of him as he rises from the chair in the film editing suite, and looks straight into the camera. He is only twenty-six years old and you can read whatever you want into his young face.

One interpretation, as valid as any, is that the young man caught in this frame is trying to square the role of his band in this new reality. These Stones, who have always been willing participants in the creation of their own folklore, who had traipsed across the US a half dozen times or more by 1969—a land that these musicians also still romanticized—were, for the moment, not merely the observers but the participants in a violent piece of its history.

Another valid interpretation is that Mick was already removing himself from the fray and moving on, just as ready to assign blame to city councilors, the Angels, and/or to Hunter, who, after all, was brandishing a pistol within easy-target range of the young singer.

"I mean, pulling a shooter out in front of acid-crazed angels, you're asking for trouble. My big fear at that point was, 'Is this going to escalate?'" writes Keith. "It was a tragedy in a way, but at the same time it was kind of a triumph. Right there you were on the abyss . . . It was almost like, 'Okay, this is civilization.' Either the veneer will come off now . . . or we'll get it back together."

Mick's words about the event have remained consistent since 1969. "Altamont was a very nasty experience," he said decades later, coming as close to accepting some responsibility as he ever had. "I guess we have to take some part of the blame because we didn't really check it out as well as we could, but it was left up to the people in San Francisco." However, he added, "Altamont was a big thing for a lot of people. They were blaming it on our image and it was some kind of 'end of the innocence.' They're still agonizing over it. 'Did it mean something? . . . Does it really *mean* something?' [laughs]. It was pretty awful but I don't think it meant very much."

It was not the band's Waterloo, just as losing Brian Jones months before was not. Just like the myriad arrests were not. Perhaps it is merely a cinematic manipulation, in this frozen frame of Mick at the end of *Gimme Shelter,* we see the still-very-young man who by 1969 had taken on sex, politics, and violence in his lyrics, often sardonically, rarely earnestly, and who more than once had been accused of courting and glorifying violence and evil. And we see the same face of the man who had been playing to and primping for the camera the whole film, now caught and frozen in a candid moment where his mask is truly off and the look on his face makes you realize why he would quickly want to reach for another.

24
Midnight Rambler

RECORDED:

March 10–11, 1969, Olympic Studios, London

RELEASES:

LP: *Let It Bleed*, December 1969

Acting Out the
Malevolent Terror of 1969

Midnight Rambler" is an opus, a modern blues-rock opera, with a subject sprung from the days headlines, but reaches back deep into the well of county and blues folklore, dating back to European mythology: the Black Rider, the Midnight Rider, the Midnight Rambler, highwaymen—the shadowy strangers who lurk in the cloak of night and pounce on innocent victims. Mick plays to our fears of those loner psychopaths like Jack the Ripper, seemingly gleeful to wear yet another mask, that of the Bogey man.

Albert DeSalvo, a serial murderer around the Boston area, served as the most direct inspiration for the song. DeSalvo was known as the Boston Strangler, with fourteen killings of women from 1962–64 attributed to him. "That's one of the most original blues you'll hear from the Stones, wrote Keith. "The title, the subject, was just one of those phrases taken out of sensationalist headlines that exist only for a day. You just happen to be looking at the newspaper, 'Midnight Rambler on the loose again.' Oh, I'll have him."

Oddly, this song was written in sunny Positano, Italy, where Mick and Keith had been taking a vacation. "Why we should write such a dark song in this beautiful, sunny place, I really don't know," said Mick. "We wrote everything there—the tempo changes, everything. And I'm playing the harmonica in these little cafés, and there's Keith with the guitar." Keith recalls the house that they rented as, "empty, barren, very cold. Huge fires and we just sat and wrote."

But by the time the song was actually released on *Let It Bleed* in December 1969, there was a more general sense of terror in the air. In August of that year, Charles Manson and his Manson Family infamously went on a murderous rampage. The Manson connections to Dennis Wilson of the Beach Boys, Terry Melcher—a producer of the Beach Boys and others'—plus Manson's claim to have been "inspired" by the Beatles' "Helter Skelter," and the "hippy commune" media label of the Manson group, all amounted to yet another nail in the coffin of the peace-and-love image of the sixties, confirming the worst fears of straight citizenry about longhairs. The Stones had an extraordinarily developed sense of the Zeitgest, and here they were tapping into a rich vein of dread and terror, and letting it bleed indeed.

The original recording was labored over, though, with Keith coming in night after night to get just the right take for the solo (slide guitar). "I think it took five nights to get the final track," said Vic Smith, who engineered on the sessions. "Once again, we're talking about erasing every performance . . . At that point when it got to the solo, it just bound the whole track together." Keith used a funky Australian-made semi-hollow guitar on this and on "Gimme Shelter."

On "Midnight Rambler" there is that classic push-and-pull of the Stones rhythm, with mapped out tempo changes, as well as fluctuations that simply could not have been planned. Even so, the original recording of "Midnight Rambler" is simply too clean, contained, and polite compared to the gritty, raging, and pulsating psychodrama it grew into live, which is why we have the *Get Your Ya-Ya's Out!* live version on the greatest hits compilation, *Hot Rocks*. While we do have a bit of leering mischief to Mick's studio vocal, along with a few unsettling laughs, it is nothing compared to how he fleshed out the role with the energy of audiences on tour. "It's when the audience decides to join, that's when it really knocks you out," Keith said in 1971. "I believe things like 'Midnight Rambler' come through better live, because we've extended it more," he explained in the same interview. "Sometimes when you record something you go off half-cocked because maybe you haven't ever played it live."

The original "Midnight Rambler" was recorded before Altamont and the Manson murders, but the subsequent live versions took the song to heightened levels of terror that are virtual rewrites of the composition. The Boston Strangler served as the original inspiration. Mick begins the last verse of the song, "Well, you heard about the Boston . . ." at which point the band wallops in on the downbeat, and he leaves the dangling ". . . Strangler" implied. Mick reportedly took some lines directly from DeSalvo's confessions. DeSalvo was known as the "Green Man" murderer before the "Boston Strangler," for the green pants he had worn during his first round of murders. Mick sings as a "green bell jangler" who "sticks my knife right down your throat."

As the band interpreted it live, the lyrics and structure of the song remained intact, but it was augmented, sped up, slowed down, peeled back, covered back up, and acted out beginning with versions as early as the 1969 tour. There is no doubt that the live dynamic alone was enough to inject a certain amount of visceral energy and urgency to the track. But it also seems that the song became informed by the immediate horrific events in California in 1969, from Altamont to the Manson murders. Just as with Mick changing the line in "Sympathy for the Devil" from "Kennedy" to "the Kennedys," one must remember that this was going down in real time.

As the years went on and the band played it live, the opus took on epic proportions, legendary interpretations, and by 1972, when the Stones were at their peak as a live band, the song became the torrid *sturm und drang* drama heard on bootlegs from the era (the so-called *Unreleased Decca Album* is highly recommended) and serves as the centerpiece of the seminal concert film, *Ladies and Gentlemen, the Rolling Stones*. Mick acts out the role of killer and victim, eventually down on his hands and knees, lashing his scarfy belt like a whip and moaning in agony, begging, "Oh don't hurt me! Don't do it! Oh, Don't do that!" After a spellbinding section where the band drones on the riff, nearly turning the beat around in the process, the song comes seemingly to a halt in the middle section, where the band just breaks the song down to bare bones, like a bump-and-grind for a big mama stripper. Jagger moans and howls, steering the song into darker depths, until he reaches the part about "the Boston . . ." (BAM!) Then Keith starts chugging the temp back up, churning up the witches' brew, until the tempo is swept back up like a tornado for the final section of the song.

The fact that this histrionic spectacle about a murderous rapist would be found enjoyable entertainment in the way that films like *Psycho* are is something that the Stones knew intrinsically. They again followed the lead of their blues heroes like Robert Johnson, who sounded eerily convincing on songs like "32-20 Blues" ("If she gets unruly, and thinks she don't want do/Take my 32-20, and cut her half in two"). Like Hitchcock compared to directors of B-movie horrorfests, Mick knew how to push spine-chilling terror to the brink and keep it gothic and believable.

25
Sway

RECORDED:

October 1970, Stargroves (Mick Jagger's house),
Newbury, England, and Olympic Studios, London

RELEASES:

LP: *Sticky Fingers*, April 1971

Not Flinging Tears for Friends on the Burial Ground

I f "Sympathy for the Devil" was a wake-up call, "Gimme Shelter" was raving reportage of current tumultuous events, and "You Can't Always Get What You Want" was a shrugging acceptance that the hopeful dreams of the mid-1960s were dashed, then "Sway" represented the beginning of a weary hangover, a theme that the Stones would explore as they wrote more of the material on *Sticky Fingers* and, particularly, *Exile on Main Street*. The band moved into the 1970s, post-Woodstock, post-Altamont, the Nixon presidency, and the height of the opposition to the war in Southeast Asia. But "Sway" was no sweeping statement about the times, such as they were; this was a personal lament about those losing their way, if not their lives, in the sway of the "demon life," something with which the band was well-acquainted, and a personal narrative they helped feed: the decadent sex/drugs/rock 'n' roll trinity, sprinkled with an aura of violence and invulnerability. But the dusty ground had been weakening underfoot.

From the beginning of February to the end of March 1969, the Stones had been recording copious reels of tape that would end up filling out not only their LP, *Let It Bleed,* but the next two, *Sticky Fingers* and *Exile on Main Street.* Trying to decide which is the "best" of the three albums is pointless. The writing and recording of all three is so consistently top-notch and intertwined that the records form a trilogy of sorts.

Much of the recording came not only from Olympic, but from Stargroves, Mick's mansion in the English countryside. This is where they recorded "Sway." The band had purchased a truck and had it fitted out with top-of-the-line recording equipment to be rented out when they were not using it. This became the Rolling Stones Mobile Unit, and it was Ian Stewart's domain to lord over. In close consultation with Glyn Johns, Stu had it stocked with a Helios console and eventually include two 24-track tape machines and fifty-eight microphone lines. Engineer Andy Johns was already "petrified" at the whole scenario: his first full album project working with his well-respected older brother, engineering a session with the Stones at Mick's manor house with their new expensive truck. "I've never used this gear before, and it's their new baby," he recalled. "Their expectations are pretty high. So I better dial it in or I'm up shit creek.

"We were having a lot of trouble with the truck because it was *brand-new,*" he explained. "So there were all kinds of bugs and the tape machine didn't work and Mick was getting pissed off at the whole thing. I think he fired me the first night. He said, 'I can record the band better with my Sony cassette machine.' I thought, *oh fuck, I'd better say something,* so I said, 'Well, it's a very small space in here, and you've got all these bloody hangers-on filling up the room, you can't listen to it properly.' There were always a bunch of fucking lowlife weasels hanging around in those days, druggies and you know, wannabes, and coattail riders. It was awful, these people were the scum of the earth. There were a lot of them there that night. The next day I waited outside his bedroom and when he came out, I said, 'Look I'll just go now, I don't want to be in the way. The Rolling Stones are more important to me and blah, blah, blah.' He said, 'Well, you're in.' It had been a bit like a test, I guess.

"Stargroves was a massive house, a big, big, big estate house, way out in the countryside, outside of London," Bobby Keys explained. "And when we worked out there, I think Mick had fairly recently gotten ownership of it, because there wasn't a stick of furniture in the place. There was a giant pool table, a snooker table, very ornately carved. But most of the place, he just set up . . . Jim [Price—the trumpet player] and I went out there to stay and Mick had sent somebody out to get cots and blankets and sheets and stuff to set up in a room for Jim and I to stay in while we were working on stuff and I remember we froze our ass off, 'cause those English ain't real fond of central heating . . . Their *castles* are *cold* and *drafty*!"

Johns described the set-up at Stargroves with the Mobile. The spot they recorded in the house was "a very large baronial hall with a gallery around it, with a grand staircase going up to the next floor where all the bedrooms were. And there was a big gigantic, sort of medieval-looking fireplace and a large bay window with latticework windows where I put the drum kit, where it sounded fabulous, nice reflections from the stone and the glass. And I just sort of hung the amps around. I think I put Mick Taylor's amp in the fireplace, with a mike up the chimney as well as the mikes up front. But [the one up the chimney] might have only been used on 'Moonlight Mile.'"

(It is the wood floors and high ceilings that give these recordings a natural sound, a warm reverberation, and other bands took advantage of this and recorded at Stargroves, including Led Zeppelin, who did material from *Physical Graffiti* and *Houses of the Holy* there. The Who recorded "Won't Get Fooled Again" in the manor house.)

In a couple of weeks in October 1970, just days back from a European tour, the Stones recorded tracks at Stargroves that would end up on *Sticky Fingers, Exile on Main Street,* and *Goats Head Soup,* including versions of "Sweet Black Angel" (with the working title "Bent Green Needles"), "Silver Train," and "All Down the Line." So yes, as legend has it, many *Exile* tracks were recorded in an old mansion, but just not necessarily the one that automatically comes to mind for Stones fans who think of Keith's house, Nellcôte, in the South of France, where much of *Exile* was recorded.

And as would be the case making *Exile* in France, recording at "home" came with thorny domestic conflicts. Mick and Marianne's relationship had started to fall apart in the previous year. The Stones had been on tour for much of 1969. Mick called her repeatedly from America, begging her to come back to him, but by the fall of 1970 she had left Mick for good. It was on the 1970 European tour that Mick met Bianca Rose Perez Morena de Macias in Paris. Bianca stayed with the band for the rest of the tour and came home with Mick. "Home" also happened to be the recording "studio" at the time, as it would with *Exile* at Keith's house in 1971. "They could hardly get any work done [at Stargroves], with Mick the way he was about Bianca," said Shirley Arnold, the Stones' secretary at the time. "She'd come into the studio and give him the eye . . . he'd leave the other Stones and follow her upstairs."

Two versions of "Sway" were recorded during that two-week period at Stargroves. The one that served as the B-side to the "Wild Horses" single was different from that which is on *Sticky Fingers.* They share the basic backing track, with Bill's bass bum note at about fifty seconds in on both versions. But the vocal take is different and there is a harmony from Keith on the verses. The sweeping strings, arranged by Paul Buckmaster, come in on the second verse on both mixes. " 'Sway' came out great," said Johns. "I think that's the first one we recorded there. Keith hadn't shown up yet. And it sounds great to this day."

The song is one of the first cases of the Jagger/Richards default songwriting credit, as apparently Keith had nothing to do with its creation. Keith, who had started falling deeper in thrall to heroin and becoming less dependable, had not yet arrived to the sessions, which had been loosely arranged now that they were not on a studio clock. Yet it has all the earmarks of a Keith tune: heavy rhythmic guitar and a lyric about finding light in the dark shadows of life—real life, not some fantastical voyage that Mick is taking you on. But the song is all Mick Jagger and Mick Taylor. Jagger had the song more or less written when he brought it in, with Taylor providing finishing touches.

After the slow, weary-sounding count off at the top of the recording, Jagger's guitar, open tuned, comes in on the right side, with the heavy downstroke, while Taylor is on the left playing the more nuanced accents until he clicks into one of his two stunning solos, a seamless mix of bottleneck slide and fingered playing.

"On 'Sway' . . . Keith doesn't play on that track," said Taylor. "Mick Jagger's playing rhythm guitar. . . . I played the slide part and the solo at the same time." Keith is generally critical of Jagger's playing: "It's not his thing. It's not everybody's cup of tea. . . . I'd never let him play electric if I could help it. He's like Bob Dylan, same thing. They thrash away at it. No sense of electric at all. Usually I turn him down." He's not joking. Chris Kimsey explained that on *Some Girls,* Keith would often do just that. Kimsey said Keith actually unplugged Mick's guitar completely a couple of times.

If you ever wondered what the big fuss was about with the Mick Taylor years of the Stones, all you have to do is pay attention to this solo at the end of "Sway." If you're not convinced there, you can move on to "Can't You Hear Me Knocking," also from *Sticky Fingers*, which out-Santanas Carlos Santana. Kimsey, who had been assisting Glyn Johns at Olympic and worked on *Sticky Fingers*, said all of Taylor's parts were recorded live, not overdubbed, to his recollection. Taylor's first solo comes in after the middle-eight. He reprises the solo at the end, but as it comes out of the chorus, you can hear him around 2:32, fiddling with the pickup selector on his guitar, setting himself up for just the perfect tone. Taylor is provided a solid foundation from Jagger's rhythm guitar and Bill's bass playing. On "Sway" his playing is almost as funky as that of Motown's in-house Funk Brothers, James Jamerson and Bob Babbitt. Bill was continuously adapting to the new directions the Stones took toward more urban R&B and funk influences, mixed in with their straighter blues and rock 'n' roll.

Nicky Hopkins is on electric piano, right up the middle of the mix. But he also has an overdub of a grand piano. His playing, cutting through with those high-octave "diamond tiaras," is typically brilliant, but it's the only track on *Sticky Fingers* that features Hopkins.*

Over this pummeling hard rock track, Mick sings about casualties from his rock 'n' roll peer group: "Ain't flinging tears out on the dusty ground/For all my friends up on the burial ground." With the Beatles breaking up officially in 1970, the Stones were perched as unlikely survivors. Brian was gone, killed by substance abuse. Mick could see his mate Keith, Anita, and Mick's most immediate ex, Marianne, falling deeper into dependency and drifting away from him. The recreational and mind-expanding drugs of the mid-1960s had given way to the harder, uglier stuff for many artists and young people in general. Jimi Hendrix had just died

---

* Billy Preston plays on a few tracks, including the sweltering gospel-soul organ on "I Got the Blues" (a personal favorite), and Jim Dickinson plays the tack piano on "Wild Horses." All told, seven people played keyboards on the album.

from an overdose of sleeping pills and alcohol that past September, and the month after Hendrix went, Janis Joplin succumbed with a heroin overdose. But Mick's point of view in the song is that if you live that "demon life," you have to expect such outcomes. Is it Mick writing from Keith's point of view? Or is he sending a bit of a message to his absent guitar player, in a song ironically so Keith-influenced? Or maybe it's for Marianne, slipping into addiction, "Someone that broke me up with the corner of her smile."

The harrowing fallout from drugs was acutely obvious by 1971. The theme started to run regularly through the band's lyrics, with a sobering message more often than a romantic one, "Sister Morphine," (cowritten with Marianne Faithful) being another such example from *Sticky Fingers*. The Stones were adding their voice to a thematic continuum of the blues: the profane/sacred divide, the women and the whiskey who sway you from the righteous path. The crossroads deal with the Devil for a good time, talent, and riches in this mortal life. And ultimately the swing of the Grim Reaper's scythe.

"It's just that demon life that's got me in it's sway" Mick incants like a rock 'n' roll rosary or blues Kaddish as the maelstrom of guitars blacken the skies.

26
Brown Sugar

RECORDED:

December 3–4, 1969, at Muscle Shoals Sound Studios,
Sheffield, Alabama
April 24, 1970, at Olympic Studios, London

RELEASES:

LP: *Sticky Fingers*, April 1971
Single, April 1971 UK, charting at number 2
May 1971 US, charting at number 1

All the Nasty Subjects in One Go

As the promise of the 1960s turned into the disappointments of the early 1970s, the Stones' approach was to "party in the face of it," to use the immortal words of music journalist Lester Bangs, describing the music of the Stones during the early seventies. "The party is obvious. The casualties are inevitable."

The casualties were covered in "Sway" and "Sister Morphine." The partying could be heard on other *Sticky Fingers* tracks, "Dead Flowers," "Can't You Hear Me Knocking," "Bitch," and "Brown Sugar." "Brown Sugar" follows the template that the Stones set on

"Honky Tonk Women" and continued through their golden era. The Stones forged a new hard R&B sound that took the best of hard rock, country, old rock 'n' roll, gospel, blues, and soul, and married that music to seemingly effortless lyrics that continued to capture and characterize the times and/or just sounded terrific. The early motto of The Who was "Maximum R&B," but as they ventured into 1970s hard rock, The Who were more about the maximum and less about the R&B. The Stones sounded funkier and sexier, and maximum R&B would more accurately describe the Stones at their peak. No song better illustrates this than "Brown Sugar," a song that lampoons some of Western society's most taboo subjects: race, sex, and drugs.

The version of "Brown Sugar" that we all know and love from *Sticky Fingers* was recorded at Muscle Shoals Sound Studios in Shef- field, Alabama. Muscle Shoals was founded by "the Swampers," who had been the in-house band at FAME Studios in Florence, Ala- bama.* FAME, founded by Rick Hall, had produced a string of early- 1960s Southern soul classics from such artists as Jimmy Hughes and Arthur Alexander, and celebrated Atlantic producer Jerry Wexler had started to bring artists like Aretha Franklin, Wilson Pickett, and Percy Sledge to record at FAME with the Swampers backing them. As Peter Guralnick points out in his book, *Sweet Soul Music*, many of America's best soul music came from these integrated bands and songwriting teams at studios like FAME and Stax in Memphis at a time when the Civil Rights struggle was in full boil. This history certainly would have attracted the Stones as they tried to catch some of that magic. "To us," writes Keith, FAME "was on par with going to Chess Records." But it was logistics as much as anything else that was the reason the band took a detour at the end of their 1969 tour to record at the newly opened Muscle Shoals Sound studio.

Stanley Booth, the author who was embedded as "official writer"

---

* Muscle Shoals is a metropolitan area encompassing these and other towns.

on the 1969 tour (resulting in the 1984 book *The True Adventures of the Rolling Stones*), called Jim Dickinson, his friend from back home in Memphis, asking if the Stones could record in Memphis at the end of their 1969 tour. ". . . they wanted to record when they were, y'know, 'hot' from playing together," Dickinson told an interviewer in 2002. "With [Musicians] Union regulations back then . . . you could get either a touring or a recording permit but not both. They were in a position where they could tour but not record and had been prevented from recording in Los Angeles. So, they were looking for a place where nobody would care and I told 'em that they couldn't record safely in Memphis at that time—'cause the Beatles had tried to record at Stax and had [been told] that there was no way—but I told 'em about Muscle Shoals."*

Dickinson said they did not fuss over the music. The whole band rolled it for a bunch of takes, "but the first time they could get through the song without a major mistake, that was the take. They played it back, listened to it and nobody said 'Should we do it again?', 'Should we do this, should we do that?'—none of that second-guessing that I was used to." The band knew the song was a winner from the get-go. A few days later, they debuted it at Altamont. Booth records engineer Jimmy Johnson's reaction to the playback: "When you got a good groove, it's lak hittin' a ball over a fence."

The guitar opening of "Brown Sugar" with a big slap-back echo is a Rolling Stones achetype†. Yet another quintessential classic from the "Human Riff," right? Well, *actually,* Mick wrote the entire

---

* Former Stax publicist Deanie Parker, who now runs the Stax Museum on the site of the studios, told *Mojo* magazine that the Beatles had a two-week session booked in April 1966 to record *Revolver.* Brian Epstein had visited the facilities, but they withdrew out of security concerns when the news was leaked. The mind reels at what the Beatles at Stax might have sounded like.

† Listen for another guitar stumble under the solo at 1:50.

song while on location in Australia filming *Ned Kelly*. "The only [riff] I missed and that Mick Jagger got was 'Brown Sugar,'" Keith admits, "and I'll tip my hat there. There he got me." Mick described what makes the music work to Jann Wenner: "I mean, it's a good groove and all that. I mean, the groove is slightly similar to Freddy Cannon, this rather obscure '50s rock performer—'Tallahassee Lassie' or something. . . . "'Going to a Go-Go' or whatever, but that's the groove."*

As usual with the Stones, they laid down a prominent acoustic guitar, providing some glue between the harmonic and percussive components of the recording. Keith plays a lot of the part accenting the upstrokes, in between the electric strums, which adds some swing to the rhythm. Ian Stewart adds his boogie-woogie riffs and a percussive one-note part from the solo section, which continues through to the end of the song. The amp for Keith's electric track was placed next to a toilet bowl in a bathroom (for a "shitty sound," as Johnson quipped).

Once the music tracks were complete, Mick set down to flesh out the lyrics so he could take a pass at the vocals. He had written only the skeletal riff and a few words in Australia. "I watched Mick write the lyrics," Dickinson remembered. "It took him maybe forty-five minutes; He wrote it down as fast as he could move his hand. I'd never seen anything like it. He had one of those yellow legal pads, and he'd write a verse a page, just write a verse and then turn the page, and when he had three pages filled, they started to cut it."

"Brown Sugar" was apparently the moderated, toned-down version of Mick's original idea. He had apparently told Booth while still on the 1969 tour, that he had started to call it "'Black Pussy' but I decided that was too direct, too nitty-gritty." There is also an

---

* The Stones recorded a version of "Tallahassee Lassie" during the *Some Girls* sessions, released as a bonus on the remastered 2012 version.

outtake from the *Gimme Shelter* film that captures Mick playing and singing a rough nascent version of the song, backstage somewhere for Ike and Tina Turner, one of the opening acts on the 1969 tour. Mick sings "Brown sugar, how come you taste so good." Ike elbows Tina, who is chatting with someone on her other side. Ike is basically saying, *Get a load of this: "Brown Sugar, how come you taste so good."* It demonstrates the absolute fearless gall this twenty-six-year-old pasty English kid in a skin-tight jumpsuit had, to sing a song that can *easily* be taken the wrong way. Even interpreting this small snippet of lyrics the *right* way could have been an invitation to a punch in the nose from a person with Ike's disposition. Furthermore, there was not even the context of the rest of the words at this point, which may or may not have helped Mick in communicating his point of view.

And just what was Mick's point of view? Less than a year after recording "Brown Sugar" in Alabama, the African-American singer-actress-model Marsha Hunt gave birth to Mick's first child, Karis Jagger Hunt. Reportedly, she and Mick had planned the pregnancy but never intended on staying together. And Hunt confirmed rumors that "Brown Sugar" was at least in part inspired by her. But decades later, he himself could not get over the audacity his younger self possessed. Here is a monster hit single, and it is about, in no particular order, the slave trade, forbidden master/slave sex, cunnilingus, and, as a bonus double entendre, heroin! "God knows what I'm on about on that song," said Mick, seemingly sincere in his bemused perplexity. "It's such a mishmash. All the nasty subjects in one go. . . . I didn't think about it at the time. I never would write that song now. . . . I would probably censor myself. I'd think, 'Oh God, I can't. I've got to stop. I can't just write raw like that.' " But there was seemingly no such inhibition when they were recording the song in, of all places, the Deep South, where those subjects were more incendiary than anywhere else.

With "Stray Cat Blues," "Let It Bleed" ("we all need someone we can cream on"), and "Brown Sugar," Mick had started to pen an envelope-pushing set of borderline, if not outright pornographic lyrics. On *Exile,* he would sing "kissing cunt in Cannes" (though that is so buried in the mix, most Stones fans have no idea that it's there). On *Goats Head Soup,* he would sing about a "Starfucker" who "keeps [her] pussy clean." On *Some Girls,* he observed, among other racial and sexual stereotypes, that "black girls just wanna get fucked all night," before lamenting, "I just don't have that much jam."

There has been much hand-wringing over Stones lyrics over the years, from well-intentioned folks, high- and low-brow both, from the ivory tower of academia on down to the pressboard pulpits of fire-and-brimstone storefront preachers. What most of these discussions seem to miss or purposefully leave out is the Lenny Bruce–style of humor. (And the Stones were self-professed fans of Bruce.) Mick and Keith, emboldened with the spirit of intellectual freedom of the 1960s and unconcerned about political correctness before that term came into vogue, continuously tested the limits of sexual taboos and commercially acceptable language.

But with concerns over the Stones' appropriation of African-American music, cultural tourism, and so on, the discussion over taboo subjects gets a bit more complicated. As early as 1965, writer LeRoi Jones (later to be known as Amiri Baraka and quoted extensively in Godard's *Sympathy for the Devil*) compared the Beatles and the Rolling Stones to minstrel shows. "Minstrels never convinced anybody they were black either." But, he said in *Downbeat,* "at least the Rolling Stones come on like English crooks." That's a key qualifier. The Stones have very rarely been accused of stealing actual songs without credit and attendant royalties; not all of their peers can claim the same thing. And as soon as they attained any leverage, the Stones used it to have their blues heroes brought out into the light. As they progressed into their career, they became more comfortable in addressing controversial subject matter head-on, though generally with humor. It was the absence of earnest sincerity that seemed to confuse or frustrate some observers. The Stones never presumed to be "authentic."

They did, however, presume to be authoritative and self-assured in their command of the idiomatic language and cultural currency of their times. Dickinson has also said that when Mick was writing the lyrics, it was clear that he had been absorbing the micro-local atmosphere and verbiage: "If you listen to the lyrics, he says, 'Skydog slaver' [though it's always written 'scarred old slaver']. What does that mean? Skydog is what they called Duane Allman in Muscle Shoals, because he was high all the time. And Jagger heard somebody say it and he thought it was a cool word so he used it. He was writing about literally being in the South. It was amazing to watch him do it."

The song was considered complete when they left Alabama in 1969. About a year later, on December 18, 1970, sax player Bobby Keys came to a birthday party for Keith at Olympic Studios (Keith and Keys share a birthday). There was an all-star jam with Eric Clapton and Al Kooper and "Brown Sugar" was one of the songs they played and recorded, with Bobby blowing a solo. The band loved the sax solo so much that they had him come and overdub it on the album version that they had recorded in Alabama, replacing the solo that Mick Taylor had played in the same break.

The horn section became an inextricable component of the 1970–1973 Stones. Keys had made his debut on "Live with Me," but it is "Brown Sugar" that became his signature solo. Bobby—who had, incidentally, once worked as a session man in Muscle Shoals—and trumpet player Jim Price, his partner in brass from the band Delaney & Bonnie & Friends, had been invited by George Harrison to come to England to play on Harrison's solo masterpiece, *All Things Must Pass*. While on some down time from the Harrison sessions, Keys was out at a London nightclub and ran into Mick, who invited the horn players down to Olympic during the end of the *Sticky Fingers* sessions. Mick invited Keys to stay at his place. Keys was "living with . . . the most eligible bachelor in the Western Hemisphere." The first thing they played on was the Memphis homage, "I Got the Blues." "We were listening to a lot of Otis Redding at the time, and I could tell Mick was really taken with using the horns to bring another dimension to their music," writes Bobby. "And I was really touting it—'Hey, Mick, listen to how great these horns are! Listen to how Otis and the horns work together'! . . . Oh man, I was campaigning like a Southern diplomat!"

Keys blasts the song home with his brassy sax lick which, along with the slapstick percussion (castanets from Mick), and the "yeah, yeah, yeah, whoo!" parts, gives the track a Moulin Rouge/burlesque feel, bawdy and fun.

Complicated, boneheaded, sarcastic, inciting, defusing, nuanced, earnest, and comic—the band owned these contradictions and reveled in the absurdity of it all. And they were pumping out hits and timeless music. As Booth observed at Muscle Shoals, "They were not good or evil, they were for better or worse artists, and all they wanted was to do their work; and for this reason they were now working through the middle of the night in Northern Alabama, after their tour was over, their money was made."

27
Wild Horses

RECORDED:

December 3–4, 1969, Muscle Shoals Sound Studios,
Sheffield, Alabama

RELEASES:

LP: *Sticky Fingers*, April 1971
Single, June 1971, US, charting at number 28

Recording the White Man's Blues in the Deep South

Keith and Mick stood at the same microphone at Muscle Shoals, lights dimmed, splitting a fifth of bourbon, and simultaneously sang the melodies and harmonies on the three songs that they had recorded over three days: "Brown Sugar," "You Got to Move," and "Wild Horses." That's your rock 'n' roll fantasy right there, pal. A six-piece band working in a tiny converted coffin factory across from an Alabama graveyard, on an eight-track recorder, with no computer editing or Autotune, recorded three songs, representing 30 percent of one of the greatest rock 'n' roll records of all time.

"Wild Horses" is often referred to as a country song, but it is simply a crushingly honest Stones ballad that just happens to have a country twang to it. The chord progression and melody could just as easily lend itself to a jazz standard interpretation or a soul treatment. Indeed, Arthur Alexander, Ray Charles, or James Carr could all have made "Wild Horses." Keith had long been fascinated with country music, growing up listening to the "cowboy songs" of Gene Autry, Jimmie Rodgers, and Hank Williams. Though you can trace some country influence back to "It's All Over Now," it showed up in earnest around the time Keith met Gram Parsons in 1968.

Parsons had come over to England with the Byrds, whom he had been taking in more of a country-rock direction. He had recently joined the band and immediately had a significant influence on their genre-defining 1968 album, *Sweetheart of the Rodeo,* which Keith says "bemused everybody at the time." When the Byrds stopped over on their way to South Africa, Keith and others went to see them play at Blaises Club, expecting to see the jangly folk-rock that Roger McGuinn et al had been known for. But the personnel had changed, and the repertoire along with it.

Knocked out by this new country-rock vibe, Mick and Keith went backstage to chat with the Byrds. Parsons left the Byrds and he and Keith became dear friends and drug buddies overnight. Parsons stayed at Redlands at least through that summer, teaching Keith how to play some country piano while explaining the nuanced distinctions between the various strains of country music— Bakersfield, as personified with Merle Haggard and Buck Owens, and Nashville, as represented by Hank Williams and George Jones.

Gram's encouragement and tutelage might have explained Keith's new confidence in taking on country music more directly, just as the band had been willing to let its soul influence show in a more obvious way. Dickinson said that when Keith would arrive at Muscle Shoals before the others, he immediately started to jam with Dickinson on country songs. This informal give-and-take greased the way for Dickinson, who was more of a rock 'n' roller, to play piano on "Wild Horses."

While Keith was comfortable in exploring country music, Mick was never as willing to throw himself into it as deeply as he would with blues and soul. "Keith and I had been playing Johnny Cash records and listening to the Everly Brothers—who were *so* country—since we were kids," said Mick. "I used to love country music even before I met Keith. . . . The country songs like 'Factory Girl' or 'Dear Doctor' on *Beggars Banquet* were really pastiches. There's a sense of humor—a way of looking at life in a humorous kind of way . . . the 'country' songs we recorded later, like 'Dead Flowers' on *Sticky Fingers* or 'Far Away Eyes' on *Some Girls* are slightly different. The actual music is played completely straight, but it's me who's not going legit with the whole thing, because I'm a blues singer, not a country singer—I think it's more suited to Keith's voice than mine."

"Mick feels the need to get into other caricatures," said Keith, referring to how Mick approached different styles of songs—not just country per se. "He's slightly vaudeville in his approach. When he sings it as a caricature . . . you expect Mick to walk out in his cowboy duds on an eighteen-wheeler set. . . . Or sing it into his CB. . . ."

Unlike the shit-kicking "Dead Flowers," though, "Wild Horses" is more like one of the pastiches Mick spoke about. But it's not a jokey send-up; it's a country-soul piece. Or a country-folk-soul-pop ballad. This is where labels fail. Just how does one characterize "Wild Horses" other than a "Stonesy ballad"? Mick called it a pop song, which may be why he sings it so sincerely. It comes out sounding like nothing other than the Stones. Country music is useful as a tool in the tool kit here, a starting point. But Parsons came up with a term for the sort of music he was after: Cosmic American music. For lack of anything better, "Wild Horses" might as well be called an example of that.

The finessed acoustic musical bed provides an uninhibited tenderness to support the lyric. The lyric idea for the chorus of "Wild Horses" came from Keith, embarking on tour and being emotionally torn about leaving behind his baby boy, Marlon, born in August 1969. Keith had the words for the chorus and Mick finished the rest of lyric, somehow managing to embrace both the original inspiration and his own feelings of leaving Marianne behind, physically and emotionally. "Childhood living is easy to do/The things you wanted, I bought them for you." That could be sung to either a child or a vulnerable lover. "Graceless lady, you know who I am." Like, "My funny valentine . . ." or "I may not always love you," it's one of those lyrics that is so nakedly honest in it's embrace of the real, the imperfect. As with those lyrics from other songs, the listener is drawn in and takes it for granted that this is a love song, by the very form and the very nature that it is being sung so tenderly.

Like many great songs, it is "about" multiple things, with inspirations both specific and general. But songs, combinations of words with chords and melodies, are rarely meant to be about one thing. They grab hold of a feeling, an elusive emotion, something that words alone fail to capture. As Keith writes, "In a way you want to stretch yourself into other people's hearts. You want to plant yourself there, or at least get a resonance, where other people become a bigger instrument than the one you're playing. . . . To write a song that is remembered and taken to heart is a connection . . . A thread that runs through all of us." There are few Stones songs more personal than this.

One influence that Mick might have taken from Parsons is how the latter treated country music as the white man's blues. Parsons had an extremely limited reedy range, but few have done more with so little. "He . . . had this unique thing that I've never seen any other guys do: he could make the bitches cry," writes

Keith. "Even hardened waitresses at the Palomino bar* who heard it all."

Similarly, Mick sounds raggedly vulnerable here, yet in remarkably strong voice for just having finished a tour (especially back in 1969 when stage monitors would be poor and so a singer would have a more difficult time hearing himself). His voice quivers at just the right time, but there is no apparent degradation of his timbre. He surrenders himself to the song. "I remember we sat around originally doing this with Gram Parsons, and I think his version came out slightly before ours," Mick recalled.† "Everyone always says it was written about Marianne but I don't think it was; that was all well over by then. But I was definitely very inside this piece emotionally. This is very personal, evocative, and sad. It all sounds rather doomy now, but it was quite a heavy time."

Before they started playing the song in the studio, according to Booth's firsthand account, Stu exited and Mick said, "We'll need a keyboard player on this one." Jerry Wexler suggested he could call a session player, when Dickinson piped up, "I'm a keyboard player." "You'll do," came the stamp of approval from Mick. The only piano in tune at the time was a tack piano, which was often heard in soundtracks of the old western movies. The soft felt hammers would literally have tacks inserted to give that percussive sound.

The tack piano fit the recording perfectly. Keith is playing his five-string open G tuning on a 12-string guitar, with the low E strings removed, making it a 10-string. There is also a 6-string with a Nashville tuning playing on one side of the stereo mix, on which Mick Taylor plays well-placed harmonics, just barely touching the strings without pressing them down, letting those ghostly notes

---

* An LA-area club where Parsons and his band the Flying Burrito Brothers would often play.

† The Flying Burrito Brothers released a version on their 1970 record, *Burrito Deluxe*.

ring out while the other acoustic does all the heavy lifting. The harmonics mesh and disappear into the same frequency range of the tack piano. On an electric guitar, Keith plays country-ish seventh licks, floating in a bit like a pedal steel guitar, with a bit of that slap-back delay also heard on Keith's guitar on "Brown Sugar." It is a very jangly song, with doubled notes chiming against each other, an autumnal sound that Keith accurately describes as "forlorn."

Although written by Mick and Keith, every player on the recording was emotionally invested in the song. This even included the stoic Charlie Watts. Charlie's playing might in fact be the most dramatic element of the song. Charlie had been on the road, too; no one in the band had a more stable domestic life than he. It would be perhaps more painful for him to leave home than anyone else. All you need to hear is how Charlie chooses his entrances and exits on "Wild Horses" to understand how much of an emotional punch he lends this music. No drummer commands an arrangement like him, coming in and dropping out at just the right moments. And then, almost as quickly, he drops out again, letting Mick and Keith carry that weight and open up their veins for you. And just as the singers are at their most vulnerable, who is there to pick them (and you) up? Charlie, like one of James Brown's Fabulous Flames, behind him all the way.

The second time Charlie enters, he rolls the snare drum in earlier on the verse than the first time he entered, when he came in at the chorus. Now he enters at the halfway point of the verse. He leaves space, an impossibly drawn-out beat number two. A deep breath. This is Charlie at his most Zen-jazz. How does he manage to lay out of that middle-eight section (at 3:00)? This is the most "up" part of the song. Most drummers would be pounding through that part first and foremost. But instead, counterintuitively, he waits until the next verse. The six-note drum fill going into the last chorus (at 5:07), is one of the most devastating of all Charlie's fills.

This is an emotional song—lyrics, music—and yet Charlie's austere choices are what provide the song the most drama.*

The whole band knew when to leave the right space. No one is looking to showboat here. Bill in particular plays no more notes than necessary, a less-is-more economy that makes the impact of the song that much more dramatic. "We want a soft warm lovely sound from you, Wyman," Booth quotes Keith as saying. "Stop donkeyin' about." There is a killer note on the bass (at about 1:33,) where Bill seems to unintentionally land just below the intended note and slides bluesily to match the actual note, like a soul singer would.

Despite the deep emotion of the recording, the session, as described by Booth, sounded like the musicians were having a good time, fueled by cocaine, pot, beer, and Jack Daniels. The band had different terms for mistakes—someone playing an incorrect note or chord—that can kill a good take. "Clams" is a common musician term. But the Stones had a whole glossary. Ruining one otherwise good take of "Wild Horses," Keith announced, "I accept the Golden Prune."

"Lights out, mouths shut," said Mick. Then they laid it down.

---

* The drums were miked with only three microphones, including a Neuman U47 out in front. "In fact, Charlie Watts wanted to buy that microphone!" said Jimmy Johnson. "But of course, I wouldn't sell it. He couldn't get over the sound we were getting."

28
Moonlight Mile

RECORDED:

October 1970, Stargroves

RELEASES:

LP: *Sticky Fingers*, April 1971

Rock 'n' Roll's Loveliest Road Song

Made a rag pile of my shiny clothes," Mick intimates on this sublime album-ender, a melancholy mood piece that fades out in a swell of strings, the band howling down "the railway lines." There are a lot of songs about being on the road. Some of them are good. A few of them are great. "Moonlight Mile" is the best.

Recorded at Stargroves, the song seems as inspired not only by the abstract notion of home, but by the place itself: "We played in this huge room with a gallery and great acoustics," said Mick Taylor. "And it was one of those sessions," engineer Andy Johns recounted. "We started at two or three in the morning and it was just that time of the night. And I think it was four or five in the morning when we got all the sounds together and everyone had learned the song and the magic started to happen, just as the sun started to come up, just a little bit of light came through the windows. I remember thinking, *boy, this is really cool,* because they hadn't done anything like that before."

"Mick first sang it to me in a first-class railway compartment on the way from London to Bristol," said Mick Taylor. Taylor has said that it is he who wrote the ending riff on "Moonlight Mile" that served as the inspiration for the string arrangement. Keith had sketched out something simple on a cassette tape, titled "Japanese Thing," from which both Jagger and Taylor built up the epic song. Keith, who is not on the track, claims, "Mick came in with the whole idea [of the song] and the band learned to play it." Keith had not yet made it to the loosely arranged Stargroves sessions.

As with "Wild Horses," Mick completely lets his guard down and offers a glimpse of the man behind the masked persona he had been building up for the sake of art or personal defense, or both. The lyric offers a view from a train, which could really be any form of transportation—tour bus, airplane, whatever—as long as it is taking him home. "In the window, there's a face you know." The face could be a loved one waiting in a window at home. But more than likely, it's Mick's own face, reflected back at him from a darkened train window. The detachment of the line, the fact that it's a face he knows but does not immediately recognize as his own, symbolizes the idea that Mick feels he is losing himself in this public character, further confused by the "head full of snow," cocaine representing the dreamy druggy existence in the band cocoon.

The double-tracked unison vocal effect, employed judiciously by the Stones over their body of work, further removes Mick from the track. We are not questioning his sincerity at all here. On the contrary, it might be one of his most personal lyrics. But the double-tracked vocal is successful in adding the aura of a dream to the song. Mick floats outside of himself looking in. He prefers the silence on his radio to "the sounds of strangers sending nothing to my mind." It would be tough to find a more romantic sentiment, a line that captures that wistful yearning, the loneliness of time away than "I am just living to be lying by your side/But I'm just about a moonlight mile on down the road." What goes unsaid in the line is what gets us the most; we know the singer is far more than a mile away. It's the kind of woebegone road poetry that we might expect from Hank Williams.

You can hear the "Japanese Thing" Asian influence in Jagger's guitar playing, an open-tuned 2-string riff on the acoustic, which he sings along with in a falsetto the second go around. It is reminiscent of a koto, a Japanese zither-like instrument, especially coupled with the piano-string plucks from trumpet player, Jim Price. "[The piano] starts off with a chord, a trick you can do with a piano," Johns explained. "You hold a chord down, then you hit the sustain pedal and . . . you get a pick and strum it across the strings." After the intro, Price settles into a lovely natural motif. Charlie plays with soft-headed mallets, summoning big gong-like splashes from the cymbals. Taylor plays an electric guitar, including some lines with a slide. When the band reaches the chorus, the ethereal vibe gets nailed down into an almost funky Stones backbeat. The arrangement reaches a climax (around 4:00). Flutes herald the return of Paul Buckmaster's sweeping orchestration to bring the song to its destination with a dramatic flourish. "That really set it off," said Johns.

Though the Stones had returned to their roots, so to speak, with "Jumpin' Jack Flash" and the songs on *Beggars Banquet*, in 1968, they were still stretching out in the spirit of experimentation with songs like "Moonlight Mile," which is reminiscent of Van Morrison's longer, vampy pieces, like the song cycle he had released in late 1968 on *Astral Weeks*. The Stones had a line of songs of this ilk, dreamy ballads that ooze and sway, spreading out for more than the usual three minutes. "Winter" on *Goats Head Soup,* and "Time

Waits for No One" on *It's Only Rock 'n' Roll* come to mind, arrangements at least partially encouraged by Mick Taylor's ability to solo compellingly for minutes, taking the songs to another level.

Johns mixed most of the record. "I had just gotten off a plane at Heathrow. I went from Los Angeles, so I had been up for about twenty-four hours. For some reason, I called in to Olympic Studios, I must have said I would. [Someone there] said 'You better get here quick. Mick wants to mix this afternoon. Get here as soon as you can.' So I got in a cab with my suitcase and drove over to Olympic and there he was waiting. And we had to do all these fucking mixes in one afternoon. I remember that despite the fact that I hadn't had any sleep, we got three or four songs in about five or six hours."

"It was great to hear [the mix of "Moonlight Mile"] because I was very out of it by the end of the album and it was like listening, really listening," said Keith. In a way, it feels like a lullaby for a junkie, a floating, peaceful nod out. This cinematic album closer that set the bar for all album closers that followed, "Moonlight Mile" drifts off in a reverie. We can imagine Mick falling asleep against the window, another moonlight mile away from home, where he would rather be, setting fire to a rag pile of his shiny stage clothes. Not a hit single, or even one of the deeper album tracks that has gotten much airplay over the years, "Moonlight Mile" is nevertheless a Stones fan's kind of Rolling Stones song, a secret handshake for those who would listen to *Sticky Fingers* continuously from start to finish.

As Johns summarized, "It's a major work of art, that particular song."

29
Rocks Off

RECORDED:

July and October–November 1971, Villa Nellcôte,

Villefranche-sur-Mer, France

(Keith Richards' rented house)

December 1971, Sunset Sound Studio, LA

RELEASES:

LP *Exile on Main Street*, May 1972

Recording on the Riviera:
The Sunshine Bores the
Daylights Out of Me

The sunshine bores the daylights out of me," "Rocks Off" proudly declares. Tax exiles living in France, recording by night in the oppressively humid basement of a decadent torn-and-frayed mansion on the Riviera, these nocturnal creatures had little in common with nine-to-five rat racers. There is no more perfect way than "Rocks Off" to start the masterpiece double album, *Exile on Main Street*.

Don Was, who produced later Stones recordings, observed in the short documentary *Stones in Exile* that at the time the band was working on the album, "There was something in the air . . . There was definitely the sense that the sixties didn't work and that you either had to blow up the system or flee from it." Given those two choices, the Stones seemed to be in full retreat, certainly in geographic exile to France, but also personally and psychologically. Mick stepped into the full embrace of the jet-setting bourgeoisie and Keith slipped into drug-aided escape, with little grip on reality. The band was creating their own fantasy world (and the ultimate rock 'n' roll fantasy of kids around the world), unmoored from normal day-to-day existence. "Feel so hypnotized can't describe the scene," goes the first line of the bridge of "Rocks Off."

It is this rootless existence—Englishmen ex-pats who loved American music living in France—that the Stones used to "fire the fucking feed" on "Rocks Off." As the lead-off track, it immediately sets the tone for the whole record. It opens with this confusing bit of noise, mixed in with the signature Stones-y riff, including Mick's humorous growl of "Oh yeeeeaaaahhh." Someone seems to be adjusting in a seat and other extraneous sounds are heard. The very fact that the record starts off like this, with these "mistakes" left unmasked, is a signal that this is to be an unusual mainstream rock 'n' roll record. The first side of the four is overweighted with an unrelenting sequence of rocking songs that pummels the listener into submission before he can get up, flip the album, and relax into the pastoral acoustic folk and country of side two.

Exile on Main Street represents the culmination of an astoundingly productive period from 1968–72. It is a four-year stretch for the Stones unmatched by any pop artist save for the Beatles, Bob Dylan, and Stevie Wonder—and the Stones *still* had a surplus of worthy material at the end of it all. The sprawl of the two-disc set, the very format, is inextricable from the material within, for the record offers a compendium of a fabled America, American music, and its Anglo, African, and Caribbean roots. And, if you're asking me, there's not a bum song on there, so don't give me the "It would have been better as a single album" argument; I am having none of that.

Suitably, creation of the record itself comes with its own mythology and represents the pinnacle of Stones lore. The primary exaggeration is that the whole record was recorded in the basement of Keith's house in the South of France. While those sessions might reasonably be considered the heart of the record and have defined it in the public consciousness, many of the album's best and most representative songs had been recorded at Stargroves, Mick's house in England. Still others date back to 1968–69 and were recorded during the same sessions at Olympic as the songs on *Let It Bleed*. The songs that were started before the band left England include "Tumbling Dice," "Sweet Virginia," "Shine a Light," "All Down the Line," "Shake Your Hips," and "Stop Breaking Down," some of which were redone or expanded on at Villa Nellcôte, and/ or later at Sunset Sound in LA. Nothing in the factual record, however, will sway many from this illusion that it's all about the South of France. The narrative fits.

Even recent quotes from Keith indicate that he still subscribes to the other main component of *Exile* mythology, that they were being "edged out" of their country, that the authorities were after them because they had enough sway over their legions of fans that they were perceived as a threat to the existing power structure, "a force to be reckoned with," in Keith's words. This theory conveniently ignores that, under the Labour government of the time, their tax rate was 93 percent and they had paid none of it. "Keith always says he was chased out of England by the cops," said Mick in *Crossfire Hurricane*. "He may believe that, but I mean it's not actually true. The real reason the *band* left was money."

The Stones had to quickly devise a strategy to save their dire fiscal situation, given their tax liability and an unfavorable contractual relationship with Allen Klein. The band had no cash with which to pay their back tax liability in the UK. The financial team—Prince Rupert Loewenstein, a merchant banker whom Mick had befriended in 1969, the band's attorneys, and their tax advisors—also discovered that Klein had assigned himself ownership of the band's master recordings and the publishing rights to their songs bought out from Andrew Loog Oldham in 1967. Klein, it came to be known, had surreptitiously been funneling untold amounts of the Stones money into a US company that happened to have the same Nanker Phelge moniker as their songwriting group pseudonym and their UK company. A settlement was reached whereby Klein retained rights to the songs through 1971, which is why some of the best songs from 1969–71 were held back from previous records, until they could be released on *Exile,* safe from the claims from Klein and his ABKO Records label.

The consensus was that the Stones would very quickly be broke if they did not relocate. France seemed like the least unattractive option. If they lived there, for a minimum of twenty-one months, it would alleviate much of their current tax burden and allow them to accumulate revenue substantial enough to pay their back taxes. As Mick points out, leaving England "for tax reasons was really not cool," in the perception of rock 'n' roll fans. Ian Anderson of Jethro Tull was one of those outspoken critics. In a 1976 interview with *Melody Maker,* he took English rock stars to task for claiming they were unfairly burdened by taxes, singling out Led Zeppelin and the Stones, to which Keith responded, "He sounded more like some provincial tax accountant. Who wants some freaky acid-head flute player teaching you about tax anyways?"

In 1970, the band had tried to make as clean a break as possible, severing their relationship with Klein, leaving their former label Decca behind, starting their own label, Rolling Stones records—headed by Marshall Chess, son of Chess Records cofounder,

Leonard—and planning the relocation to France. They individually ended up in different locales, Keith renting a decadent Belle Epoque mansion on the Riviera not far from Nice, for about $10,000 a month. Its glory long faded, Villa Nellcôte was the name of the house in Villefranche-sur-Mer.

After scouring the South of France to find a suitable studio in which to work, Stu, Miller, and Andy Johns came up empty. "We tried various cinemas or halls that one might rent," said Miller. "We never found a suitable site and in the end we chose convenience over sound." It was decided that working at Keith's house with the Rolling Stones Mobile Unit would be the best option and would also be most likely to guarantee his presence. He and Anita were slipping deeper into heroin dependency, a habit that started in earnest in late 1970. Given that Keith was becoming far less dependable, working on "Keith time," a "bohemian" schedule, in Charlie's words, became a necessity if the band was going to get anything accomplished. "The idea was to find another place to record like a farmhouse in the hills," said Keith. "But they couldn't find anywhere, so eventually they turned around and looked at me. I looked at Anita and said, 'Hey, babe, we're gonna have to handle it.' Anita had to organize dinner sometimes for something like 18 people."

Meanwhile, more ex-pat-rock-star domesticity was celebrated when Mick and Bianca were married in May 1971 in St. Tropez. It began a summer rotation of rock stars coming in and out of Keith's home. Dominique Tarlé's photos of the summer, compiled in his excellent collector's-item book, *Exile,* show John and Yoko, Clapton, Parsons, Stephen Stills, Ringo, Paul and Linda, and others. "Many of them had nothing to do" after the wedding, says Tarlé. "So, as usual, it ends up at Keith's house." Tarlé himself remained at Nellcôte for six months, taking photos that add romance to the specific mythology of *Exile* and decadent 1970s rock 'n' roll lifestyle.

Even with such a tranquil and exotic setting, there on the French

Riviera, a sense of unease ruled the day. Bianca, who had clashed with Keith and Anita, was in the late stages of her pregnancy over that summer and went back to Paris and Mick divided his time between the two locales. Keith's drug use was also contributing to the personal distance. Mick and Keith were writing separately more often. Since there was no set schedule, the band members were spread out geographically (Charlie was a six-to-seven-hour drive away), and work was sporadic, band members would stay for a few days at a time. No one seemed to be in control. ". . . Winging it. Staying up all night . . . Stoned on something; one thing or another," is how Mick described it. "It was this communal thing where you don't know whether you're recording or living or having dinner; you don't know when you're gonna play, when you're gonna sing—very difficult. . . . Everyone was so out of it. And the engineers, the producers—all the people that were supposed to be organized—were more disorganized than anybody." As Jimmy Miller said, "We just couldn't seem to get started."

When they did end up working, the basement kitchen formed the hub of a warren of rooms turned into a makeshift studio. Keys described the basement to me:

> It was like a catacombs, a lot of compartmentalized rooms. . . .
> It was a very makeshift, experimental atmosphere that we were
> recording in. You know, sometimes Jim and I would be down
> the long hallway away from all the other guys and we couldn't
> see anything . . . it was hotter than hell in there and we were
> wearing bathing suits, shorts, and flip-flops and drinking lots
> of whisky and beer. It was a very primitive setup as far as re-
> cording goes. There was no eye contact between Keith or
> Mick, and Charlie, and Jim and I, 'cause we were out in a hall-
> way and we couldn't see Jimmy Miller, and we couldn't see
> anyone. It was sort of a science project, but it worked.

Charlie's drums were set up in the wine cellar. Price and Keys set up in a hallway. The piano remained upstairs. Acoustic guitars were tracked in the kitchen. People communicated over mikes and headphones. The guys in the truck had to continuously run in and out of the house. "Plus . . . someone had the bright idea to say, 'Oh, let's save money and tap into the mains out in the road,'" said Johns. "And of course that was going up and down. And they were running the amps off the truck. Once it got below a certain voltage or amperage the breaker would go off. And this was happening all the time. Plus it was so damn humid, the guitars would go out of tune. It was a real problem."

Getting through a take with guitars going out of tune resulted in understandable frustration. The band would work on tracks for weeks, Keith running through guitar riffs continuously as he searched for just the right feel and sound. The two main guitar tracks heard on "Rocks Off" were overdubs recorded by Keith. He had one version of the rhythm part down on tape, with the basic tracks of the band recorded in one all-night session. Everyone headed for home or upstairs to bed as dawn broke. But Keith felt the track just was not grooving sufficiently and he came up with the other guitar part in a burst of inspiration. When Andy Johns rolled into the villa he was sharing with Price, about a half hour's drive away, the phone rang. Keith was on the line. "Where the fuck are you?" he asked Johns. "Well, you were asleep," explained Johns. "Oh, man, I've got to do this guitar part. Come back!" said Keith. Johns obeyed and Keith recorded the second part, both with a '57 Telecaster, "and the whole thing just came to light, and really started grooving," said Johns.

The twin clean guitars enter, chugging in an extreme stereo spread, louder than anything in the mix, as drums, horns, piano, and bass all make their way into the track. Keith is also playing that high, somewhat distant sounding guitar in the middle. He recalls in his book that he had turned an amp around, away from the microphone, to face the corner of a tiled room.*

Everything else sounds crisp and present, including Nicky Hopkins's piano, which comes in with his commanding right-hand on the chorus playing it's own rhythm up in a high-enough octave to cut through. He again demonstrates why he was the best piano player for a hard rock 'n' roll band. No other piano player could fit an acoustic piano into a full rock arrangement better than Hopkins. Though "Sympathy for the Devil" is often cited as the pinnacle among his Stones contributions, it is on songs like "Rocks Off," where he would have to carve out his own space in a dense arrangement, that Hopkins truly shined. By 1971, the Stones were effectively an eight-piece band: the five actual members, plus two horns, and Nicky was one of the band. They came off the road from the European tour as hot as a pistol, and kept on rolling through reels of tape at the studio. "We were invited to go and we *went*," said Keys. Keith said: "It's us against the world now. Fuck ya . . . We're all gonna do this, boys, we're all just gonna move out and be a family, and here's the place. And in a way it was energizing."

It was an unusual way to record, as horns were generally overdubbed on sessions by the early 1970s. Now they were a part of the ensemble. "Normally you would not have a horn section hanging around with you the whole time you were recording," Mick said. But they "became an integral part of the record."

"You can't have horns, I guess, wall-to-wall, from beginning to end on everything, on every song," Keys lamented. I replied that *Exile* comes pretty close to that dream of wall-to-wall horns "Well, I'll tell you, we had a lot of time for overdubs," he laughed. "Yeah, that was a good album to play horns on. For one thing, Jim and I were there and nothing was written down or arranged and such.

---

* The band was using mostly Ampeg amps during the sessions.

We had time to sit down and go over the tracks and Jimmy Miller had ideas, and Keith had ideas, and Mick had ideas, and you know, I think even *we* had some ideas. But we had plenty of time to work stuff out because hell, it was in Keith's basement and we weren't in a studio, punching a time clock, or anything like that."

With the full ensemble running on all pistons on "Rocks Off," Mick is fairly buried in the mix, somewhat by design. When a vocal is too up-front in the mix, a track automatically becomes less rocking and loses its drive. The ear gets taken away from the guitars and drums. The band learned this especially early, when mono mixes would bring the vocals to the fore more readily, and when combined with the compression that radio stations would add, would jump out to even more prominence.* Miller and Johns might have overcompensated by bringing his vocals so low on some of these tracks. "On the 'Rocks Off' mix we put on an echo effect on Mick's voice and got lucky," said Johns. "It ties together."

"Mick and I always fought a bit over his vocals," Jimmy Miller said in Richard Buskin's book *Inside Tracks*. "I thought they should be up-front but whenever we were mixing he would come in and say, 'Too much voice, too much voice.' I'd say, 'You're kidding! You can hardly hear it!'" Miller asked Mick once why he wanted his vocals so low all the time and Mick explained he wanted it to be like the old blues records he grew up with, always trying to decipher the words. Mick explained that he would buy the records and listen to them repeatedly. Miller said that Mick wanted to sell more records to those interested in learning the words, which were not printed in the packaging of Stones albums.

On "Rocks Off," the "buried" effect works well. The listener has to bend his/her ears to try to discern what Mick is singing. For the

---

* It is for this reason that, during the mixing sessions, Stu brought an acetate of the "All Down the Line" mix to an LA radio station to play while the Stones drove around LA one night, listening on the radio.

Stones, the words are inextricable from the music. Repeated listenings reward the listener. The title being slang for getting off orgasmically, the song is "splattered on the dirty road" with sex and violence. Mick's "dancer friend . . . comes every time she pirouettes on" him. It's an extreme wet dream. The music is indeed kicking and does not stop, but the dream images open the album in a surreal way. The fact that Mick can't see a person's mouth moving but can hear them speaking, or that he himself wants to shout but "can't hardly speak," could reflect the frustration of the band as they receded—or withdrew—further from normal life.

The song comes to an even more druggy half-time halt during the middle-eight, where it feels like we are moving in slow motion, under water. "Jimmy would actually have very good ideas," Johns told me. "I learned some sonic tricks from Jimmy over the years. For example, in the song 'Rocks Off,' you know there's that middle-eight reprise part, you know, it's phased [modulating one sound against another for a sweeping effect]. Jimmy said, we have to do something with this, why don't we phase it? And I said, okay we can do that, and then I came up with the idea for the lower pitch on Mick's voice with the tremolo on it . . . I used a low-frequency oscillator on it. That was Jimmy's idea and I just edited it in."

Through it all, throat-straining harmonies from Keith occasionally miss their target word or note—in a good way, of course. There are ghostly voices even under the parts other than the intentionally creepy middle-eight, where surreal vocals float in backward and are swept up in a vortex. Mick Taylor breaks free at the very end of the arrangement, with the band vamping on the horn riff, similar to the end of James Brown's soul revue. Charlie pounds out a start-stop-catch-up drum fill before he clicks back into the backbeat. The background vocal part also sticks to a funky percussive pattern: "Only *get* 'em off, only *get* 'em off, *get* 'em off!"

As Taylor just starts to add his bluesy soloing, the mix fades out. Taylor had plenty of the spotlight to solo on *Sticky Fingers,* as he would on the next two records, as well as during the live shows. But *Exile,* even as it sprawled out, offered very little opportunity for him to rise above the band and soar like he does on "Can't You Hear Me Knocking" or "Winter." It is all about serving the song, the ensemble and the rhythm, on this most soul-influenced of Stones records. As Peter Guralnick writes about those studios that were sacred ground to the Stones, "Much like Stax, FAME had no flashy lead guitarist in their studio group; rhythm was the key component."

Rhythm was also such a key component for Keith Richards that he had summoned Johns back at the crack of dawn that day to record his new rhythm guitar idea. Who was Johns to turn him down? "I'm twenty-one years old and there I am in the South of France working with the best band on the planet," said Johns. "It was my initiation into how you could actually live . . . *rock 'n' roll.*"

The Stones were not only living rock 'n' roll, but living life as theater, continuing to cultivate, in Marianne Faithfull's words, the "patina of aristocratic decadence" that had first appeared when Brian met Anita. With model girlfriends, servants, drugs, and a swirling vortex of hangers-on ensconced in a Riviera waterfront mansion of faded glamor, they were creating *the* template for seventies rock stars.

Long past their status as mere sixties pop stars, the Stones were rock gods, slumming in the enigmatic mythology of American roots music. "A sad little poem right out of America," is how Jack Kerouac described Robert Frank's photos in the introduction of the Swiss émigré's 1958 collection, *The Americans.* That epigram might as well describe *Exile.* It was these photos, as well as some new ones commissioned by Frank, that the Stones used for the packaging of the album. The mere act of choosing Frank indicates the mindset of the band. They were quite willingly subscribing to an outsider's skewed romantic vision of America that they had accumulated from years of listening to blues, rock 'n' roll, country, folk, and jazz. And they were also consciously contributing to that tradition, creating contemporary apocrypha, such as glorifying Angela Davis in "Sweet Black Angel," say, or name-dropping Pat and Dick Nixon and the obscure Dallas groupie, the Butter Queen, in "Rip This Joint."

It fits the romantic lore of the album that while Keith was a kid in England listening to early rock 'n' roll on Radio Luxembourg, good ol' boy Texan Bobby Keys, same age to the day, was experiencing the birth of the music firsthand. As a kid Bobby had watched Buddy Holly and the Crickets practicing in his aunt's neighbor's house. And Keys had himself played sax with the Crickets after Holly's untimely death. Bobby, who had met the Stones way back on their first US tour in 1964, was now living the dream with them in the South of France as they recorded this record of Americana. The Texan's background added some authenticity to the American references on the *Exile,* ringing, as it does, with juke joints on dusty roads and moonshine fueled hell-raising at the union hall.

But by 1971, the band was not delusional or blindly nostalgic about what America was really about. The Stones had seen enough of the ugly reality of America to shoot a hole in the inflated-cartoon-balloon version. And yet, as artists, they aspired to create something akin to what is captured in Frank's photos, "that crazy feeling in America when the sun is hot on the streets and the music comes out of a jukebox or a funeral," as Kerouac wrote. Their job was not to report reality; their job was to give it shape. They did not shrink from the dark and ugly; they embraced it. And this is why *Exile* needed to be two records. It consists of music that could have come from a jukebox, and music that could have come from a funeral.

But it's really about that body of work dating back to '68. *Exile* was just the final couple of chapters. And this may be why they ended up disappointed with this flawed masterpiece. There was no stated concept going in. Mick says that "the writing process was very loose." The sessions at Nellcôte were sprung from jams. "As unrehearsed as a hiccup," is how Keys described it. Keith himself says that he never plans anything, but "Mick needs to know what he's going to do tomorrow. Me, I'm just happy to wake up and see who's hanging around. Mick is rock. I'm roll." Mick in particular has repeatedly stated that it just should have been better. "It was frustrating, and it took quite a long period of time," Mick has said. "A lot of the tracks were not made in the South of France. They were tracks we'd made or hadn't finished, or hadn't released on the previous album . . . *Exile* was recorded under a lot of difficult circumstances, and in what was not a very good recording place. It was a bit uphill . . . And there were so many drug problems. . . ."

But by 2010, when the Stones remastered and rereleased *Exile* with bonus tracks and an accompanying documentary film, even Mick had come around a bit and questioned his past memories and frustrations. "Yeah, there was outside trouble of all different nature, it was a time of change—but what time isn't?" he asked, as if in a conversation with his past self. "People getting married, like me, other people having loads of children. A lot of things happened. It was like a three-year period, you know? . . . [I]t wasn't all bad. Some of it was fantastic. It was very full of incident, but it wasn't all angst, when you see the photographs everybody's having a wonderful time. You can paint it as this degrading experience, but it really doesn't look like that when you look at it."

Had he fallen prey to the Stones mythology? Was he consciously feeding it? If so, was it for purely commercial reasons or had he finally succumbed to personal nostalgia? *When you see the photographs . . . when you look at it.* Now even Mick had reduced the record and the era to a series of snapshots, willing to forget all the mundane daily iterative struggles that went into creating the whole.

There's no need to retrofit "Rocks Off" into the mythology. This one is pure unadulterated French Riviera *Exile on Main Street.*

30
Tumbling Dice

RECORDED:

July and October–November 1971, Villa Nellcôte,

Villefranche-sur-Mer, France

(Keith Richards' rented house)

December 1971, Sunset Sound Studio, LA

RELEASES:

LP: *Exile on Main Street,* May 1972

Single, April 1972, charting at number 7 in the US

and number 5 in the UK

Shuffling Out of the Sixties and Finding the Holy Grail of Grooves in the Seventies

They would play very poorly for two or three days on whatever song and then if Keith got up and looked at Charlie, then you knew something was about to go down. And then Bill would get up and put his bass at about that

84 degree angle, and you went 'ah, here it
comes. They're gonna go for it now.' Then it
would turn into this wonderful God-given
music.

—Andy Johns in *Stones in Exile*

That shuffle, the perfect tempo, that slight drag—"Tumbling
Dice" is the Holy Grail of grooves and was so coveted that
Rod Stewart later took a tape of "Tumbling Dice" into his
Foot Loose & Fancy Free (1977) sessions to play to the band he had
assembled to record "Hot Legs." The Clash's Joe Strummer said of it:
"It surges forward, but it's not a straightforward tempo. It's halfway
between a slow and a straightforward rocker. It has a mystical beat."

But this perfect, supple feel took years of finessing, beginning
in 1970 as a generic upbeat blues tune called "Good Time Women."
It was "like pulling teeth," said Johns. By the time it got to Nellcôte, it still took hours and dozens of reels of tape (Johns has
claimed anywhere from thirty to one hundred reels) before it
clicked in and finally hit that pleasantly buzzed and relaxed take.
"They would play for days without coming in and listen to anything," Johns told me. "When they would go and do a record, the
first few days were just horrible, because they hadn't played with
each other for a while and they would sound just dreadful."

"I remember writing the riff upstairs in the very elegant front
room," said Keith, "and we took it downstairs the same evening
and we cut it." Still, Keith played that riff on the reprise for six
hours one afternoon. As Charlie has said, Keith likes to "marinate"
something and come back to it later. When you think about it that
way, "Tumbling Dice" does have that well-marinated sound, like it
had been pounded out, then soaked in aged marsala for days, before being taken out and grilled crispy and served on a platter.
Johns told me that he had assumed that it was a new song that

Keith had been playing in France and it wasn't until years later, when someone played him a bunch of bootlegs dating back into the '60s, that he realized it had been an idea kicking around for years.

But even this album version required some studio magic. Speaking of the final piece, Johns explained, "There was a big gap to punch in there [on the tape]. And for some reason Charlie was having a mental block. Every now and then, Charlie would get a mental block, especially if Mick or Keith were giving him a really hard time about something that could be quite simple. And Jimmy said, 'Well, I can fucking do this.' And I said, 'Oh, you've done it before, why don't you go and do it now?' I'd already persuaded Charlie to double-track the drums on that part." Johns thought it could really fatten up the beat, so he punched in Miller playing the two parts and he reckons it couldn't have taken more than a half hour, if that. You can hear the difference in styles.

By the autumn of 1972, when summer was over and everyone had packed up the moveable feast, the strung-out Keith and Anita were left alone in that grand waterfront house with their budding family. It was clear that the sessions at Nellcôte had run their course. Miller and Johns gathered up all the tapes and brought them to LA to sort through and mix. It is when they started unreeling the recordings at Sunset Sound, playing the music for friends of the band, adding background singers and guest players, that the Stones realized what they had in "Tumbling Dice." The song, and the rest of the album, started to come to life.

The backing track was complete, but Mick did not have most of the lyrics written yet. It is tempting to believe the inspiration for the lyrics of "Tumbling Dice" had been influenced by the gambling in Monte Carlo, a stone's throw from Nellcôte, where some of the musicians were making occasional excursions. And this might be true in an indirect way. But despite his outlaw image, Keith is not a gambler. Often, Johns, Jim Price, and Bobby Keys would spend some nights gambling at the tables in Monte Carlo. "Sometimes Keith came with us," said Johns, "but he refused to gamble. I guess it would look bad if he lost. Keith wasn't into being a loser."

However, as with many, if not most, of the songs on *Exile*, "Tumbling Dice" was taken to LA for mixing without having lyrics beyond a few phrases. Keith and Mick even employed Beat author William Burroughs's (whom they had met in the '60s) famous "cut-up" technique for inspiration on some songs ("Casino Boogie," for example), snipping words and phrases from newspapers and other sources and randomly reassembling them. But the lyrics for "Tumbling Dice," which grew out of the 1969 "Good Time Women" song sketch, was inspired by a housekeeper in LA. "I sat down with the housekeeper and talked to her about gambling," said Mick, who also did not gamble. "She liked to play dice and I really didn't know much about it. But I got it off of her and managed to make the song out of that."

The Stones were students of Americana, the traditions of the blues and folklore. They knew where to cast their nets. The fact that Mick had cast his in the direction of the housekeeper was not pure kismet. He was consciously turning over rocks, looking for something specific. He might have already had the idea to use the well-worn lover/gambler/rambler trope, but he needed the particulars to come up with something like, "I'm all sixes and sevens and nines."

His bruised voice sounds like he has just rolled out of bed after trying to sleep off a hangover. He sounds vulnerable and soulful, full of regret, at odds with the unconvincing braggadocio of the lyrics. It sounds like he is shaking off his Jack Flash persona. He may be "playing the field every night," but he is losing. Even if this is just another character, it sounds like there's a whole lot of Mick himself invested in this performance.

His vocal is so exceptionally low in the mix as to be almost overwhelmed by the arrangement. He is just part of the ensemble. "I really like that thick mix where Mick is working hard to impose himself on the track," explained Keith. It adds an edge of urgency, like a live soul singer. He is selling the song, but he is not much louder than a horn in the horn section. When the single was released, there was a contest in one music newspaper that had listeners offering their best guesses at the indecipherable lyrics.

Mick has often disparaged the sound of the mixes on *Exile*. "I started mixing that in like October or November and it was going very slowly, *reeeeeallly* slowly," said Johns. "And I got four or five mixes and then there was a Christmas break and Mick was getting really impatient." So they replaced Johns with Joe Zagarino to finish mixing, but he also had difficulty and the Stones were still not satisfied. "So Mick called me up and told me to come back," said Johns. "I got it all done in a marathon three-day session. And it was pretty much on my own. Mick said, 'Here are the tapes, go and do it.'" The difficulty in mixing stemmed from the murky source sounds they had recorded in France. "It was just tough to get a good sound in that basement," Johns explained. "It really was. If they had been playing spectacularly, it would all come together and the sound would be good too. Otherwise it would take a long time to get anywhere."

Mick later claimed that he was certain that the version on the record was the wrong mix of "Tumbling Dice." Robert Greenfield, who was present for the mixing session, recalls Mick telling Miller that he was okay with either of two mixes. Rather than taking a hands-on role in the mixing, "Jimmy was a set of ears," Johns said.

No matter, the sound of "Tumbling Dice" is that particular *Exile* gumbo: open-tuned and slide guitars churning away, some baritone sax and/or trombone, Charlie and Jimmy pummeling out some tribal beats, and Nicky's piano somehow finding a home in it all. Mick Taylor played the bass, while Mick Jagger played second guitar with Keith.*

While Mick had this vision of the finished vocal arrangement in his head, most of what he was doing in France was steering the tracks along. When they got to LA for vocals and overdubs, they added the backing ensemble of Venetta Fields, Clydie King, and (possibly) Merry Clayton.† "A little bit of those girls goes a tremendously long way," Mick said. The women singers add a gospel soulfulness. There is a palpable ache to this song—not just the particular *Exile* recording, but something that also comes through in subsequent live versions. By the time that Miller sets down into the crestfallen old coda, we are left with an acute yearning, waxing nostalgic—for what? For lost summers? Lost romances? The unrealized optimism of the sixties? Marianne notes that their idea of the sixties ended with the 1967 busts: "In the sixties we were rebelling because we still had hope." But as hope turned to disillusionment, she, Anita, and Keith all turned from mind-opening acid to mind-numbing heroin. The Beatles were officially broken up by 1971. The Stones had survived, but not unscathed; Brian was dead and it appeared that perhaps Keith, too, was slipping away. "[I] don't see the time flashing by," denies Mick as he sings.

If there was any message, it was roll on. "I never stop to worry," Mick sings about whatever might be pressing concerns: The Nixon years, the war, the shootings at Kent State in 1970, the busts, the fallout, the band's precarious finances—whatever it was. "Baby, I can't stay/You got to roll me/Keep on rolling." You can see the attraction, why Keith had to play that reprise riff repeatedly; like the last sunset on a summer holiday, all slightly burned out from the sun and in-

---

* On live versions, Taylor didn't seem to know quite what to do and added a repetitive riff that plays off Keith's main. But it undercuts Keith's part and is distracting. When he breaks out into solo lines, it restores equilibrium.

† Clayton declined to confirm or deny her presence on the album.

dulging too much, we don't want that melancholy part to end either. We know we have to go home, but we are not quite ready to leave. We linger and savor this moment. The assured swagger of the song's lyric is subverted by the song's ultimately bittersweet coda.

The theme of survival is sustained across the lyrics of *Exile*. With the Beatles gone, it was up to the Stones to carry the torch. Dylan was transmogrifying into a far less relevant version of what he had been a decade before. Of the big three, the Stones had not only lasted, but improved leading into *Exile*. By 1971–72, the Stones had been around long enough that, for some people, attending their shows might have started to attain a feeling of a high school reunion, checking in with some old friends. Reviewing the "Tumbling Dice" single, *Melody Maker* proclaimed, "it's impossible to see their names on the label and not undergo inner convulsions in which joy, mirth, tears, nostalgia, and deep emotion are inevitably interwoven."

Johns counted himself as one of those fans. "The Rolling Stones were the center of the bloody universe for rock and roll," he recalled for *Goldmine* magazine. "And rock and roll back then meant a little bit more than it does now. It had social significance, breaking down the establishment and all that. It represented the way a generation felt about things."

They were still the center of the rock 'n' roll universe, to be certain. But there were exciting new acts like Bowie and T. Rex vying for the attention of the younger siblings of Stones fans. As Bowie wrote in the 1972 Mott the Hoople hit, "All the Young Dudes," "My brother's back at home with his Beatles and his Stones/We never got it off on that revolution stuff." Though the so-called glam acts were ostensibly futuristic, the rock 'n' roll they sang was self-referential and, in their own way, they were as self-conscious as retro acts like Sha Na Na. Both strains were about escaping the present and giving up on the power of rock 'n' roll to change anything significant, fiddling while Rome burned.

The Stones managed to combine both the earthy and old with the forward-leaning and theatrical. Unpretentious *Exile* is more about celebrating the heritage of American music and betrays an early concern for maintaining rock 'n' roll's relevance in the face of rapid change. Real escapism would come later, in the mid-1970s, with disco, and to some extent, punk rock,* at a time when radio formatting also became more fragmented. In 1972, you would still hear "Tumbling Dice" on contemporary top 40 radio next to, say, "The Candy Man," from Sammy Davis, Jr., "Let's Stay Together," from Al Green, or "Burnin' Love," from Elvis.

A big hit while the Stones were recording in 1971 was "American Pie," in which Don McLean sings melodramatically about the death of rock 'n' roll, taking with it all his guileless youthful dreams. McLean comes across as one of those obsessive fans who turns on their idols, seemingly embittered by what rock music turned into and, interestingly, taking the Stones to task with his lines, "Jack Flash sat on a candlestick," before moving into weak allusions to "Sympathy For the Devil" Altamont: "No angel born in Hell Could break that Satan's spell." On Don McLean's Web site, "American Pie" is described as "the funeral oration for an era." The song's producer, Ed Freeman, earnestly explains its significance as follows: "Without it, many of us would have been unable to grieve, achieve closure, and move on. Don saw that, and wrote the song that set us free. We should all be eternally grateful to him for that."

I reckon for most others—at least the rank outsiders that were hipper than those driving their "Chevy to the levee" and drumming the steering wheel on the one and three beats as they sang, "Bye bye, Miss American Pie . . ."—"Tumbling Dice" and *Exile* provided a real New Orleans–style funeral, instead of McLean's uptight "oration" for the death of an era.

---

* I am referring to the more nihilistic strain of punk (Sex Pistols) than the engaged and socially conscious (the Clash).

The rest of that Lester Bangs quote, about "partying in the face of it," summarized the contemporary reaction to *Exile* for those who understood the record upon release: "The party is obvious. The casualties are inevitable. It is the search for alternatives, something to *do* (something worthwhile even) that unites us with the Stones continuously."

31
Let It Loose

RECORDED:

July and October–November 1971, Villa Nellcôte,

Villefranche-sur-Mer, France

(Keith Richards' rented house

December 1971, Sunset Sound Studio, LA

RELEASES:

LP: *Exile on Main Street*, May 1972

The Gospel of the Rolling Stones

Who's that woman on your arm?/All dressed up to do you harm" begins "Let It Loose," perhaps the most gut-wrenchingly honest and emotional song that the Stones have recorded. "I think Keith wrote that, actually," recalled Mick, referring to the opening lines. "That's a very weird, difficult song. I had a whole other set of lyrics to it, but they got lost by the way-side. . . . I didn't really understand what it was about, after the event." Mick has called "Let It Loose" "rambling" and in hindsight was unsure of the song's meaning. But there was clearly something personal in there. The recording sounds like Mick is a raw nerve, turning in one of his most passionate vocals on record.

It makes complete sense that Keith wrote those opening lines. Like much of *Exile,* "Let It Loose" is almost certainly Keith and Mick writing about themselves and each other, like the opening lines of another stellar gospel song on the album, "Shine a Light," for example, where Mick is singing to Keith, "Saw you stretched out in room ten-oh-nine with a smile on your face and a tear right in your eye . . . Just seen too many flies on you/I just can't brush 'em off." While the earlier Glimmer Twins of *Let It Bleed* were brothers-in-arms in romanticizing the hedonistic lifestyle of "Live With Me" and "Monkey Man," on *Exile,* Mick and Keith sent messages back and forth to each other through the songs, something they would continue throughout the rest of their career. (Keith's style poetically captured in "Shine a Light" with the "Berber jewelry" image). At this point, who was more fascinating than the Rolling Stones for subject matter, and who better to write about them than themselves? But now the lyrics often had to do with the fallout, the damage created by drugs and bad relationships, mistrust, and betrayal.

Much of the lyrical matter on *Exile* reflects that increasingly insular world that the members retreated to, mentally walling themselves off as the exterior world and outsiders spilled in physically. That's who the seedy "flies" are. Keith might see a woman taking advantage of Mick, but Mick sees some more insidious characters around Keith. *Exile* is the Stones' *Great Gatsby.* There's a constant party going on upstairs at this decadent waterfront mansion all summer, with hangers-on and parasitic people of dubious reputations coming and going seemingly at will, while down in the catacomb-like basement, like the darkened lonely rooms in which Gatsby took refuge in his own mansion, the band tried to get to work in following their muse, their Daisy Buchanan—if you'll continue to indulge the metaphor. But both Mick and Keith see themselves as Nick Carraway–like observers, "hip to what she'll do" to their own Jay Gatsby friend.

If Keith only wrote the opening lines of "Let It Loose," worrying about some woman taking advantage of his friend, then the next lines seem to be Mick answering, admitting: "Bit off more than I can chew/And I knew, I knew what it was leading to." So if Mick didn't cop to consciously understanding what the song was about, or figured it out only later, then he either tapped into the same subconscious wavelength that Keith was on, or Keith wrote the whole thing as a dialogue between two friends, characters that bore an awfully close resemblance to Mick and Keith circa 1971–72.

Mick's flight as a social butterfly fluttered upward after he married Bianca, which Keith commented on caustically in public interviews. "Since she married Mick, Bianca is *enormous. Everyone* knows Bianca," he said. "She's in *Vogue,* the newspapers, but it's not something you do, it's not a job, it's not an art to get yourself in the papers. What have you created?"

Mick, who considered the gossip and hobnobbing with the upper strata of society good publicity for the band, nevertheless was fully aware of his mate's disapproval. "I don't think Keith particularly *liked* any of it," he reflected in the late 1970s. "He didn't think it was good for me." Keith elucidated, though, pointing to a more specific problem with Mick marrying Bianca, who simply was not compatible with Keith and Anita: Suddenly, Mick and Keith were not spending as much time together and, as a result, not writing as steadily. This became a more pressing concern while they tried to work through *Exile.* "Mick marrying Bianca stopped certain possibilities of us writing together because it happened in bursts; it's not a steady thing," said Keith. "It certainly made it a lot more difficult to write together and a lot more difficult to just hang out."

"At first I thought Bianca was just some bimbo," Keith writes in

Life. "She was also quite aloof for a while, which didn't endear her to anybody around us." This was a common problem in other bands, notably the Beatles, as the young men who grew up in these musical posses together from adolescence now reaching their late-twenties and finding that "Wedding Bells Are Breaking Up That Old Gang of Mine," as the old song goes.

Much of the intra-band drama is played out in "Let It Loose," the most stirring gospel production that the Stones ever produced. The fact that it comes out of the revival-tent voodoo chant of "Just Want to See His Face" is somehow appropriate; Jesus is not mentioned anywhere, but by the end of "Let It Loose," I feel like I have seen the face of God. After thirty five years of listening to the song, it still reduces me to rubble. It opens with a guitar arpeggio played through a fast Leslie organ speaker, giving it that church feel right off the bat, as if a preacher might intone a voiceover, "Brothers and sisters, we are gathered here . . ." Then Mick comes in with those lines. The vocal sound raw, like it was done live at the basement sessions, which according to Johns, is possible; they did some keeper vocal tracks in France.* But one can hear what seems to be the original ghost vocal of Mick singing with the band leaking into the open mikes in the background. There are other extra noises, whistling, off-mike hollers, distant sounding, adding to that swampy, layered feel of the album.

The arrangement builds and rests at various points, with Charlie laying down his signature dramatic entrances and exits on the drums. When he comes in for the first time on the second verse, it's like a punch to the sternum. The guitars have been augmented by little breaths of strings via Nicky's Mellotron, and his piano parts that weave around Keith's lattice of fast-vibrato-Leslie guitar.

---

* In my earlier book on *Exile*, I had apparently come across some errant bit of research that places the recording at Olympic Studios. But every other bit of research points to it being recorded at Keith's house.

When Mick sings, "I give her just about a month or two," he gets a call-and-response of a six-person gospel vocal ensemble who answer him as he hits the last word of his phrase. They come in at least as loudly as Mick himself. The session singers were assembled in part by Dr. John, who is singing with them, and include Joe Green, Venetta Fields, Tamiya Lynn, Clydie King, and Shirley Goodman. Some had worked variously with Billy Preston, Quincy Jones, Dr. John, and/or had hits of their own. Goodman had been part of a New Orleans duo in the 1950s called Shirley & Lee, and later had a 1974 hit with "Shame, Shame, Shame," as Shirley & Co. Tamiya Lynn (misspelled "Tammi" on the record credits) said that Mick wanted a "funk feeling, this real honest church feel . . . He had an appreciation for black music, and he said it openly, so that was out of the way. We knew he had this affinity for the blues and where it came from . . . Mick came out of a respect for black experience, or black music. The greatness comes from the spirit."

After the song builds to one of its peaks, the band drops and Mick remains silent for a full minute, as the mini-choir sings a soothing, lush, sacred-feeling vamp, "oooh," repeated like a mantra, against only Keith's guitar figure, like the song is being reintroduced. It is the sort of gospel arrangement you might hear on Stevie Wonder's 1976 *Songs in the Key of Life*. The voices are richly layered, warm, and well-recorded, like Wonder's "Have a Talk with God." Nicky starts to play them out of the break with some country-gospel-like trills. Charlie lashes out an elongated fill that brings us to the song's climax, as the majestic horns coming in. It's just one of the most emotional moments on any record. The horns just elevate the song to an almost sacred level.

This is what people who love *Exile* are talking about. This is what went missing from a lot of later Stones records. I am not saying that the Stones should have remained some bastardized gospel band. And having recorded a dozen records over a twenty-five-year career in a band and as a solo musician, I am under no illusions that any artists should repeat themselves. But I simply miss the gospel and true soul elements from this period more than any other component, more than even Mick Taylor's fabulous guitar playing or the singular bass playing of Bill Wyman. *Exile* is about a depth of feeling and less about any intellectualizing that came before or after. Pretense and artifice are not present on the album. Nothing speaks to this emotional power more than the influence of gospel as represented on *Exile*.

Keys and Price were a big part of this, having come over from the Delaney & Bonnie scene. "Right," replied Keys. "And Billy Preston brought a lot of that influence too." Preston played on "Shine a Light" from *Exile* and "I Got the Blues" from *Sticky Fingers,* as well as other mid-1970s Stones recordings. Preston took Mick down to a gospel-heavy church or two in LA to see authentic music in the proper setting.

"When you think about it," Chuck Leavell told me, "rock 'n' roll piano comes in large part from the church and gospel. Little Richard, Jerry Lee Lewis, Ray Charles, Billy Preston, and more owe a lion's share of their styles to gospel. That goes for myself as well."

Keys was happy to be part of this era of the Stones' return to rootsy music. "The parts that appealed to me have always come from the very beginnings of rock 'n' roll, you know the Muddy Waters, Bo Diddley, Holly, Presley. . . ." he said. "All of those elements were present in the Stones' music. Maybe not sounding exactly the same, but the *feeling* was the same. That's what rock 'n' roll has always been, as far as I'm concerned, it's a *feeling*."

That feeling, and the spirit that Tamiya Lynn pointed to, is what we hear after those horns kick in and Mick is inspired enough to give the performance of a lifetime. I cannot point to another vocal performance of his that I prefer. Granted, it may just be *too* raw and emotional for some listeners. He returns to the arrangement at about the 3:00 mark and, over one particular drum break, in the call-and-response with the chorus, he draws out a deeply arresting line: "Mayyyyyyyyy-be your friends think I'm just a stranger/Your face I'll never see no more."* This increasing distance between two people that he is wailing about is so obviously personal and heartfelt, it sounds like he has broken down, and he turns it over to the backing singers, who ad-lib their own inspired parts. Keith reintroduces the guitar riff on the penultimate repeat, which signals the final retarding end of the song, with the backing singers drawing the song to a close as the music fades, as if they are laying hands over poor old Mick's slumped and sweaty shoulders, like his heroes James Brown and Solomon Burke, all drained out.

---

* This line is actually lifted from a traditional ballad Man of Constant Sorrow, made famous by Dick Burnett in 1913, covered later by the Stanley Brothers and others.

32
Happy

RECORDED:

July and October–November 1971, Villa Nellcôte,

Villefranche-sur-Mer, France

(Keith Richards' rented house)

December 1971, Sunset Sound Studio, LA

RELEASES:

LP: *Exile on Main Street*, May 1972

The Tao of Keith Richards

I did [heroin] basically to hide. Hide from fame
and being this other person. Because all I
wanted was to play music and bring my family
up. With a hit of smack I could walk through
anything and not give a damn.

—Keith Richards, *Stones in Exile*

Here is Keith Richards' signature song, his calling card, his manifesto. If "Let It Loose" was a tender rumination of the increasing yawning distance between the friends and partners, then "Happy" is a more raging reaction to the yin-yang lifestyles of Keith and Mick. There's Mick's jet-set life and Keith, who hated this lifestyle. And if *Exile* is the Stones' *The Great Gatsby,* then "Happy" is a rock 'n' roll update of Cole Porter's Jazz Age "I Get a Kick Out of You."

Porter got "no kick from champagne," Richards "never got a flash out of cocktails." Where Porter got "no kick in a plane," Richards "never got a lift out of Lear jets."

There might be nothing but coincidence in the similarities of these lines, and Keith himself writes about not knowing from where or what source the lyrics poured out (although he had been known to cover Porter's song in later years).

In between the Porter-esque lines of "Happy," Keith adds some good old blues and rock 'n' roll sawhorses about not working for the boss, and just needing a love to keep him happy. But it's lines like "Always took candy from strangers," that simply ring true to Keith's persona, as he is promulgating this rock 'n' roll Gypsy/ pirate image. But we gladly accept it as an honest self-assessment; the song is pure joie de vivre that represents the flipside of the desolation heard on "Let It Loose." Keith knows what he wants out of life. A rented mansion on the Côte D'Azur, a house full of partying friends, and his band around all summer making a record, with a little jab of smack every once in a while, and he is happy; a junkie bon vivant.

"I got to know Keith very well," said Bobby Keys about this time at Nellcôte. "And the way he plays, and I could identify the way he plays guitar is where I've taken a lot of my horn licks and his rhythm." Bobby and Keith form the basis of the main "Happy" riff. Keith had been going over the guitar part in the basement of Nellcôte, while Bobby was blowing on a new baritone sax, mimicking the lick. It can be heard clearly in the break (around 2:09–2:15), though a trombone in the same range was also added as an overdub.

Keith has always displayed a unique sense of rhythm, playing parts that can sound like false starts or sometimes turning the beat of a song around.* For example, Keith's riff at the top of "Happy" seems to start in the "wrong" spot. It is this sort of tricky bit of bopping and weaving around the downbeat, creating tension. If you try to count off in 4/4 time, (four beats per measure), you'll never get a grip on this slippery fish of a lick. The first measure of the song is in 6/4 time (count to six before resetting to one) before the drums arrive to steer it into a more standard beat. You're waiting for the elusive thing to just land and lock in at some point. But even then, as Keith goes into that slide solo at around 1:13, the arrangement gives it five measures, which is quirky, as usually solo breaks are in blocks of four.

The song came to Keith all at once, in a flash of inspiration. The only other musician present was Keys. Jimmy Miller sat in on the drums, and those three formed the basic track. Keith overdubbed a bass part. Though the backing track had been finished by the time the rest of the Stones arrived, the song was further layered with overdubs: Wurlitzer electric piano from Nicky, Jim Price on trumpet and trombone, and it sounds like Bobby added a tenor sax in addition to his baritone. He also played maracas. In addition to a thumping bass, Keith added a second slide part on the other side of the stereo mix.

There was never any doubt that Keith would take the lead vocal on the song. Andy Johns says that Keith had taken a stab at the

---

* To "turn the beat around" in a song means something that starts off playing on, say, the second and fourth beats of a particular rhythm, starts worming its way to the other side of the beats, the one and three, while still in the same tempo. Just as the disco song that takes its name from the concept, you "turn it upside down."

lead vocal while still in France, as opposed to waiting until they went to LA to overdub it. "I was sitting watching the thing build, there going, *wow, this is going much easier than usual,* because that album was slow going, I can guarantee you. And then Keith said, 'Why don't you let me sing?' Why not indeed? So he did a vocal very quickly and I think we kept that vocal. I think that's the one that ended up being used." Mick and Keith overdubbed backing vocals in LA. Mick starts taking over the ad-libs at the end, for which Keith seems to gladly step away from the mike.

The effect is raucous and loose, a rave-up that might have been more at home on side one of *Exile*. It sounds like what the Faces were doing, which in turn had been deeply indebted to the Stones. (By this point, the Faces had released their first two LPs, which were all about fun, soulful rock 'n' roll, with a big heaping of Sam Cooke influence, mainly via Rod Stewart's vocals.) Ronnie Wood had been looking like Keith and sounding like him on guitar for a few years. Now, on Keith's second lead-vocal album track, he had a little bit of Stewart's sandpaper hoarseness, mixed in with a little Dylan nasal twang, to his high tenor. And Hopkins pounded the keys on the Wurly, instrument of choice for the Faces' Ian McLagan. Maybe the Faces were a kick in the ass to the Stones, reminding them to stick close to the core of what they have always done best.

It is significant that "Happy" was done without any input from any of the Stones other than Keith. There was Mick's overdubbed vocal parts, but it was all Keith, as author and behind most of the instrumentation. Since everyone was far flung, and there was no stated recording schedule, there were relatively few recordings that feature the traditional Stones lineup, with all five members on their proper instruments. Mick was often in Paris with Bianca. By the end of their stay in France, it was apparent that the gulf between Mick and Keith had widened dangerously and that each had their perceptions about the band and what it should be. And people who worked with them started to feel they had to be pulled into one or the others' camp. Miller noticed this shift, stating: "The basic material for songs used to come out of a beautiful collusion between Mick and Keith. But then it became Mick's song or Keith's song, which started even on *Exile,* which is why I think it's Keith's album."

Back in the 1970s, Keith was still bitter about the genesis of the Keith/Mick split. "The fact is that Mick spent most of his time during *Exile* away, 'cause Bianca was pregnant; you know, royalty is having a baby. So what am I supposed to do? *I'm* supposed to be making an album. But I never considered it *my* album." Keith, though was glad that it had gained so many converts over the decades. From initial critical pans and mixed reviews to *one of the greatest albums of all time* is a long arc, but it is what he might have foreseen. Around the turn of the '60s into the '70s, he felt like the band was writing finally for more than the here and now. These were albums that would be digested over years and appreciated later on. He said, "*Exile* . . . may be the best thing we ever did."

33
Coming Down Again

RECORDED:

November–December 1972, Dynamic Sound Studios,
Kingston, Jamaica
May 1973, Island Recording Studios, London

RELEASES:

LP: *Goats Head Soup*, August 1973

The Flipside of "Happy"

I f the band had been in a more literal mood, "Coming Down Again" would have been a more fitting title for the record than *Goats Head Soup*, which was a silly idea that came from recording the album in Jamaica, goat being, as Mick pointed out by way of explanation, "the national dish." "Coming Down Again," another Keith-sung number, is a bittersweet album track that few people aside from die-hard fans recall, like a secret gem "hidden" in clear view, begging for rediscovery. Keith wonders, in bruised voice, "Where are all my friends? Coming down again." But it reflected the prevailing attitude of the band at the time.

The Nellcôte summer was in the rear view, the party was over, the tour finished, and all the hangers-on had split. The baby boomer counterculture was left wandering in the desert of the mid-1970s, wondering what the hell happened to it all. Looking back during the mid-1980s, Jagger told an interviewer: "To use a cliché, the sixties never really ended until later on in the seventies. I sort of remember the album *Exile on Main Street* being done in France and . . . after that going on tour and thinking, 'It's '72. Fuck it. We've done it.' We still tried after that, but I don't think the results were ever that wonderful."

Mick's quote refers to the 1972 tour, one of the most fabled rock 'n' roll tours of all time, recounted in all of its debauched detail in Robert Greenfield's *S.T.P.: A Journey Through America with The Rolling Stones,* and in the Robert Frank film, *Cocksucker Blues*. While Mick was hanging out with an entourage of Truman Capote, Lee Radziwill, and other society types for much of the American leg of the tour, Keith had the likes of William Burroughs and filmmaker Kenneth Anger showing up. If the Stones were defining the very notion of decadent glamour, or recreating it for a new generation, then Mick was the glamour and Keith was the decadence. In the film, whenever there was a party scene in a hotel room, with Keys or Frank and groupies, it was Keith you'd see, not Mick. "Elegantly wasted" was the term being used to describe Keith in the seventies.

The band was at its absolute zenith in the 1972 tour, never sounding as great before or since, with incendiary performances, especially in the well-oiled two-guitar engine that Keith and Mick Taylor had become. For proof, there is *Ladies and Gentlemen, the Rolling Stones,* the concert doc that was released on DVD in 2010. Frank's footage was initially intended to be folded into the concert portions filmed for *Ladies and Gentlemen,* but the Stones put the kibosh on that idea once they saw the raw footage of drug use, groupie fun, and general mayhem. The band sought to ban the film outright, but an arrangement was struck, with a court decision that allowed the film to be screened once a year as long as Frank himself was present.

The two-month tour was an absolute circus, legendary for its hedonism. The pace was grueling, fifty shows, with two shows a day on many dates. "At the end of the 1972 tour I said, 'I've just had enough,'" said Charlie. ". . . I just wanted out. I needed a break, and then I was okay again." To another interviewer he said, "I got off the plane in '72 and said *No fucking more* because I don't actually like touring and I don't like living out of suitcases. I hate being away from home. I always do tours thinking they're the last one, and at the end of them I always leave the band." Charlie is legendary for resigning from the band after each tour.

The tour completed, the band did not waste much time getting to work on the next LP. *Goats Head Soup* was the doomed follow-up to the brilliant four-record run that had started with *Beggars Banquet*. And by all accounts, the band was at one of its lowest personal ebbs, certainly the lowest to that point. Drugs had started to take a grave toll, including on Jimmy Miller, who had produced the band's greatest run of material, and engineer Andy Johns, who had been responsible for most of the actual sonic and technical aspects of the previous three albums. The two had succumbed to abject heroin addiction and Miller was ineffective. The Stones had learned all of his production techniques and felt they no longer needed him. Not coincidentally, this would be Miller's last record with the Rolling Stones. Johns worked on one more, *It's Only Rock 'n' Roll*. Miller, said Keith, "went in a lion and came out a lamb. We wore him out completely . . . he ended up carving swastikas into the wooden console . . . It took him three months to carve a swastika. Meanwhile, Mick and I finished up *Goats Head Soup*." Johns said, "They were no longer listening to poor old Jimmy."

For business, legal, and taxation reasons, the Stones ended up recording the album in Kingston, Jamaica, at the relatively primitive outpost Dynamic Sound Studios, pictured in the Jimmy Cliff 1972 film *The Harder They Come*. They had to consider this venue primarily because they could not be in England or America, and now they could add France to the list, as arrest warrants were hanging over the heads of Keith and Anita for drug offenses. Anita had gotten clean from heroin for her second pregnancy, the one that produced their daughter, Dandelion. But once the baby came, she picked up where she had left off. Now they were living near Montreaux, Switzerland, one of the last places that would allow them residence. If the Stones had considered living on the French Riviera an exile for tax reasons, Jamaica must have seemed like asylum for junkies hounded by the police in multiple countries. Mick, who was now very much involved with the band's business matters, would visit Keith from time to time to discuss the financial details. "Mick picked up the slack, I picked up the smack," admits Keith.

Dynamic Studios was a bare-bones eight-track studio with small rooms and amplifiers bolted to the floor. It was fortified behind gates with an armed guard in violent Kingston. Johns had gone down to advance the place and requested some changes and additional equipment. "The recording room was great," he said. "Had a nice sound to it. The control room needed some changes. . . . The speakers—there was one way down the end of the wall, about ten feet away from you and another one that was a little way off to the right of your head. So there was no way you could work that way. So I asked them to change one or two things. . . . Of course, by the time we got there, they hadn't done anything. Jamaican time!"

The band and crew were all holed up at the Terra Mansion, a hotel that had been the family estate of Chris Blackwell, founder of Island Records. They found out that the concern for security shown at the studio was not out of proportion, with stories of guys getting into fights at the studio with machetes. And the Stones family had to deal with their own experiences of brutality. According to Johns, about a month and a half into the recording Bill and Astrid's room was broken into by a knife-wielding intruder. "Oh man, that was awful," said Johns. "Poor old Bill and Astrid. . . . It was a really violent place, Kingston. And some guy just came in through the sliding glass doors, made Bill get under the bed, raped Astrid. He's got this whacking great knife that he's got up to Astrid's neck. Bill has to hear all this . . . It's just awful. And then he took money.

"She [Astrid] told me what had happened. She was more worried about poor old Bill than she was about herself. . . . So I put on a pair of pants, jumped over the back wall and went running after this—I had presumed this guy would have gone down the back alley, you know. And I had a knife with me, or a broken beer bottle or something, and cut my feet to ribbons. There was all this broken glass in the street. And he'd gone completely the other direction."

For having been recorded in an unusually violent atmosphere, "Coming Down Again" is a gorgeously rich musical tableau, with Keith's voice supported with a soft low harmony from Mick throughout the refrains. The vocals are intimately close in the mix. On the digital remaster from 2009, you can hear Keith's off-mike noises, lip smacks and all. At the top of the track, you can hear him purr something like, "Well . . ." sotto voce.

On "Shine a Light," Mick had sung, "And your late night friends will leave you in the cold gray dawn." Now Keith, who wrote "Coming Down Again" himself, answers, affirming Mick's alarm, waking up as if in a daze. The music has the sound of sober cold gray dawn itself. "Coming Down Again" could certainly be read beyond a mere drug comedown, but the drug haze is at the very center. Indeed, the music itself is a hazy cascade of wah-wah and Leslie-speaker guitars, atmospheric vocals, a sad sax solo from Keys, a prominent melodic bass from Mick Taylor. Charlie once again demonstrates his jazz finesse, sliding in and out of the arrangement. Primary to the song, though, is the motif master, Nicky Hopkins's piano, which starts the song with one of his loveliest vamps. He continues to provide the form of the song throughout the arrangement. The guitars hang and flutter around it like a tattered cape on a scarecrow skeleton.

This would be the penultimate album to prominently feature

Hopkins. The Stones had decided his schedule as a solo artist and session musician was incompatible with theirs after *It's Only Rock 'n' Roll*.* Additionally, Billy Preston's involvement with the Stones was dovetailing with Hopkins's (they toured together on the 1973 tours, with Billy mostly playing organ and Nicky piano), and the band believed Preston's African-American gospel upbringing, as well as his solo career as an R&B hitmaker, lent the Rolling Stones' "act" a bit more authentic soul, particularly in live performances; Preston was a showman, and Mick often played off of Billy's energy in concert. "Billy produced a different sound for us," writes Keith. ". . . it was like playing with someone who was going to put his own stamp on everything. He was used to being a star in his own right." However, upon reflection, Keith said in 1983 that the mid-1970s Stones were in danger of "studio musicians and sidemen taking over the band. The real problem with those albums was the band was led astray by brilliant players like Billy Preston. We'd start off a typical Stones track and Billy would start playing something so fuckin' good musically that we'd get sidetracked and end up with a compromised track. *That* made the difference."

While Nicky remained friendly and continued to work with the individual members, he was hurt by the end of the relationship with the Stones. They could be cold in their dealings. The 1973 tour for *Goats Head* was also the last for more than a decade for Keys. But that was more directly his own undoing. He had sunk deep into junk, saying of the time, "I wasn't a musician, I was a junkie." He felt that he had gotten so bad, after an incident where he crashed a car into a canal in Holland, nearly killing his wife and himself, that he had to leave during the tour. When he got back to England, he felt Keith would be the person to call. But Keith only answered, "Keys, *nobody* quits the Rolling Stones. *Nobody.*" He did not play with them again until 1989, and even then, Keith had to sneak

---

* He played on two songs on *Black And Blue*.

him back in and Mick did not say a word to Bobby the whole tour. To this day, Mick has few words to say to Bobby.

Bobby was just one of those friends of Keith who got caught up in trying to keep pace and be like the cool outlaw with the legendary constitution. But the music was starting to suffer. The band was becoming as known for Keith's drug abuse as for their records. Multiple papers and magazines had morose celebrity death watches, with Keith regularly coming in at the top of those most likely to die first. And it's curious to read reviews and reactions to the band's 1970s albums, from critics and the band itself, over the years, from the immediate time of release, into later reassessments. *Exile*, in particular, went from being panned to lauded within a year of its release. Bud Scoppa, reviewing *Goats Head Soup* in 1973 for *Rolling Stone,* neatly makes this very point with his opening sentences: "History has proven it unwise to jump to conclusions about Rolling Stones albums. At first Sticky Fingers seemed merely a statement of doper hipness on which the Stones (in Greil Marcus' elegant phrase) "rattled drugs as if they were maracas."

Scoppa goes on to make a similar observation about *Exile*'s initially cold reception, only to become more beloved as years went by.

Lenny Kaye—who later was a founding member of the Patti Smith Group and a sought-after record producer—had given *Exile* a mostly negative review in *Rolling Stone,* but once fans had time to live with it and make sense of the record, it grew and continued to grow in appreciation and gain adherents. Conversely, *Goats Head Soup* was more or less initially embraced by the critics, judging by the old reviews. Scoppa called it the "antithesis of *Exile*," a positive critique pointing to the growth of the band and desire to move on as artists. But since then, it has often been unfairly slammed and held up as representative of the slide into formula and mediocrity the band was taking—the drugginess, the sense of entitlement as rock aristocracy.

Drugs had become a more frequent topic with each album—directly and metaphorically. "It was getting pretty hairy in Jamaica," said Johns. "Keith was way into it and by now I was and so was Jimmy Miller. And Mick [Jagger] used to do some every now and again. He would call me up and say, 'Why don't you come to my room and bring something with you.' He'd do it, like, Tuesdays and Fridays. I never really got into it with Mick Taylor. I think that was later. He was probably sampling it.

"But I remember Jimmy did this historic run to LA to cop for us, 'cause we'd run out of it and Keith and I were jonesing madly. And I recall Keith calling me from the bar and saying, 'Come on down to the bar, Andy, we can drink our way through this.' And I went down to the bar, had a Bloody Mary and immediately threw up on the floor. And looking back on it, Keith had obviously gotten something from somewhere and wanted someone to hang out with, and he didn't offer me anything.

"And then I figured Jimmy probably left something in his hotel room. And I said to Keith, 'You know, I bet there's something stashed in Jimmy's bathroom.' 'Well, let's go find out.' So Keith had me crawl through the window of Jimmy's bathroom and I open the medicine cabinet and there's an electric razor there, and I look inside of that and sure enough, there are two grams of smack. And I'm very pleased with myself and I go, 'Keith, look, I got these.' And he immediately takes both of them and goes, 'Great, that'll do.' And I go, 'Wait a second, ho ho! One for you one for me.' 'Oh, well, hmm [mumbles an approximation of Keith].' He was just going to walk off with the whole thing, the bastard!"

The arrests, hearings, and visa problems were a constant background noise and distraction to the band, and obviously well-publicized. By the time they rolled into the mid-1970s, Keith was the poster boy for bad behavior. But it was no longer an image of outlaw cool. Young punks smelled blood when they pounced on their former hero, who by the Toronto bust in 1977 just seemed like a pathetic, weak version of his former self.

Yet even before it got to that, Lester Bangs offered his dissenting view on *Goats Head Soup* for *Creem*: "There is a sadness about the Stones now, because they amount to such an enormous 'So what?' The sadness comes when you measure not just one album, but the whole sense they're putting across now against what they once meant . . . "

"I said not long ago that I wouldn't have written it without heroin," says Keith about "Coming Down Again." "I don't know if it was *about* dope. It was just a mournful song—and you look for that melancholy in yourself." He goes on to discuss the belief from some listeners that the song was about him stealing Anita, which Keith dismisses as "water under the fucking bridge." But it is difficult not to read that into a song, which contains the brilliant lines "Stuck my tongue in someone else's pie . . . Being hungry, it ain't no crime." The sex and pain; the humor and sadness; the cleverness, and the heartfelt—all wrapped up in an eloquent verse, delivered in a brutally expressive vocal take. Keith's voice somehow managed to sound strong in spots, but weary overall, like a long, defeated sigh.

While there is little dispute that the band had peaked in 1971–'72, that peak was so extraordinary and sustained that it eventually had to come to an end. Rather than a precipitous drop-off in quality, though, *Goats Head* is an easy comedown. What makes the record so beloved by certain fans are the ballads and Van Morrison-esque impressionistic lyrics in songs like "Winter," "100 Years Ago," "Angie," and Keith's lament, "Coming Down Again." The moody tone of the album set forth with these liquid, gauzy ballads are only slightly offset by the token raunchiness of "Starfucker" (a.k.a. "Star Star"), the violence-sick "Doo Doo Doo Doo Doo (Heartbreaker)," the Halloween-cartoonish funk of "Dancing with Mr. D," and so on. Yes, these are all good songs, but the best of *Goats Head* is heard in the ballads. The rockers feel a bit rote and unconvincing.

"And by then I'd worked a lot in the country field, especially with Gram Parsons," explains Keith, "and that high lonesome melancholy has a certain pull on the heartstrings." Though an early version of "Coming Down Again" seems to have been attempted in the November–December 1972 sessions, the album version was likely recorded in May 1973. In the interim, Keith's good friend and inspiration, Gram Parsons, overdosed and died a sad death in a cheap motel out near Joshua Tree. Parsons is thought of as a country-rock singer-songwriter. But with his solo albums *GP* and *Grievous Angel,* he had been showcasing songs that were similar to the ballads by the Stones and Van Morrison. In fact, the doleful "New Soft Shoe" or "Brass Buttons" could be direct musical influences on "Coming Down Again."* "Where are all my friends?" asks Keith mournfully in "Coming Down Again."

"This was a terrible period for casualties," adds Keith, who had now lost another friend to drug abuse. He had never really dealt with losing Brian. The Stones plowed right through, working at a fevered pace. Marianne Faithfull has called Brian's death a "slow-motion bomb. It had a devastating effect on all of us. . . . Anita went through hell from survivor's guilt plain and simple. She developed grisly compulsions. . . . Keith's way of reacting to Brian's death was to become Brian. He became the very image of the falling down, stoned junkie hovering perpetually on the edge of death."

"Everybody's got a different way of dealing," said Keith in 2012, looking back at this time. "And I didn't for a while [laughs]. I took to the stuff." There was indeed something quite sad about the Stones in 1973, a palpable sorrow and acknowledgement. And that emotion fills the ruminative "Coming Down Again" with a yearning regret and momentary sobriety, a pause before the next hit.

---

* Though it is was on the posthumously released *Grievous Angel* album of 1974, "Brass Buttons" was a song that dated back to the mid-1960s. Surely Keith had heard it, if not the actual recording.

34
Angie

RECORDED:

November–December 1972, Dynamic Sound Studios,
Kingston, Jamaica
May 1973, Island Recording Studios, London

RELEASES:

LP: *Goats Head Soup,* August 1973
Single, August 1973, charting at number 1 in the US and
number 5 in the UK

Ain't It Good to Be Alive?

It would be tough to blame anyone who finds this classic Stones ballad a prime example of what Ian Stewart had in mind when he called *Goats Head Soup* "too bloody insipid." It certainly is a wimpy MOR (middle of the road) pop song by most definitions of "wimpy"—treacly strings arranged by Nicky Harrison, the latest in the fine tradition of young, talented engineers to cut their teeth at Olympic Studios, and a lyric with an undefined inspiration, just a mournful sentiment about the end of a vague relationship. But are the Stones supposed to be rough and tumble all the time? Are they not allowed just a small bit of Elton John–like '70s-AM-radio schmaltz from time to time? In fact Mick postulates that the prominent strings and piano are "probably why it was so popular in Latin countries at the time. It was definitely a change of pace for us, almost like a reaction to the harder sounds of *Exile*."

While I much prefer—and considered writing instead about—"Winter" as a song, "Angie" marked another undeniable milestone for the band. Here they were scoring a number one hit in the US, number five in the UK, and remaining on the charts in the US for thirteen weeks, competing with the likes of Donnie Osmond, the Carpenters, and Cher. And they didn't have to compromise their sound too much to do so. Mick was frustrated with how *Exile* turned out as an album, but he was equally alarmed at the relatively modest radio play, with only "Tumbling Dice" breaking the top ten and the album coming in at 176 on the *Billboard* Top 200 for 1972. Mick became far more commercially conscious and calculating from 1973 onward. *Goats Head* might have been more Mick's record than *Exile*, but the reality is that "Angie" is hard-guy Keith's progression, melody, and title.

Contrary to the mythology, it is not about Angela Bowie. But an ode to his friend's wife would certainly have been some juicy material. Look at the mixing of rock couples from the era: Eric Clapton and Pattie Boyd (George Harrison's partner); Keith with Brian's girlfriend, Anita; Anita with Mick; Keith with Marianne. As Keys writes, "The English are strange about switchin' wives. They really are. And then the guys go on and remain friends. I don't know if the wives stay friends or not."

Alas, we have both Mick and Keith saying that "Angie" was not written about Angela Bowie. For one thing, Mick says he had probably not yet met Angie, as she was known, at the time of the recording. Furthermore, we have Keith's own harrowing account of going cold turkey after finishing *Exile* in LA. He "loaded well up" before he got on a plane to Switzerland, knowing full well that he was headed for the rehab clinic, and had to be taken from the hotel to the clinic in an ambulance in an overdosed state. While he was kicking it, Anita was giving birth to their daughter, Dandelion. Once he could sit up and move his fingers, Keith started with the tentative chords of "Angie," fitting in the name he and Anita would give his daughter (they had not yet known the sex of the baby). When the Catholic hospital insisted on a Christian name, Angela was added. As Angela Dandelion grew up, she refused to be called by that floral appellation, or its nickname variant, "Dandy." She preferred Angela. When she was married, "Angie" was played at the wedding ceremony.

It is the placement of the inspiration in the clinic, though, that certainly makes one wonder if it is heroin itself in the lyrics, especially in such lines as "Everywhere I look, I see your eyes." In fact, you could pick out many of the lyrics and read the addiction struggles that Keith and Anita were going through. But it was Mick who wrote most of the lyrics. One has to wonder if again he was tuned in with and giving voice to Keith's struggles. Or, perhaps Mick is singing, "Ain't it good to be alive," and "They can't say we never tried," to Marianne, who had dramatically attempted suicide, miscarried a pregnancy, and surely had that sadness in her eyes. Maybe it contains all of these concerns in the lyric. As with "Coming Down Again," there is a sense of genuine regret. The problem is that it is just kept slightly too generalized, not giving us quite enough to latch on to. But it is just that level of open-endedness that might have contributed to the commercial embrace of the single, a roomy vessel to carry listeners' own meanings.

The music itself leaves no doubt about the intended mournfulness, heavy on the strumming interplay between acoustic guitars from Keith and Mick Taylor. With *Goats Head*, the third full Stones album added to his discography, Taylor brought the band a new level of musicality. While he adds soaring melodic solos on "Winter," and dense textured layers to "Can You Hear the Music," on "Angie" he is content to add a elegiac 12-string bed to Keith's minor key arpeggios.

Nicky plays one of his most inspired parts on "Angie," a gentle country-soul motif that nevertheless asserts itself and weaves itself into the guitars to form the main force of the song. Bill adds his typically understated and underappreciated bass lines while his partner in the rhythm section, Charlie, again employs his stop/start approach, underscoring the drama of the lyric at the right moments, laying out at others. It was Mick's idea to add the strings, arranged by Nick (credited as "Nicky") Harrison, who also worked on some Joe Cocker arrangements.

Underneath the whole recording are those ghost vocals, from Mick's original guide track, singing as the band recorded the basic tracks. The remnants of his guide vocal are as loud on this as almost any other Stones track one can recall. Judging from these original vocalizations in the background, it sounds as if Mick's ideas about where the words would go in the arrangement were drastically different before he actually wrote the lyrics and overdubbed his vocal. On the final vocal track, his voice sounds youthful, at the top of his natural tenor range. He sounds like a wistful boy with a broken heart.

He plays up that part as he sings it in the promo video clip for the song. In the days before MTV, record labels started to put together short promo pieces to screen on syndicated television shows, among other outlets. "Angie" was one of the first that made an impression on me. These were typically clips with the band miming to a backing track while the vocalist sang live. The Stones are seated around the lips of a flower-petal-strewn stage, in heavy makeup, Mick and Charlie in white suits. Poor Mick Taylor, in his rouge and eye makeup, with an open-necked blouse and necklace, looks like a young Margaret Thatcher. Mick sings the live vocal over the existing vocal.

It was the first hit Rolling Stones single I recall hearing contemporaneously, hitting number one and ending up at 85 overall for the US for 1973, the year that saw Tony Orlando & Dawn's "Tie a Yellow Ribbon 'Round the Old Oak Tree" and Jim Croce's "Bad, Bad Leroy Brown" as the numbers one and two. Elton John's "Crocodile Rock," Marvin Gaye's "Let's Get It On," and Paul McCartney & Wings' "My Love" were also all in the top ten for the year. I believe it was the first year, at age seven, that I was fully aware of all the radio hits. Doleful "Angie" stood out. I had already obtained some '60s Stones LPs and 45s from neighbors, but "Angie" was one of the first songs I learned how to play on guitar. It was a good one to learn if you wanted to try to win the hearts of the girls. I should have practiced a little harder or learned to sing earlier in my career.

35
It's Only Rock 'n' Roll (But I Like It)

RECORDED:

December 1973, the Wick

(Ron Wood's Home Studio)

April–May 1974, Stargroves and

Island Recording Studios, London

RELEASES:

LP: *It's Only Rock 'n' Roll,* October 1974

Single, August 1973, charting at number 16 in the US

and number 10 in the UK

Ronnie Wood Checks In

Maybe some people liked *Goats Head Soup, It's Only Rock 'n' Roll,* and *Black and Blue,* but basically, those albums did not represent the best of the Rolling Stones. . . . We were complacent, which is what critics were saying, and while I didn't believe that at the time, looking back, I can accept the fact that we were coasting.

—MICK JAGGER,
mid-1980s interview

B y the middle of 1973, Anita and Keith were a complete train wreck. In June, Anita got arrested again for drugs, this time in Jamaica. In July, there was a raid at Keith's place in Cheyne Walk, London, which resulted in his arrest for possession of pot, heroin, a pistol, and a shotgun. Also in July, there was an enormous fire at their Redlands house. It had not even been the first fire there that year. Fire was a recurring theme for the couple. Staff at Nellcôte had rescued the passed-out nude couple from their flaming mattress in the fall of 1971. When Bill had called Mick to tell him the news about the latest Cheyne Walk arrest, "Mick said he couldn't believe it but in truth, we all could," writes Bill. ". . . We were all sad and disappointed at what was happening to him."

As the band soldiered on through an uneven middle period, Mick was largely holding the whole thing together. But even at this low ebb, the band was still coming off a number one smash in the US with "Angie." Many big Stones fans—mostly people who were kids in the 1970s and bought these spotty records upon release—still consider these few records from 1973 to 1976 solid, with some genuine high peaks. Yet most agree that the period was pocked with mediocre songs and too much filler on the albums. I am one of those 1970s kids who loves these records, despite their flaws. Of course, they were not as great as 1968–72, but what is?

It's Only Rock 'n' Roll is a very solid good-time record in the way that the Faces co-opted the good-time vibes from the peak years of the Stones themselves. And here, the Stones started mixing, literally, with the Faces, jamming with Ron Wood, Kenney Jones, along with Willie Weeks as the rhythm section on this track (no Charlie Watts or Bill Wyman on this song). Along the way, they maintained or reclaimed some of that purist rock 'n' roll mojo.

In 1971, Ron Wood had purchased his twenty-room mansion, called "the Wick," in Richmond Hill and he installed a professional-level home studio in the basement. It immediately became a rock 'n' roll club house, with a revolving door of musicians going in and out, crashing there, recording between jaunts to the local pub, and contributing to Wood's solo records. In December 1973, Mick had stopped by and helped out on Ronnie's "I Can Feel the Fire," and in turn, Ronnie helped put together a recording of "It's Only Rock 'n' Roll." Mick and Ronnie were on guitar, and David Bowie joined Ronnie on the "But I like it" backup parts. Weeks and Jones as the rhythm section were overdubbed later. Mick was so excited by the jam session that he phoned Olympic engineer George Chkiantz (who had worked on *Let It Bleed*) late in the evening and virtually begged him to come to Ronnie's house to record it. Chkiantz had just become a father and told an interviewer that Mick, "was very serious about my coming down . . . he even offered to pay for a babysitter." Chkiantz did come down and also later transferred it at Olympic, ushering the track to its next stages, which were produced by the Glimmer Twins. The album is the first record that Mick and Keith produced themselves. The Jimmy Miller era was officially over.

Mick took it to the Stones for their own overdubs, including replacing all of the backing vocals with Mick, Keith, and Mick Taylor. And, Keith playfully informed Ronnie, "I took the precaution of removing your guitar parts," though he did leave the galloping 12-string acoustic from Ronnie. Keith plays very loudly mixed licks off to one side, and less loudly mixed riffs off on the other side. Mick's vocal is an urgent growl, with a low harmony added by himself throughout the song, verses and choruses. Stu, who "quite liked *It's Only Rock 'n' Roll*," is here with the sort of piano he was born to play, hammering out sixteenth-note figures on the outro vamp. But modest Charlie, upon hearing Kenney Jones, said he wouldn't have done the drum part any other way and left it. Indeed, Jones is one of the most underrated drummers in rock 'n' roll history. He truly grooves this funky rhythm on "It's Only Rock 'n' Roll."

And that's what the recording is: a funky take on the Chuck

Berry oeuvre that the Stones were known for. It's the first truly exciting up-tempo Stones song since the *Exile* sessions. But is it a
Stones song? It's more like a Jagger song that includes some overdubbed Keith riffs. "It's Mick's song," writes Keith, "and he'd cut it
with Bowie . . . it was damn good. Shit, Mick, what are you doing it
with Bowie for? Come on, we've got to steal that motherfucker
back. And we did, without too much difficulty."

It mattered little. Keith was happy with the feel of the track
and Ron Wood—credited on the album as "inspiration"—was already making his way into the band. In fact, he didn't find out
until years later that the Stones had called him in 1969 to see if he
would be interested in replacing Brian Jones. "Sod's luck, Ronnie
Lane answered the phone," Ronnie recalled, referring to his bandmate in the Faces. "Mick asked, 'Would Woody join the Stones?'
Lane told him, 'Ronnie is quite happy where he is, thank you very
much.'"

So, in a way, the single presages the Stones Mach III, when Ronnie joined them a couple of years later, while finishing up *Black and
Blue,* and recording the full *Some Girls* LP. "It's Only Rock 'n' Roll"
sounds fun and loose, feelings one associates with Ronnie. They
were now in that mid-'70s era of the Stones where they had become
so famous, flamboyant, and self-referential that they morphed into
a sort of cartoon version of themselves, self-caricatures. But that's
meant in the best possible way. The Stones were fun again, by design. Mick's new mission is the message of the song: Don't take it so
seriously. Loosen up. We like it, yes, but after all, it's only rock 'n'
roll, kids.

The mood being far lighter on *It's Only Rock 'n' Roll,* the heavy
winter blanket of *Goats Head Soup* was lifted. The album has the first
cover song since *Exile,* a scorched-earth deconstruction of the Temp-
tations' "Ain't Too Proud to Beg." We get a nihilistic dance number
simply entitled "Dance Little Sister," with a world-negating, ass-
shaking, insistent rock 'n' roll beat that predates the escapist obliv-

ion of disco by a year or two. And there's the boogie-woogie burlesque raunch of "Short and Curlies," with the classic refrain "It's too bad, she's got you by the balls," yet another buddy song that seems to be directed from Keith to his pussy-whipped pal, Mick. "Luxury" is the first of the band's pseudo-reggae/ska songs, with a lyric about a gold digger and the man who aims to please her. In between the bar-band happy-hour fun, we have some lovely ballads and brilliant moments of musicality, including the best Mick Taylor solo on a Stones record, on "Time Waits For No One."

But it is on "It's Only Rock 'n' Roll" that Mick might have the most fun of all. *What more do you want from me, people?* he asks. "If I could stick a knife in my heart/Suicide right onstage/Would it be enough for your teenage lust?" While it is ostensibly addressed to a woman who thinks that she's the only girl in town, this time, it's not some heavy statement. It is not about war, rape, murder, or Satan. It's not, as he mocked in a 1973 interview, the band's "definitive album. That's the sort of thing a reviewer says 'This is the DEFINITIVE NEIL DIAMOND ALBUM.'" No, it's only rock 'n' roll. But he likes it, still, after ten years in the game.

Yes, the Stones had only been around ten years and critics were again wondering if the band had already overstayed their welcome. Few bands had lasted so long. They were pioneers, venturing into their (gasp!) thirties. But they were still vital. The reviews for the album tended to be very positive. "The idea of the song has to do with our public persona at the time," Mick said in the liner notes to the 1993 compilation, *Jump Back*. "I was getting a bit tired of people having a go, all that, 'oh, it's not as good as their last one' business. The single sleeve had a picture of me with a pen digging into me as if it were a sword. It was a lighthearted, anti-journalistic sort of thing."

The cartoon image was being promulgated by the Stones themselves, with the single sleeve that Mick mentions, a big-lipped caricature of him impaled by a pen, and the video, which remains the funniest music video of all time, or at least until the Beastie Boys' "Sabotage" came out. First of all, the entire band is dressed in white sailor suits. The only one who is not laughing or containing a laugh from the opening on is Mick himself, who remains in this sort of pre-punk spastic persona he developed. But the rest of the Stones are all grinning and laughing from the start. But when the little circus tent they are in starts to fill up with soap suds, eventually overtaking Charlie completely, they are in hysterics. "Poor old Charlie nearly drowned," Keith said ". . . because we forgot he was sitting down."

36
Time Waits for No One

RECORDED:

January 1974, Musicland Studios, Munich

April–May 1974, Stargroves and

Island Recording Studios, London

RELEASES:

LP: *It's Only Rock 'n' Roll*, October 1974

Mick Taylor Checks Out

I f the *It's Only Rock 'n' Roll* album was about escapist rock 'n' roll, losing one's self in the music, then "Time Waits for No One" was a momentary pause and reflection. "Time can tear down a building, or destroy a woman's face/Hours are like diamonds, Don't let them waste," sings thirty-year-old Mick with yet another stylistic variation, an oddly affected faux Caribbean patois. He inhabits the role of a sage, as he warns that no one will escape death or the ravages of time, even those who are sated in leisure," which he certainly was.

The bulk of *It's Only Rock 'n' Roll* had been recorded right after the band had gotten off the road, with the idea being that they were in hot playing shape. The songs were being written quite quickly, though the partnership of Jagger and Richards was not in full synch. Still unable to work in England (tax issues) or the US (union issues), the band was now working at Musicland Studios in Munich, owned by disco king Giorgio Moroder, who discovered Donna Summer. "The sessions went reasonably well but I can't say that they were the most inspired sessions that I've been around for," recalled Johns. "I guess someone had suggested the studio, which wasn't that bad. The control room was pretty cool. I remember they had these great monitors in there." The studio facility itself was located in the basement of a hotel, so the musicians could just roll out of the elevator. Queen, Led Zeppelin, David Bowie, and Munich-based Summer (whom Moroder made a global superstar) also recorded tracks at the facility.

Keith had relatively little to do with "Time Waits for No One," which may have started with one of his riffs but "got taken up by others in the band," he said, "turned into something I didn't even imagine." It's one of Mick Taylor's finest moments, a song that he maintains he cowrote with Jagger. This, however, is apparently not how Jagger chose to view it. Journalist Nick Kent broke the news to Taylor, recounted in a devastating passage in Kent's *The Dark Stuff*: "I'd seen him a few days earlier and he'd spoken excitedly about some songs he'd written with Jagger and Richards that were to appear on *It's Only Rock 'n' Roll*," wrote Kent. "When I told him that I'd seen the finished sleeve with the songwriting credits and that his name wasn't featured, he went silent for a second before muttering a curt 'We'll see about that!' almost under his breath. Actually he sounded more resigned than anything else. . . ."

Taylor says that Keith was often absent and that he and Jagger had been spending a lot of time together in the studio, collaborating, which was why Taylor was heartbroken when he did not receive credit. Jagger likely had the bigger picture in mind, however, and knew what effect a Jagger/Taylor credit or two would have on the fragile nature of the band as a team, choosing to take his chances with an embittered Taylor over a wrathful Richards.

The beginning of the end for Taylor had started back in 1972 when he left England for France with the Stones. Taciturn, married, but lonely in France, waiting around for the band to get some traction, with very few live shows and a lack of songwriting recognition—it had all started to nag at the young star who believed he had more potential than to just stew in bitterness while lost in the unreality (or parallel reality) of life in the Stones.* He had even called up Bill and Charlie at one point to see if they'd be interested in doing some projects on the side, but he was quickly and quietly relieved of those delusional ambitions by the rhythm section.

Taylor had a difficult time adjusting to the uncertainty of the Stones' schedule. "The whole band seemed to be falling apart," he told an interviewer. ". . . for a whole year we just really didn't do anything. We didn't see each other . . . I think there were all sorts of things going on, that were absolutely nothing to do with the band and being on the road and making records, which interfered with relationships within the band. . . . It was a constant struggle to keep the band going . . . They had all sorts of financial problems and drug problems." He has said that he does not regret having left the band, but in almost the same breath admits, "If I'd been a bit older, I don't think I would have left."

But in 2012 he admitted in the documentary *Crossfire Hurricane* that he feared he might die from drug abuse if he had stayed in the Stones. The idle hands and the easy access to dope in the world of Keith, combined with musical dissatisfaction, caused him to start seriously consider resigning. By *Goats Head Soup*, he was complaining

---

* Though Taylor vehemently denied in a 1975 interview that the lack of songwriting recognition had anything to do with his departure, in 1991 he told another interviewer, "I was told I would get credit for those songs—that's one of the main reasons I left. They don't write songs like that now, do they?"

openly about his desire to move on from the Stones. He told Andy Johns, " 'I don't think I'm going to be able to do this much longer.' And I'm going, 'What are you, crazy?! You're going to quit the Stones? You're out of your fucking mind!' "

But the album marked the end for Johns himself, and the start of a brief working relationship with Keith Harwood, who later died in a car crash leaving Stargroves after a session. "I'd known Keith [Harwood] since he'd first started at Olympic," said Johns. "Keith was very good, I wouldn't say he was stellar or the top of the mark, but he was very good and was a nice fella. I got on fine with Keith. I just had some problems with the Stones, and I was getting too high. And they'd hired this lady, Anna Menzies, to run the Stones office, who *hated* me. She'd hated me since I was about seventeen years old. So she had them get rid of me and had me replaced with Keith. And the funny thing was, in '78 or something like that, Mick called me up and asked did I want to go to Paris and record an album with them. And I would have liked *nothing more* than to do that. *Absolutely nothing.* I still have Rolling Stones *dreams,* for chrissakes! But I had just signed a contract with CBS and so I was bound. And I said, 'Mick, if only you'd had called forty-eight hours ago, I'd be on the next fucking plane.' But he didn't understand that, you know, *but it's the Rolling Stones and we want you to come and work with us how could you say no?* So I don't think he ever forgave me. Oh, I've seen Mick since, but not like I've seen Keith [Richards] and Charlie and Ronnie. I mean, Ronnie and I go back to when he was in the Faces. But Mick doesn't really want to have much to do with me. I even saw him at a gig and he kind of blocked me out."

Taylor and Johns were united for another post-Stones project soon after *It's Only Rock 'n' Roll.* When Taylor was offered the chance to collaborate in a Jack Bruce–led project, which Johns was engineering, he jumped ship. Both Johns and Taylor were gone from Stones World. Taylor had arrived in the Stones as a fresh-faced cherub and left with a drug habit of his own.

Before his split, though, Taylor capped off his remarkable legacy within the band with some of his personal-best contributions. Whether or not he actually deserved a songwriting credit on "Time Waits for No One"—the first song recorded for the LP sessions—will only be known to the band members themselves, but his indelible mark on the song via jaw-dropping guitar lyricism is undeniable. Never again would the Stones reach the sheer musical heights heard when Taylor was soaring alongside Nicky Hopkins. Sure, more great songs came, as well as one more album of sustained excellence with *Some Girls* in 1978, but when Taylor, Hopkins, Keys, et al were with the Stones, there was a potent combination of superior songwriting, one of music's great rhythm sections, and restrained, tastefully melodic musicality from Taylor and sidemen that enhanced what the original core of four brought to the table. What, for example, would "Time Waits for No One" be if not for Taylor's parts?

Rarely did the Stones stretch out so long on a studio recording to allow one player to shine. This has never been a jam band, thank heavens. "There was going to be a space for a guitar solo, it was a first take," Taylor recalled. "I mean the backing track and the guitar solo is the first or second time we actually ran through the song, so the guitar solo was done live. It's got a long sort of extended guitar solo at the end, which is because it was a good solo and it's peaking. That's how long the track goes on for." Taylor flies for three glorious minutes, elevating the two-chord vamp to vertiginous, soul-stirring heights. It is astounding that it was one take, live, with no punch-ins to repair. "I was in awe sometimes listening to Mick Taylor," wrote Keith. "I guess that's where the emotion came out. I loved the guy, I loved to work with him, but he was very shy and distant. . . . I always found it very difficult to find any more than the Mick Taylor I'd met the first time. . . . He was fighting himself somewhere inside."

On this song, Taylor didn't plumb his usual bluesy pentatonic scales. He credited a trip to Brazil prior to the recording for a bit of the Latin influence. As with "Can't You Hear Me Knocking," there is some suggestion of Carlos Santana. Taylor's playing brought out the best in Hopkins, who sounds like he is raising himself off the bench with excitement by the end, swept up in the improvisations.

The band as a whole is heard expanding their roles on "Time Waits for No One," a mesmerizing tapestry that represented as much of a departure as almost any previous Stones song. Charlie, who starts and ends the song cheekily with a ticktock beat, plays in a more jazzy, finessed style, jettisoning the usual backbeat for something more nuanced. Splashy exoticism is provided by renowned English percussionist Ray Cooper (The Who, Elton John, Paul McCartney)—who had been brought in by Mick during the overdub sessions at Island Studios—meshing with the track that Charlie had laid down. Bill adds some synth, and Keith grinds out a swirling rhythmic part that was played through an EMS Synthi Hi-Fli guitar synth. Taylor also plays a 12-string acoustic, mostly heard on the verses.

It would be easy to forget what a change of pace such ballads as these, as well as those on *Goats Head Soup,* represented, which in part accounts for a bit of the backlash the albums have received. However, in hindsight it becomes clear that this was the natural evolution of the band. Though they put out one more convincing rock 'n' roll record, the main growth of their songwriting became their ballads. *Black and Blue,* which followed *It's Only Rock 'n' Roll,* contained some bittersweet slow songs. After *Some Girls,* the band's attempts at writing up-tempo rockers started to produce ever-diminishing returns, to the point of outright embarrassment. ("You Got Me Rocking," anyone?) But their ability to write satisfying and, at times, sublime ballads continued through even their most recent albums.

The song brings side one of the vinyl LP to an ecstatic close, the second of two ballads after three rockers (two of which actually have the word "rock" contained within their titles). The penultimate song on the side is actually the last recording to feature Taylor, "Till the Next Goodbye," fittingly.

The Songs

Part 3
THE RON WOOD YEARS

37
Memory Motel

RECORDED:

March–April 1975, Musicland Studios, Munich

October–November 1975, Mountain Recording

Studios, Montreux

RELEASES:

LP: *Black and Blue,* April 1976

Thirtysomething

O ne night, late in 1974, I found myself . . . sitting between the two Micks, Jagger and Taylor," writes Ronnie, "when MT leant over and told MJ 'I'm leaving the group.' . . . I just laughed. But Taylor looked at me and said, 'I'm serious,' and just like that, he got up and left the party."

Jagger turned to Ronnie right there and then and asked for his help, if not as a permanent replacement, then as a possible temporary touring guitarist for 1975. Wood agreed to help out if the Stones needed him. They did, and they called Ronnie in for their next recording sessions.

Famously, *Black and Blue* was the Rolling Stones' guitarist-audition record. After Taylor left the band, the Stones had to find a replacement. We had heard it ever since the sixties: the Stones were always a two-guitar band and it has always been the interplay between two guitars that turned Keith on. However, it is specifically the weaving in and out of rhythm and lead parts that defines the Stones sound, not one guy soaring melodically above the rest of the band, as Taylor had done fairly regularly. The Stones hadn't fired Taylor, but now that he was gone they didn't so much as blink before setting out to find a new player.

In December 1974, a month or two after Mick Taylor left, the Stones started new sessions for *Black and Blue* in Munich, with their old pal Glyn Johns back on board engineering. He was thrilled that he was back with the core of the Stones, with Nicky Hopkins. More thrilling to Johns was that the band seemed to be back in the productive swing they had been in during the 1960s. In Munich, they recorded eleven songs in less than two weeks. When they broke for the holidays and reassembled at a rehearsal facility for orchestras ("Mick Jagger's idea of saving money," explained Johns) in Rotterdam in January, they started trying out guitar players.

Seven names are commonly mentioned as those that jammed and/or recorded with the Stones on the album, including two Americans, Wayne Perkins and Harvey Mandel. Jeff Beck also recorded some parts but the band erased them. Neither side saw it as a good fit in his case. Also not on the album were fellow prospects: Eric Clapton; Small Faces and Humble Pie founder Steve Marriott; or Rory Gallagher, an Irish blues player little known in the US but who had sold many millions of records worldwide. Perkins was mostly known as a session guy at Muscle Shoals. Mandel was a respected blues player who had been in Canned Heat and in an early-1970s version of John Mayall's band.

Ronnie, though, claims he had no idea there was an audition going on and thought he was coming in merely to help on the sessions. And he didn't treat it that way once he saw all the other players filing in and out of the studio. "Clapton said to me in Munich, 'I'm a much better guitarist than you.' I responded, 'I know that, but you gotta live with these guys as well as play with them. There's no way you can do that.' Which is true. He could never have survived life with the Stones."

Keith says it came down to Perkins and Wood, who was still playing with the Faces. But when Ronnie picked up a newspaper with the announcement that his buddy, Rod Stewart, was leaving the Faces (Ronnie Lane had left previously) it made Wood's and the Stones' choice starkly clear. It was a personality-based decision more than anything else. Everyone in the band loved Ronnie. He was virtually family. In 1974, Keith had lived at Ronnie's house for four months, rarely venturing out. Mick had started recording "It's Only Rock 'n' Roll" with Ronnie at his basement studio prior to that. Charlie and Bill also both got along well with lovable Ronnie. In fact, Charlie had played in a band with Ronnie's older brother, Art, before joining the Stones. By all accounts, Ronnie came in like the job was his already, immediately bringing out the song "Hey Negrita" for them to cut. "He's only just walked in and he's bossing us around already," said Charlie. Though he toured with the band in 1975, the choice of Ronnie as a replacement would not become official until 1976.*

For all of these auditions of hotshot guitarists, one would be forgiven for expecting to hear a showboating guitar spraying out blistering leads and riffs on *Black and Blue*. But it has very little in the way of conspicuous rocking guitar parts. In fact, the two best songs on the unfocused album are ballads. "Memory Motel," a sprawling travelogue set to a washy Fender Rhodes electric piano and warbling guitars, is a nod to the blue-eyed soul and soft rock sound of the mid-1970s. The Beatles had not been the Stones'

---

* Not until 1990, at the insistence of Wyman and Watts, was Wood made a full partner in the Rolling Stones.

competition for six or seven years. Now they were trying to elbow aside acts like Hall & Oates for airplay.

The baby boom generation was now in their mid-thirties, raising families, probably not paying as much attention to new records from the bands with whom they grew up. In his *Creem* review of the album, the ever-passionate Lester Bangs called *Black and Blue* the first "meaningless" Stones album, while also noting the band was not only in step with, but probably ahead of their time. But see, *that's* the meaning. The band was reflecting their thirtysomething milieu. Listening to these soft rock, light funk, and faux reggae songs you feel like you're at a grown-up baby boomer's party, like the one that Carly Simon sings about on "You're So Vain." When Simon's song was released, with Mick's backing harmonies, there was much speculation that it was Mick who was the song's vainglorious subject.

Perhaps coincidentally, many fans have read Hannah, the subject of "Memory Motel," to be a stand-in for Simon, a "peachy kind of girl," whose "eyes were hazel and her nose was slightly curved." There were rumors of a fleeting affair between the two, as there often were in gossip pages regarding Mick and other women. "I don't worry about the future," Mick declared in 1975, comparing himself to others in their thirties. "I'm living out my adolescent dreams perpetually."

Jagger sings about meeting the woman out at the real-life Memory Motel in Montauk, Long Island, New York, where band friend Andy Warhol had a summer place. The Stones were rehearsing for their 1975 tour at Warhol's house in April and May of that year. They also rehearsed in Baton Rouge, Louisiana, in May, which is where they kicked off their tour on June 1, followed by a show in San Antonio, Texas. All of these places figure into the song.

Mick can't shake the memory of "Hannah" as she drives off in a limping pickup truck to Boston, while he has to fly "on down to Baton Rouge" for the concert dates. While it is a long way from "Satisfaction," it also speaks to a restlessness. This time, it's in the form of an existential pre-midlife crisis. It's as if Mick would rather be the one "singing in a bar" in Boston than traveling "ten thousand miles" with his superstar band. He pines for this woman—surely younger—for her age, beauty, and perceived freedom, all things that seem to be slipping from his grasp. The inspiration for her character was "a real, independent American girl," said Mick. The "back up to Boston" part could certainly fuel speculation in the direction of New Englander Simon.

"Memory Motel" has more in common with "Moonlight Mile" than the double-M alliteration of the title. Both are epic laments from the road, but "Memory Motel" finds an older, wiser, more mature Mick holed up in hotel room on the twenty-second floor, while some friends of his "are bustin' down the door," trying to pull him out of his funk and back into the fun of a rock 'n' roll tour. As he said, he was living out his adolescent fantasies, but here we bear witness to his ambivalence about the life he is living, just as we do on "Fool to Cry." You get the feeling that Mick has just outgrown it all.

It wasn't planned out as such, but Keith plays the part of a one-man Greek chorus, singing two bridges in the song that are so substantial that the part turns the song into a duet of sorts. Keith interjects with a warmly present, in-your-face, weary second lead vocal (double tracked, or with a delay to approximate the same effect), as if he is conversing with Mick. Or he is playing Mick's inner voice, offering support. "She's got a mind of her own and she uses it well." Keith also adds deeply emotional backing harmonies to accent certain phrases, crushing those lines out of the park.

What's also fascinating about the Mick and Keith interplay is that it's the only track I am aware of where they are both on keyboards. Keith is on the Fender Rhodes electric piano, riffing off his partner, who is playing the acoustic piano. At the early April 1975 sessions in Munich, Mick had started to show Keith a bit of what he had written, when Keith joined. ". . . I like to get everything finished, done, written on paper, typed up, all written out," said

Mick. "But [Keith] doesn't like that so he says, *I've got a middle bit here,* and he sits down at the other piano, the electric piano, and he plays the middle bit. Then I learn that and he learns my part, and then we make the track, and I sing what I've got. And then I go and finish the words. They're all done in a day. And in fact, when Keith wrote the middle bit, he did those words . . . he goes . . . *mmmm . . . she's got a mind . . . of her own. . . .*"

Also unusual is that there is no Rolling Stone, past or present, on either of the guitar tracks. Instead, there are two parts, an acoustic by Wayne Perkins and an electric from Harvey Mandel. With neither Keith nor Ronnie on the track, though, Mandel and Perkins do an admirable job of making "Memory Motel" sound, well, *Stonesy.* It is really a continuation of the Keith/Mick Taylor dynamic, with Perkins playing arpeggios and strums on the acoustic, and Mandel slipping in mournful, tasteful melodic runs non-intrusively between the two poignant piano parts. With the neo-doo-wop call-and-response and "sha la la" backup vocals, the synth string pad from Billy Preston, and Bill's bass runs, the recording sounds less like the early 1970s epic "Moonlight Mile" and more like the Philly Soul that the band had started to explore on *It's Only Rock 'n' Roll,* with Blue Magic singing backups on "If You Really Want to Be My Friend." Groups like the Delfonics, the Chi-Lites, and Harold Melvin and the Blue Notes had been burning up the American charts in the early to mid-1970s. The Stones successfully incorporated certain elements of that vocal-group soul into the overall Stones sound, just as they had with their early influences from Stax and Motown. Charlie adds his well-chosen dramatic entrance and exit points, as usual.

The sonics of "Memory Motel" and *Black and Blue* in general are strikingly more clear and crisp sounding, with a flat dryness not ordinarily heard on Stones albums up to this point. Like the highly defined cover shot by fashion photographer Hiro, the mix brings the vocals to the fore while allowing a featured spot for each element, from the scaffolding Charlie builds to undergird the arrangement, to the snaky bass line that explores its own melody, right on up to the spiky spires of Preston's gleaming synth. Principal engineers Glyn Johns and Andy Johns both exited the Stones orbit on this album, leaving Keith Harwood to handle the project with the Glimmer Twins, including recording "Memory Motel." Harwood had worked on *It's Only Rock 'n' Roll,* and some significant Led Zeppelin records. Glyn had not worked with the Stones since early *Sticky Fingers* sessions and had in the interim gone on to great success with Steve Miller and the Eagles. Glyn had been one of those pioneers who had started in the very early 1960s with primitive systems, ushering record production through all of its stages, and was still working in 2012.*

With the revolving door of engineers, guitarists, and multiple studios, it is no wonder that *Black and Blue* lacks an overall focus, consisting of some barely fleshed-out jams to round out the high points. Like "Tumbling Dice," "Memory Motel" combines that end-of-summer melancholy—that sexy slow ballad feel, Mick singing about leaving the Long Island beach town over those synthy strings and fluid guitar lines that wring out a nostalgia for those late 1970s summers, like Elvin Bishop's sultry summer of '76 single "Fooled Around and Fell in Love."

"Memory Motel" is a modern epyllion, a romantic mini-epic. Set over this wash of instrumentation, Mick sings the song within the song, as if enchanted by the siren song Hannah sang for him on the beach that "stuck right in [his] brain." It's a captivating vignette about how a man could become ensnared in an affair that nags at him as something more than a road fling.

---

* Recording technology continued a rapid improvement through the 1970s, arguably peaking before the advent of early, brittle versions of digital recording. Though digital technology improved greatly, and the flexibility of digital tools is inarguable, many still measure late-1970s analog as the sonic high point.

38
Fool to Cry

RECORDED:

March–April 1975, Musicland Studios, Munich

October–November 1975, Mountain Recording

Studios, Montreux

RELEASES:

LP: *Black and Blue,* April 1976

Single, April 1976, charting at number 6 in the UK

and number 10 in the US*

Daddy, What's Wrong?

The very title of *Black and Blue* reflected the spirit of the band at the time. It felt more like the hungover *Goats Head Soup* than the "get up and dance" vibe of *It's Only Rock 'n' Roll*. On "Fool to Cry," Mick let on the fact that he was a father going through a crisis of confidence. He was reflecting the early-midlife funk felt by many in their thirties, as they realized they were not

---

* An odd choice for a single from an album with no clear choices, the song was brutally edited down from the LP version for the single release.

kids anymore, taking stock: *What am I doing with my life?* Even if the song was not intended to be purely autobiographical, one cannot help but think of Mick as he sings: "When I come home baby, and I've been working all night long/I put my daughter on my knee, and she says, 'Daddy, what's wrong?'"

"It's surprising, eh?" he said to an interviewer in 1976. "It's the family side. Well it is true. The Stones are getting on. . . ."

But it's more than the family bit that's surprising; it's the personal vulnerability displayed by Mick. Like a good soul singer, he knows vulnerability can be sexy and works it here. He knows we would ask: What's Mick Jagger got to cry about? Yet there's a deep ache and a hunger, as he searches to fill the void with a woman who "comes from the poor part of town." Who is the real Mick Jagger? Is he just this empty aging Don Juan rock star stereotype that he simultaneously embraced and considered stabbing pens and knives into on "It's Only Rock 'n' Roll (But I Like It)"? The image of a father crying noticeably in front of his daughter resonates as perhaps one of those relatively rare views into Mick Jagger, the person. He offers a moving blue-eyed soul performance of the simple lyric, remarkable in its candor and self-awareness. He said in 1993, "This dates from the period when I had a young child, my daughter Jade, around a lot, calling me *daddy* and all that. It's another of our heart-melting ballads." Nothing like a kid to hold a mirror up to your face.

Recorded in December 1974 in Munich, Mick opens with the electric piano, joined by Nicky Hopkins with note-perfect accompaniment on grand piano, playing a shimmering flourish around the 2:20–2:40 range. Those sustained synth melodies, suspended over the chord changes, offer their own plaintive hook. Bill's evolution on bass continues, adapting to the bass-up-front mixes associated with seventies soul and funk. And like a funk player, he slides up the string on the post-chorus refrains of "Oooh, Daddy you're a fool to cry." The backing parts are breathy falsetto, all layered on overdubs by Mick. He adds some affecting ad-libs in the middle break and funky ending vamp. At the ending, after a spoken-word, half verse and chorus—which is very much in fitting with the Philly Soul of Harold Melvin and the Blue Notes, and the Manhattans—the band hits a turnaround blues chord and goes into a three-chord funky blues, with Charlie playing a double-time pattern on the hi-hat, his drums in that improbable mixture of flat and crisp, like those on a Sly and the Family Stone album such as *Fresh*. Keith and Wayne Perkins trade the weaving-style parts Keith was so fond of.

With the lyric, "All my friends call me a fool," the Chi-Lites' smooth single, "Oh Girl," which hit number one in the summer of 1972, was likely an inspiration for "Fool to Cry." Mick, sounding as if he is singing informally into a handheld mike, carries the song with his passionate vocal. While he could very easily lapse into the sort of lampooning he reverted to for country music, perhaps with a spoken-word soul man caricature, he instead thankfully plays it straight—with an American accent of course, but sincerely. His command brings to mind one of his heroes, Solomon Burke, himself a big daddy who was not afraid to shed a tear or two to get a song across.

39
Respectable

RECORDED:

October–December 1977, Pathé Marconi Studios,

Boulogne-Billancourt (suburban Paris)

RELEASES:

LP: *Some Girls,* **June 1978**

UK single, September 1978, charting at number 23

Talking Heroin with the President

All the slick balladry of the last few records had amounted to much wallowing and navel gazing with not enough rave-up rock 'n' roll for most Stones fans. It was a bit of a seesaw ride after *Exile. Goats Head Soup* felt mostly down. *It's Only Rock 'n' Roll* seemed like focused upbeat rock 'n' roll by comparison, though still missing the high-water mark set by *Exile.* And then the Stones were sloshing about again in mid-tempo funk and downbeat balladry on *Black and Blue.* On the *Some Girls* LP, however, the band came roaring back with arguably one of the top five records of their discography, stripping their sound down to an essential core, with an unrelenting three-guitar attack, Mick's aggressive and soulful vocals, and the top rhythm section in rock 'n' roll circa 1978. This concentrated reclamation was fully realized with the enlisting of Ron Wood from the Faces for his first full studio album as a Rolling Stone. Essentially a love letter to the gritty mid-to-late-1970s version of New York City, as well as an answer to the burgeoning punk rock, new wave, and disco trends in pop music, *Some Girls* demonstrated that the band remained a vital force with a deep well of great songs left in them, not merely a touring circus cashing in on nostalgia. That would come later.

From the churning sleazy funk of "Some Girls"—a button-pushing number with a hilarious litany of sexual and racial stereotypes that landed them in controversy with the Rev. Jesse Jackson—to the trucker-country burlesque of "Far Away Eyes," the album consists of all winners, songs that span a wide breadth of styles. But it is the gutter-guitar-rock on *Some Girls* that constitutes the pumping heart of the LP: the stripped-down punk-funk of "Shattered," the amped-up Velvet Underground–informed, two-chord gay-hustler ode "When the Whip Comes Down," and "Before They Make Me Run," which is Keith's bookend anthem to "Happy" in spirit, if not attack, a cool middle finger to those who had written him and the band off and listed him as number one on the death watch year after year.

Included on this list of essential tracks is the punk-meets-Chuck-Berry of "Respectable," a classic kiss-off, partially to Bianca Jagger, but generally to everyone else declaring them dead, or worse, irrelevant. Along with the lyric of "Before They Make Me Run," the message was partially directed at the young punks of the mid-'70s nipping at their heels, some of whom supposedly felt betrayed by their onetime heroes—new leaders like the Clash's Joe Strummer, who declared in song, "No Elvis, Beatles, or the Rolling Stones in 1977!" Well, he was two-thirds correct. Bloated Elvis died on the toilet. The Beatles had split eight years prior and the individual members seemed to be meandering in mediocrity by the late 1970s.

But again, *Some Girls* is a New York record, even beyond the lyrical references. Regarding English punk rock, Mick said in 1977, ". . . they're getting really boring, that's all. . . . I'm afraid this country is so stagnant, so fashion conscious that everything can just fall to pieces." Rather than directly answer the English challenges of the Sex Pistols (anyone could see that flash in the pan coming a mile away) and the Clash (Mick: "I can't listen to the Clash when I wake up in the morning . . ."), the Stones continued to take influences from New York bands such as the Ramones, Lou Reed, and maybe even a bit from the Talking Heads ("I like David's stuff. I love his stuff," Mick told interviewer, Bill Flanagan, about David Byrne of the Talking Heads).

While Mick soaked up all the contemporary music he could find, from disco uptown at Studio 54, to punk rock downtown at CBGB, Keith was the one who seemed to take a lot of the brunt of the young turks' ire. After all, Mick had long been seen as a jet-set sell-out, while Keith had that tough-as-nails buccaneering image to uphold. Through the floundering mid-1970s, however, he was seen as a pathetic junkie. He didn't seem to worry about it, though. In 1979, reflecting back a couple of years, he told an interviewer, "I'm probably a little out of touch with the music here [England], but most of the stuff that's happening here has lost touch with itself anyway. It's back to fads. One minute it's Bay City Rollers, then it's punk rock. . . . I think punk rock was great theatre, and it wasn't all crap."

If anyone was going to make fun of the Rolling Stones, it would be the Stones themselves. "Well now we're respected in society/We don't worry about the things that we used to be," Mick sings coyly on "Respectable." "We're talking heroin with the president. . . ." Much had happened to the Stones, not only from their humble beginnings in an Edith Grove flat, but even in the two years between

Black and Blue and *Some Girls,* leading up to the major drug trafficking arrest that truly nearly ended the band and was a looming dis-
quiet hanging over the sessions for *Some Girls.*

With the addition of Ronnie and the subtraction of Taylor, the
band discovered a new fire that stoked up the tours of 1975 and
1976, an energy well captured on the live album, *Love You Live,* particularly the fully live* side recorded at the El Mocambo Club in
Toronto. Around this time, Keith called Mick Taylor a "cold fish."
Regarding Ronnie, "Woody's strength, as is mine, is to play with
another guitar player. None of that virtuoso clap trap." Soon after
the *Some Girls* recordings, Ronnie noted, "These Paris sessions have
made me realize how much of a Rolling Stone I always have been.
It's really weird. I feel like I've been with them right from the start."

However, there was some dissent about the quality of the shows.
Nick Kent, the journalist who had covered the band for years said,
"The shows . . . were terrible. There was no mystery and no momentum anymore; just an ill-focused blur of a sound buffeted by
Wood and Richards's frankly clumsy guitar interplay." Glyn Johns
said that Ronnie was "the worst choice they could have made . . .
musically I don't think he fits with the Stones at all." Johns felt
that Ronnie's talents were being wasted in the Stones, what he had
to offer was redundant to what the band already had, and that he
was being treated as a "court jester."

Between tours, the band members again dispersed. Ronnie
moved to America for tax reasons. Bill was living back in France.
Charlie was back and forth between his houses in England and
France. Mick, still unable to live in England full time, had been
spending a lot of time in New York in 1975 and was living there by
1976, purchasing an apartment, clubbing with Warhol and Bowie.
"I'd moved to New York at that point," he told Jann Wenner. "The

---

* There seem to have been a fair amount of vocal and guitar overdubs, redoing the
original live parts on the other three sides.

inspiration for the record was really based in New York and the ways of the town. I think that gave it an extra spur and hardness."

By 1976, Keith and Anita were growing more isolated from each other, and in March of that year, she gave birth to their third child, a son they named Tara, after Tara Browne, their "A Day in the Life" friend from the 1960s. Anita was a more hopeless junkie than Keith was at this point, so he took their son, Marlon, out on the road with him (Tara was only a month old at this time, so he and Angela [a.k.a. Dandelion] stayed with Anita). By all accounts, though, the amount of dope that surrounded Keith at this time was mind-boggling, to the point that multiple dealers had their own tour passes. Mick and the rest of the band had a laissez-faire approach toward Keith's life in a drug cocoon. Like most things in the band, they did not talk much about it, never mind stage some sort of intervention.

While the Stones were playing a concert in Paris in June 1976, Keith's two-month-old infant son Tara died in his crib at the home the couple had been renting in Switzerland. "I got the phone call as I was getting ready to do the show," writes Keith. "And it's a 'Sorry to tell you . . .' which hits you like a gunshot." Rather than cancel the show that night, Keith once again found it best to do what he does and soldiered on. But Kent witnessed a much more harrowing scene when Anita arrived in Paris. Far from being a soldier marching forward, Keith joined his grieving junkie wife, looking like the walking wounded. "He was crying too and looked all of a sudden to be impossibly fragile . . . they looked like some tragic couple leading each other out of a concentration camp. I honestly thought I'd never see them alive again."

Keith writes that the cause of death was listed as "respiratory failure, cot death. Anita found him in the morning. I wasn't about to ask questions at the time. Only Anita knows. As for me, I should never have left him. . . . It's as if I deserted my post." Their daughter, Angela, was taken to live with Keith's mother, and he kept

Marlon on the road with him, and when that round of touring ended, sent him off to boarding school. "Keith was very calm and very protective and very normal and loving," said Anita. "He just said, *Forget it*. And everybody else told me the same thing. They all said, *Forget it. Look after your other children*. I am sure that the drugs had something to do with it. And I always felt very, very bad about the whole thing." But Keith writes that he had started to look for an exit strategy from the relationship at this point.

There continued to be Keith's arrests, car crashes, and so on, all well documented in other books. After his early 1977 court appearance for a drug bust resulting from an accident he had on the M1 motorway, Keith observed, "What is on trial is the same thing that's always been on trial. Dear old *them and us*. I find this all a bit weary. I've done my stint in the fucking dock. Why don't they pick on the Sex Pistols?"

But 1977 proved to be the fateful year that almost broke Keith. The band had planned the gigs at the El Mocambo in Toronto specifically for some material for *Love You Live*. The idea was to capture that small club feeling, bringing the band back to its roots. They performed two shows on March 4 and 5 of that year, and the set heard on the album is freewheeling and inspired. The band had arrived on February 20 for rehearsals, but Keith and Anita got there four days late. When they arrived at the airport, customs found a blackened spoon in Anita's pocket, from a hit of smack that Keith had taken on the plane over, as well as some hashish. The Mounties had intercepted an advance package Keith had ordered sent to the hotel and they set up an elaborate arrest, which was set in motion on February 27. He had an ounce of heroin with him, which amounted to trafficking and "an automatic jail sentence for a very long time," Keith realized.

"Are you asking me if I knew it would happen, like . . . sooner or later?" Mick asked Kent. "Well, yeah, of course! Christ, Keith fuckin' gets busted every year. . . . But I'm not judge and jury."

"I have to say that during the bust in Toronto, in fact, during all busts," writes Keith, "Mick looked after me with great sweetness, never complaining. He ran things; he did the work and marshaled the forces that saved me. Mick looked after me like a brother."

As they did whenever faced with adversity, they went on with the show, recording music so energetic and vital at the Toronto club that it sounded like they were playing for their lives. While faced with their biggest drug scandal, with rumors of massive bribery to make what looked like a police set-up, which bordered on entrapment, go away, the Stones were far from the doe-eyed boys they were at the time of their 1967 bust. While this was all going down, Margaret Trudeau, the May–December wife of Prime Minister Pierre Trudeau (she had been twenty-two when she married the fifty-one-year-old politician), was seen gallivanting with Mick, taking a ride in his limo to the gig from the hotel. She had ensconced herself at the Stones' hotel in a room next to that of Ronnie, who later wrote, "We shared something special for that short time." The scandal of her presence enflamed the already out of control situation. "I have to pay for the Rape of Canada," Keith said in 1979, noting that the bust and L'Affair d'Trudeau were simultaneous. Later, he wrote, "You shouldn't be a prime minister's wife if you want to be a groupie."

The Stones had a tough criminal lawyer, Bill Carter, who had gotten Keith out of trouble in a previous brush with the law in Arkansas in 1975, had negotiated visas to tour, and generally smoothed over various speed bumps with his political connections. He once again came through, this time going to Jimmy Carter's (no relation) White House. (Bill Carter had started his career as a special agent in the Secret Service.)

Jimmy Carter's administration was in the process of developing drug policy that encouraged treatment over punishment. Bill Carter negotiated for a US visa that allowed Keith to come to the US for a treatment using a "black box cure," which used an electronic pulse on strategic pressure points of the body, like electronic acupuncture. During the time between the arrest and the trial (nineteen months in total) Keith substituted Jack Daniels for smack, and came out of his drug fog, getting more involved in the business side, and choosing tracks for the *Love You Live* LP in May 1977, a process that caused a serious conflict between him and Mick, who had gotten used to being the one in charge. Keith continued to fall off the wagon, though. It was not an immediate and permanent cure from the addiction. But for the most part, he was off heroin by 1978.

Though the charges were the most serious he had ever faced, Keith instinctively believed he could again slide out of trouble. It was this survivalist energy that carried over into the *Some Girls* sessions. Keith called it "a rejuvenation." The band started rehearsing new songs for *Some Girls* in the side room, the Studio B of Pathé Marconi in a Parisian suburb called Boulogne-Billancourt, with engineer Chris Kimsey on board to handle the recording. Kimsey had done some engineering on *Sticky Fingers* in 1970 when he was just beginning his career. "And he would," noted Keith, "on the basis of this [*Some Girls*] experiment, engineer or coproduce eight albums for us. . . . He wanted to get a live sound back and move us away from the clinical-sounding recordings we'd slipped into." The studio was an EMI-owned facility and the Stones had just signed a major $14 million, four-album record deal with WEA in the US and EMI for the rest of the world.

They booked the studio with the idea that they would start in the massive rehearsal space there and then move into the main studio when it was time to actually record the album. "The recording area of both studios was vast," Kimsey told me. "It was the control room that was a big difference. The control room in the cheaper studio was absolutely tiny and angled and in an odd shape and then with an EMI TG1234 desk with quadrant faders, but only a 16-track tape machine. The studio next door had a brand-new

Neve desk which, you know, you needed two people to operate it, it was so big. When we got set up in the smaller space, it just started to sound *so good*. It got to the point where Mick thought it would be better if we went into the more expensive room, which makes a change for him, because normally he likes to save money. And I said to Keith, 'We're crazy to move from here. It sounds great in here. Why go and change it all?' Keith agreed and so we stayed in that room. And we went back there many times. A lot of *Emotional Rescue* was done there, *Undercover* . . ."

The band set up in a semicircle more or less like the old days at Olympic. Each amp had a makeshift three-sided booth set up around it so that the musicians could change what they heard by simply moving themselves around. There is a hilarious chart of the set-up at the Web site for *Sound on Sound* magazine, showing a bar off to one side of the performance area, sub-mapped by category: "Food"; "Tea and Coffee"; "Ice Machine"; "Vodka, Jack Daniels, and Soda." Kimsey was particularly pleased that the control room was so small that Mick and Keith could not comfortably fit themselves in it, never mind the rest of the band, keeping them out of his hair, allowing him to concentrate on the recording end, while they spent their time working on the music. "It was quite strange, I could be in there for six hours and the band would play and I would be recording," recalled Kimsey. "There would be a take of something and they would say, 'Okay, let's go have a listen,' but it would only ever be Mick and Keith who came in to listen back. Really, though, the comments would always be like, 'Yeah, that's pretty good,' or, 'That's too fast.' But there was never, ever, a discussion about sound. That was just completely left to me.

"The nature of the room was such that I had to put this little PA up," Kimsey continued. "This just gave them more freedom to not wear headphones. Charlie would have had to have worn head-phones, obviously. But it was only a little Shure PA, with the vocal and the kick and snare coming through. Mick would sing, I don't think we ever recorded a song without Mick singing. You have to have the singer singing, even though he didn't have all the lyrics completed. He's got the melody and he's pretty much got the rhythms of what the vocal is going to be. I would imagine it's about 60 percent live and 40 that we would have patched up or over-dubbed. You can almost tell on some, because if you listen on head-phones on some tracks, where he changes his words and phrasing, you can just hear it in the ghost, 'cause it's coming over the PA through the overhead mikes. You can just hear it in the background. It's kind of a weird, ghostly thing . . . It was like a club gig." Kimsey told another interviewer, "The PA was aiming at the drums, so the snare would actually come back through the overhead mike and create this quite unique sound."

Mick had a few song ideas, but Keith came in with no material prepared and just started hammering it out, just the core band, with new-guy Ronnie thrilled to be aboard, giving the proceedings a visceral, enthusiastic energy. "You know it's a good room when the band is smiling," said Keith. "The flow just seemed right from the get go."

Kimsey said that the psychology of the band was ripe for expression as well. "Because of the situation with Keith, with the impending [legal issues]—and he was still using [heroin] at the time," he said [which Keith confirms]—"it was quite amazing, because Mick supported him 110 percent, in so much as he wouldn't get on his case about [it]. And he really helped Keith and nurtured him through that whole period. And in doing that, he also made a lot of business decisions, not really with Keith, but keeping the whole thing going. This created quite an energy in the recording because you really didn't know if this was going to be the last Stones re-cord, if he was going to go down. I think that almost gave it a mo-mentum, a drive."

The band admitted that they felt like they were getting kicked around. "A lot of it was, we've got to out-punk the punks," said

Keith. "Because they can't play, and we can." But on "Respectable," and other *Some Girls* material, the looseness recalls Ron's old band, the Faces, as much as any new bands. "Respectable" is just a 12-bar basher, revved up to a breakneck pace. Mick had originally intended the tempo to be slower, but he and Keith argued over it and Keith won out with the faster pace. Kimsey said that Mick actually sped everything up all the time. "He can't even count in time!"

Each of the three guitars is distinct in the mix, Keith and Ronnie doing their weaving, panned on each side of the stereo, while Mick strums away lower in the mix, straight up the middle, all playing through small, but powerful Mesa Boogie amps. "Another factor [in the rejuvenated feel of the record] is that Mick was playing a lot of guitar," said Kimsey. "Mick was bringing songs in and wanted to play the electric guitar. His energy is very different than to that of Keith or Ronnie in playing guitar. It is more, I suppose you could say punk rock. It's just a very animalistic, basic way of bashing out the chord sequence . . . which kind of fits with his energy as a person, the way he moves and sings anyway. And that is what lends it the energy that people think of as punk rock." Kimsey states that he never heard any talk of needing to answer punk rockers. "There was never a conscious effort like, *oh, we have to sound like this,* or *we have to make something like this.* It just sounded like it sounded. That was it. There were never any references at all to anything."

Keith was not always thrilled with Mick adding the thrashing to Keith's finessed latticework with his new guitar mate, Ronnie. I told Kimsey that I had read where Keith had actually unplugged Mick's guitar. "Yeah, he did!" he laughed. "And he actually did that—one of the very few times . . . Ron was doing a solo, you know, eyes closed. Keith ran and unplugged the amp. And Ronnie kept playing but realized suddenly there was no sound. And he turned around and there's Keith laughing his head off, saying, 'You played too many fucking notes, you see the power's gone off!'"

This looseness and thrashing away all at once in a small room was counterintuitive to the direction record production had been taking in general. It was an era where you had producers and engineers starting to get clinical about recordings, which would only increase as recording technology went digital. Did Kimsey feel any pressure from the recording fraternity, perceived or otherwise, with such a huge commercial band, to fight the thrashy live sound and get a cleanly engineered product? "No, none at all," he replied. "I was just so happy to have boxes and boxes of U47s, U67s [laughs], all these beautiful [expensive, vintage Neumann] mikes. I mean, I was using these beautiful old U47s on the guitars! Can you imagine? On the Boogies? [loud amps]." Kimsey was not afraid of overloading these fragile and expensive tools. "The [mixing] desk just said to me, 'Yeah! What else you got, just give me more!' It was a real global thing capturing that album. I mean, I'm sure it would have sounded quite different if they hadn't had Boogies, if they'd had a mixture of Ampegs and Fenders [amplifiers]; it all just sounded really good in that room. That was the magic thing."

Over that raging wall of guitars, Mick spins a tongue-in-cheek, self-referential lyric. With all that was going on with the band, he outrageously jokes about talking heroin with the president and getting laid on the White House lawn. The latter alluded to a visit Bianca had with President Gerald Ford's son, Jack, at the White House. There is a great photo of Warhol taking a Polaroid of them. There were three shots taken of Jack and Bianca in the Lincoln Bedroom. On July 14, 1975, *Time* magazine reported:

They met several weeks back, danced at a Manhattan discothèque, and he invited her to his home for a drink. With Husband Mick Jagger on the road with his Rolling Stones tour, Bianca Jagger, 30, last week took Jack Ford, 23, up on his invitation. Jack's home, of course, is the White House, and Bianca arrived with artist Andy Warhol and plans for a Jack Ford story in Warhol's *Interview* magazine. "This must be the meeting of the Weird Washington Photo Club," joked the President's son nervously. . . .

Mick, who had demurred on the chance to visit the Ford White House, had spent the previous summer trying to salvage his relationship with Bianca, but he ended up spending Christmas with Jerry Hall at the Savoy Hotel in London. He had also met Jerry Hall while touring London in 1976 and started flirting with her while she was engaged to Roxy Music's Brian Ferry. Bianca filed for divorce in 1978. It's this "rag trade girl" and "the queen of porn" who bears the sarcastic contempt of her soon-to-be-ex-husband on "Respectable."

40
Miss You

RECORDED:

October–December 1977, Pathé Marconi Studios,
Boulogne-Billancourt (suburban Paris)

RELEASES:

LP: *Some Girls*, June 1978
Single, April 1976, charting at number 1 in the US
and number 3 in the UK

The Rolling Stones Four-on-the-Floor Dance Number

Miss You" was the band's biggest hit in years, a rock 'n' disco number, more Sly and the Family Stone funk than Bee Gees pop, more R&B than Tavares, more guitar-driven than all of them. The Stones had been incorporating funk since the *Goats Head Soup* album, if not earlier; something like "Live With Me" had a certain bass-led funk to it, and the band had long been influenced by James Brown. But with "Fingerprint File" in 1974, and "Hot Stuff" and "Hey Negrita" from 1976, the band was taking on dance-funk directly. Billy Preston demonstrated the four-on-the-floor beat to Mick while they were rehearsing at the El Mocambo Club in Toronto, which formed the foundation for "Miss You."

While "Hot Stuff" had a few shout-outs to New York, about its citizens being tough and broke, it was really not much more than a sketch, a jam. But on "Miss You," rather than just some fluffy faux-disco lyrics about dancing this, shaking that, or being "hot," Mick sounds like a cuckolded lonely man longing to break free—presumably from Bianca—and "holding out so long" for Jerry Hall, the striking, leggy blond Texan model he stole away from Brian Ferry. Mick shed any leftover midlife introspection from the *Black and Blue* album, and on *Some Girls,* it's as if he has entered a new era of Jaggerhood, where he has doubled down on a libertine Lothario persona, much as he had embraced whichever lecherous and dissipated devil role he had thrust upon him leading up to *Beggars Banquet* ten years, and a seeming lifetime, prior. And much as he had fed vicariously off of the energy of 1960s street protests and general urban sociopolitical turmoil on *Beggars,* he absorbed the street energy of funky mid-1970s New York City, an era of pronounced poverty, violence, and filth as well as the accompanying escapist soundtrack that marked the era, with punk and disco reigning supreme in the clubs of the city.

Bill pumps out a commanding funky bass line, again flashing remarkable growth and incorporating new elements into his playing. He had been touring the dance clubs in Paris as "research," for the right, um, *feel.* "The whole thing with 'Miss You' and the bass," Kimsey explained, "Bill would go to nightclubs a lot, but I think Bill was more the person *to go* to a disco—well, Mick would go, obviously, to pick up girls, and Bill, too. But you'll never see Keith in a disco, or Charlie."

The band had cut a version with Preston playing the bass, playing those upstroke octaves, and it was that demo that formed the template for what Wyman expanded into for the record version.

"There were a couple of times where Mick would walk over to Bill, as they were running through a track and Mick would sort of shout in his ear what he wanted to hear on bass, but it was not specific notes," Kimsey said. "It was more like [makes a boom boom sound] percussive ideas. Bill would look up at Mick and go, 'Yeah, yeah, yeah, yeah!' But then he would just keep on playing the same thing he had been playing the whole time."

The band called Kimsey after not having worked with him for about seven years because they had always had engineers who had come up through Olympic, for every album since 1967: an unbroken chain that included Glyn Johns, George Chkiantz, Andy Johns, Keith Harwood, and Kimsey again. Kimsey said that he thinks they liked working with him partially because he had not been a big rock 'n' roll fan and was not fazed by the Stones' celebrity status even when he was just starting his career. "You see, when I was working at Olympic, it was mainly film scores I was working on," he explained. "My musical background was not rock and roll. I listened to the radio a lot and the pop music of the time. The Beach Boys I liked. I wasn't into the rock scene that was going on in the UK. I was more into classical music, film music, and musicals. So when the Rolling Stones walked in and I was on the session, I wasn't impressed at all. They were just musicians. And that stayed with me through the whole relationship working with them. I think they kind of appreciated that."

Nevertheless, Kimsey said he treaded carefully interjecting his opinions during the sessions. "Ron and I were both the new kids on the block," he explained. "Insomuch as I got brave at suggesting, something like, an MXR pedal had just come out, a new analog delay pedal, and I would say, 'Why don't you try that?' and things like that." Keith had started to use a couple of compact MXR effects pedals on "Some Girls," one of which was a green analog delay, which Keith refers to as a "reverb-echo" and one was an orange phase shifter, which is a dominating sound on *Some Girls,* especially "Beast of Burden." It is a bit of that slap-back echo that you can hear Keith playing off of on "Miss You," though. It was like a new color in his palette, a function he compares to the Gibson Maestro fuzz box on "Satisfaction." But he kicks on the phase shifter for the middle-eight "Oh, baby why you wait so long" part (around 1:55), modulating at a watery fast rate.

The sessions for *Some Girls* would begin, as usual, after midnight. "Miss You" has that summer late night vibe. "I remember being in Munich and coming back from a club with Mick singing one of the Village People songs," said Charlie, " 'YMCA,' I think it was—and Keith went mad, but it sounded great on the dance floor." Charlie dug a lot of those classic disco songs, naming the O'Jays, Trammps, and George McCrae as records he and Shirley would play at parties. So Charlie and Bill bring some heavy thumping bottom to "Miss You," while the guitars stick up on the high strings. The band layers on the vocals, Mick sounding deep and rich on the spacious verses, especially the fever-whispered, "I been walking Central Park" breakdown. In between the lines, his ghost guide vocal is prominent, sounding like some shouting from the next room, adding to the urban atmosphere. Keith and Ronnie join him on the wordless vocal riffs. Mick bellows the amusing imitation of some friends who call him to break him out of his lovelorn funk, much as his friends had in "Memory Motel": "Hey, whassamatta man? We gonna come around 12 with some Puerta Rican girls das just dyin' to meetchoo."

"We didn't think much of 'Miss You' when we were doing it," Keith writes. "It was 'Aah, Mick's been to the disco and has come out humming some other song . . . We just thought we'd put our part in on Mick wanting to do some disco shit, keep the man happy." Keith represented many rock fans who were hostile to disco. It is funny to recall how much of a threat the dance genre was perceived as to the future of music. In Chicago, a rock radio station went so far as to stage a "Disco Demolition" night, an event between a baseball double-header at Comiskey Park where a crate of disco records was blown up in the center of the field. The "disco sucks" crowd quickly slipped out of control, resulting in a riot of sorts. It was difficult not to see such a backlash, led predominantly by white suburban males, as having some roots in racism and homophobia. Was rock 'n' roll really so fragile that it would be threatened with extinction accelerated by a different style of pop music? In hindsight, the kids should have been more fearful of trash like REO Speedwagon and the insipid, "California rock . . . complacency," in Keith's words. Kenny Loggins and his "yacht rock" ilk could do more to bring down rock 'n' roll, and it is that strand—some of it, like the Eagles, a bastardization of the country rock started by Gram Parsons—that the Stones were kicking against.

Though no one in the Stones copped to consciously setting out to record a "disco" song per se, the band found this groove and laid into it, taking it somewhere beyond disco. It sounds like what it is: a garage band trying to play a disco song, not to cash in necessarily (though it was a big hit and they certainly capitalized on that with a 12-inch dance mix), but as an experiment.

Ronnie's mate, Ian McLagan of the Faces, is on Wurlitzer electric piano and Sugar Blue on harmonica. Sugar Blue was an unknown busker from New York who came over to perform in the more hospitable subways of Paris, "one of the greatest stages in the world," he says. People would come just to hear him play. "I met this cat whose name I can't remember, who said, 'Hey, man, we really like the way you play—why don't you come on over and play with the Stones?' I said, 'Sure, Mack . . . uh-huh . . . give me the telephone number.' The guy said, 'Hey, man, this is no jive.' . . . So that cat gave me the number, and I said, 'Well, what the fuck have I got to lose? I'll give 'em a call.' I called the number and said, 'Hey, man, can I speak to Mick Jagger?' A couple of minutes later a guy says, 'Hey, mate, how are you?' He invited me down to the studio. . . ."

Sugar Blue had been a fan of the Stones' records since he was a kid. He had learned about the blues from their albums. He says for the entire session he was "on cloud nine. . . . They were nice to work with, they were damned nice to work with, because they were patient. . . ." His wailing harp is distinctive from Mick's more traditionally blues-based howls. Blue plays it with long sustained notes here, fitting into the minor-key blues mesh consisting of the three guitars and electric piano playing simultaneously. His sound on the track resonates more like a violin, with note choices on his ending solo that are more jazz-sax-like than, say, a Little Walter–like flurry of notes and chords. Blue sticks to the main riff, the melody that Mick sings on the verses and in falsetto, the main hook of the song. Out of nowhere comes a staccato squeal of an actual sax, played by Mel Collins picking up the cue from Mick, who screams out of that quiet break.

Kimsey's mix on the album is actually an edit, drastically cut down from a much longer take that the band played. There is a single remix from Bob Clearmountain, as well as an extended dance mix by the latter.

"I think I mixed all of *Some Girls*. I know Bobby Clearmountain did a mix of 'Miss You,' a single mix," Kimsey said. "But I think I did mix all of *Some Girls*. I mixed at Electric Lady, I think. There's a funny little story there. Earl McGrath, who was the president of Rolling Stones Records, lovely Earl, he said to me, 'I just discovered this young kid, Bobby Clearmountain, at Power Station. We should let him have a go at mixing "Miss You." I think he's a good talent.' So Bobby did that, and this is before mixers really came into the business, before remixing was happening. And my pride was a bit put out, I was a bit pissed off, but thought, 'what the hell.' And then about six months later, when the album was out and the single was number one or whatever it is, I was working in the States and 'Miss You' came on the radio. I driving down PCH [Pacific Coast Highway] and it came on and I thought, 'Wow, this sounds *amazing!* It sounds f-ing great! Oh, gosh, Bobby, it's really, really cool. I love

this. Well done, Bobby!' And I think the difference in the two versions—my mix was for the album and his mix was for the single—is that there is no sax solo on the single. But driving in the
car, all of a sudden, the sax solo came on. And it was my frigging
mix! And after that I thought, well shit, if it's in the grooves and
you've got it, you'd be an idiot to fuck it up."

In large part due to the crossover success of the single, *Some
Girls* was a monster hit, with over six million copies sold in the US
alone, making it the band's all-time biggest selling non-compilation
LP.* As early as the 1970s, there was a serious discussion among
rock 'n' roll fans about aging: Can the generation who declared "I
hope I die before I get old," and "Never trust a person over thirty,"
indeed continue to maintain relevance into their late thirties? This
was a big deal at the time. The Stones, though, never made such
pronouncements. They assumed that they might grow old playing
music, just as their blues heroes had. But rather than shrinking
back down to smaller blues or rock 'n' roll venues somewhere, the
band shot straight to the top of the charts.

---

*   *Hot Rocks* sold more than 12 million records.

41

All About You

RECORDED:

January–February 1979, Compass Point Studios,
Nassau, Bahamas
November–December 1979, Electric Lady,
New York City (possible overdubs)

RELEASES:

LP: *Emotional Rescue*, June 1980

Hanging Around with Dogs: The Stones Slip into Another Valley

A perfectly fine LP, *Emotional Rescue* has some good songs, a few genuinely hilarious ones like the title song, ("I'll be your knight in shining armor . . . on a fine Arab charger . . . ."), and at least one great one, the ballad "All About You." Virtually spit out by Keith, it is a bitter lyric about being "sick and tired of hanging around with dogs like you." As with many Stones songs, it could be viewed as a breakup song with a lover, but was more likely a vitriolic reflection of bad times between Keith and Mick. Though their relationship was given a bit of a jump-start as Mick helped

Keith through his trial and rehab, tensions became acute as the two clashed over business and the direction the band should take.

Overall, though, the *Emotional Rescue* LP marks the real drop-off in quality of new material by the Rolling Stones. Many will argue that the next record, *Tattoo You* is among their best, and I would agree that it is an excellent collection. However, let's set that aside, as that record consisted purely of outtakes from their golden period, rescued from the dustbin, fleshed out, and polished, mostly by Mick and Chris Kimsey. "*Emotional Rescue* started in the same place in Paris," Kimsey explained. "It started where we'd left off [with the *Some Girls* sessions]. There were quite a few tracks left over from *Some Girls* that we didn't use and *Emotional Rescue* was a strange album for me. I don't remember much of [the sessions] because it didn't seem very good to me at the time. [The sessions] spawned *Emotional Rescue*, which was a very different-sounding record. It was a little haphazard, that album. And then we sort of moved off to Nassau to do more tracking and overdubbing, and then went to New York. The great thing about *Some Girls* was, it was Paris and then we mixed it in New York. That was it. And I think it sounded better for that rather than hopscotching all over the place."

As Peter Silverton wrote in his review of *Emotional Rescue* for *Sounds* in 1980, "*Emotional Rescue* is the least committed Stones record ever. . . . It's the most obvious way of dealing with your own myth. Just pretend it doesn't exist. And do the best you can. The cover would maybe have you believe otherwise. The thermographic photos (of the Stones and who else?) hint that there's a little looking below the surface."

And that was a *good* review! Which is sort of the point. Mick more or less stopped investing himself in Stones songwriting around this time, chasing after hits and putting in less personal inspiration. The album as a whole is laid back, as if the band needed to express their stored-up aggression on *Some Girls* and, having accomplished that, they went back down to the islands and Paris to record a chill collection of light Euro-disco, faux reggae, cartoonish new wave, and polite pop-rock. "Mick is a great flavor-of-the-month person," said Charlie. But if "Miss You" was a heavy throbber, then "Dance (Pt. 1)" was a skinny-bottomed boy's chardonnay-sipping pose at a passé Paris discotheque. The dance material just sounds like a flimsy version of the obvious influences of Chic and early Prince. But the songs seemed to become exercises in Stones-like posturing for Mick, as the band struggled to keep it all together as a unit, even while reaching ever-stratospheric heights as a money-making touring entity. "My attention span is so limited," said Mick in 1980. "You know, I just love to make up songs and I don't even like to finish the words. I just like to sing *ooooh* all the way through. And then I'm happy after that. I don't want to do anymore. That's *it*. I don't even want to hear it again." By his own admission, songs were disposable.

For those looking for actual humanity in Stones records after *Some Girls,* a good place to start would be the Keith-sung ballads, like this one. They might not always be the "best" songs, and they were almost certainly never considered possible hits, but the heart and soul of the band could usually be found hiding in those booze-besotted, nicotine-fogged corners of the records where an increasingly raspy Keith stepped up to the blue-spotlighted mike to offer his take on matters. "[Mick and Keith] fought a lot during that album because Keith thought Mick was getting his way too much," Kimsey told an interviewer, "and Keith had to fight for what he believed. Keith *fights* for his half of the Glimmer Twins." The biggest source of tension at this point did involve that musical cliché, *musical differences*. According to Bill, Keith accused Mick of "listening to too many bad records."

Kimsey expanded on the fraying band dynamic: "It was different [than working on *Some Girls*]. To me, it was like Keith was waking up. I think he had missed quite a few years. I didn't feel that there was much energy or determination with [*Emotional Rescue*].

It's an album with my least favorite songs. It's a real odd mixture."
Kimsey noted that Mick and Keith were working separately more
often. "It was almost like doing a Mick album and a Keith album.
Keith had started really digging into himself and enjoying his own
songs more. There was a lot of time spent on his songs, with him
overdubbing vocals, vocals, vocals, vocals."

By the spring of 1978, Keith had more or less kicked junk for
good, with the nursing of Mick and Jerry as they stayed up in Woodstock, New York, along with Keith's personal manager, Jane Rose.*
By getting off the stuff, Keith effectively drove the final nail in the
coffin of his relationship with Anita, whom Keith might have been
with forever had she cleaned up along with him. Instead, she
plumbed lower depths, including the scandalous affair with a
seventeen-year-old would-be suitor who shot himself in the head
with a revolver while playing a game of Russian roulette at her
rented house in suburban New York with her son Marlon present.

In October 1978, Keith had his trial in Toronto and was given a
sentence of one year's probation. The government of Canada really
did not want to imprison a popular rock star on the trumped-up
charge of trafficking, which they knew full well was not his intent.
The fact that Margaret Trudeau had been hobnobbing with the
band at the exact moment and at the location of the bust only sul-
lied the matter politically. But it was a Stones superfan, a young
blind woman named Rita Bedard, from Quebec City, who gave the
presiding judge an elegant exit from the controversy. She convinced Judge Lloyd Graburn to show leniency for Keith. She explained that she had followed the Stones from gig to gig and that
Keith asked the truckers that hauled their stage rigs to take her with
them and assure she got to the next show safely. "She came forward
and went to the judge's house, after office hours and at night,

---

* Rose had previously worked for the Rolling Stones organization.

knocked on his door and told him this story," writes Keith. "Two days later I had the next hearing and it was, 'Okay, you're sentenced to perform a concert for the blind,' which we gladly did." The Stones and Ronnie's side band, the New Barbarians, Keith taking part in both acts, performed the show for the Canadian Institute for the Blind in April 1979.

The outgoing Ronnie was also the catalyst for a general new-found appreciation that the band found for each other. "There's such a great rapport going now between the band that people actually say to each other, *You played great tonight!*—which we'd never say," said Bill Wyman at the time of the 1978 tours. "That's never been said in twelve years. I've never been told, ever, *You did a great set tonight*. I've only been told, *You were out of tune tonight*."

But Ronnie was also speaking up for himself at this time. "Ronnie [was] trying to claim a stake in the songwriting," Kimsey continued. "Because he would come up with bits he never got credited for. I mean, Ronnie would always say, 'Chris, make a note. I wrote that! I wrote that! That's my bit!'"

Things between Mick and Keith continued to vacillate between love and hate. Keith had written the *Some Girls* track "Beast of Burden" for Mick, ". . . to say, 'Thanks, man, for shouldering the burden,'" according to Keith. "The weird thing was, he didn't want to share the burden anymore." By 1980 it was now a control issue, and Mick did not want to relinquish that aspect of his power. "The phrase from that period that rings in my ears all these years later is 'Oh, shut up, Keith,'" he writes. It cut him badly. So while there is undoubtedly some of Anita in "All About You," it seems to have more in it about Mick, who Keith felt was condescendingly treating him like a child.

"That song was hanging around for three years," Keith told *Rolling Stone* in 1981. "After researching to make sure it wasn't somebody else who wrote it, I finally decided that it must have been me." While Keith was recording vocals for "All About You," he asked Earl McGrath, who was running Rolling Stones Records, to come up to the roof of Electric Lady Studios. There, Keith said he threatened McGrath that he would throw him off to the pavement below if he did not act to somehow repair the damage being done between Mick and Keith. "I said, you're supposed to be the go-between with Mick. What's going on," writes Keith. "I wanted to let him know how I was feeling about this. I couldn't bring Mick up there and throw him off, and I had to do something."

Such urgent desperation can be heard in the lyric of "All About You." It's a killer R&B ballad, a devastating and deeply emotional track, raw, stark, savage, and tender, one of the most soulful songs since *Exile*. And like the gospel-informed ballads on *Exile*, part of what makes "All About You" so affecting are the backing vocals, rough-and-tumble harmonies layered on by Keith and Ronnie. The overlapping phrasing, off-mike mumbling, the drunken horns, and late-night weariness amount to a stripped-down deconstruction that echoes like the lonely hollows in the space that Keith remembered hearing as a kid coming over the midnight airwaves from Radio Luxembourg, the "end of Lonely Street" darkness heard on the sparse "Heartbreak Hotel." In addition to guitar, Keith filled in missing space left after the original basic tracks with piano and bass. "I never knew what Keith was going to [put] on it, I never knew what he wanted . . ." said Charlie soon after a very sparse sketch of a track was recorded. "But it was a great track to play. That's being a drummer, you know? . . . How he made a song out of it, I don't know."

"It had a little bit of sentimental input there about his feelings for Mick at the time. Just listen to the lyrics," said Bobby Keys, who was back on his first Stones album since *Goats Head Soup*. Keith has said that "All About You" was just one of a few songs with at least some of the barbed lyrics aimed at Mick. He writes, "It was at that time when I was deeply hurt."

42
Start Me Up

RECORDED:

October–December 1977, Pathé Marconi Studios
Boulogne-Billancourt (suburban Paris)
April–May 1980, Rolling Stones Mobile Unit
at a warehouse on the outskirts of
the Paris Peripherique (ring road)

RELEASES:

LP: *Tattoo You*, August 1981
Single, August 1981, charting at number 2 in
the US and number 7 in the UK

Making a Dead Band Come

Perhaps a more accurate title for this song would be "Jump-Start Me Up," using Mick's car metaphor, for it seemed, before this album, like the Stones' engine had permanently stalled. But that is exactly what *Tattoo You* did: It gave the band a new breath of life, the last gasp of artistic relevancy, allowing them to capitalize on the growing significance of the new MTV music video network, embark on a hugely successful stadium tour, and release a subsequent live LP and concert film, also successful. This set the stage for the latest period of the Stones, a billion-dollar touring juggernaut cashing in on nostalgia, an exceedingly deep back catalog, decades of good will, a storied past, and suburban fans who were now parents and grandparents with a lot of disposable income.

The Stones had recorded two albums' worth of material during the sessions for *Emotional Rescue,* which itself had some material carry over from *Some Girls.* They needed to tap this well of reserves as they had signed an enormous $14 million record deal leading into *Some Girls.* They had two more records due per the contract. But Mick and Keith were not speaking. "We had a period where Mick and Keith were not getting on at all and there was no way they were going to go into the studio together," Kimsey said. "And so Prince Rupert [Loewenstein] called to ask if there were any tracks we could use. I said, 'Well, there's pretty much two-thirds of an album; stuff from *Some Girls* and *Emotional Rescue.* And if there is stuff there, there was probably stuff from the previous albums as well.' I spent four or five months going back through everything and found a couple of things from *Black and Blue,* that was 'Slave,' actually, that was from Rotterdam with Glyn and the Mobile. And I found 'Waiting on a Friend' from *Goats Head Soup.* The rest of it, I think was from what I had recorded."

In fact, "Start Me Up" had been recorded the same day as "Miss You." The band had been slogging away at a reggae version of the song without coming up with a workable take they felt confident with. "After they cut it, I said, 'That's bloody great! Come and listen,'" Kimsey said. "However, when I played it back, Keith said, 'Nah, it sounds like something I've heard on the radio. Wipe it.' Of course, I didn't, but he really didn't like it, and I'm not sure whether he likes it to this day. I don't think it's one of his favorite songs, although it's obviously everyone's favorite guitar riff; his guitar riff. Maybe because Keith loves reggae so much, he wanted it to be a reggae song."

Keith was probably less worried that he had heard something

like it on the radio than he had heard something like it on one of their own records. It is a quintessential Stones lick. The band had an embarrassment of riches, or riffs, as the case may be. Keith recalls that he simply threw the rock version of the riff out there in between reggae takes, to break up the monotony and Charlie instinctively just thwacked in with the snare beat. In the end, they only did a couple of takes with the rock version before sliding back into the reggae. Last I checked, there was a reggae-style outtake on the Internet under the title "Never Stop."

Kimsey said the band had worked on the song for about six hours. The style of writing, arranging, and recording had not altered dramatically over their career, but there was a gradual evolution and different songs called for different approaches. "You see, if they all played the right chords in the right time, went to the chorus at the right time and got to the middle-eight together, that was a master," Kimsey explained. "They would never sit down and work out a song. They would jam it and the song would evolve out of that. That's their magic." This is consistent with how Jim Dickinson explained "Brown Sugar" going down in 1969. Once they had the song arrangement from top-to-bottom with no major mistakes, that would be the take they went with. Kimsey explains that this method kept everyone on their toes, particularly Charlie, who could never be certain if Mick would change where a bridge or chorus came in the song from take to take. Mick would simply try to influence the direction and arrangement over the guide vocal, either with actual snippets of lyrics, or actual spoken or shouted directions, like, "Okay, here we go! *Don't make a grown man cry. . . .*"

This also explains some of Charlie's sometimes odd fills and entrances to songs or choruses, like "Honky Tonk Women." And here on "Start Me Up," he comes in on the one beat at the beginning, then he catches up. He is once again playing the four-on-the-floor kick drum similar to what he had played just previously on "Miss

You." Charlie is cracking here, and it is truly hard to believe that they just tried the song spontaneously in this tempo and non-reggae beat once or twice before abandoning it. It sounds like the whole drum part was charted out beforehand. "Throughout the recording, Charlie kept it very straight ahead and Keith just went for it," Kimsey explained. "It was like 'Oh, I remember this,' as they played along, and it just stuck together with a lot of space. That's the song's magic, really."

"I had to be ready for a lot of stuff, because all of a sudden they would get fed up and Mick would say something like, 'Let me try this now on piano,'" said Kimsey. "And so I had everything set up and ready to go. You had to be on your toes. You've only got 16 tracks and you had to have everything miked up and ready to capture it. A live vocal on piano in a big room could be [problematic in terms of sound leakage into the piano mikes]. But if the vocal was the magic then it didn't really matter because the leakage is your friend, as it were."

When it came time to review the album material in general, Kimsey sent around tapes to the band of the outtakes he proposed finishing off for their approval. He had spent those five months or so assembling and preparing the tracks (mostly back in London, at Olympic) in between a few sessions with other artists, but it proved to be a daunting job.

Once the songs were gathered and the tapes prepared, Mick proposed they take the Rolling Stones Mobile back to Paris to overdub the needed vocals. He found a ridiculously cheap Paris warehouse where they parked the truck and set up a booth. "But when I'd assembled everything and sent it to everybody, Mick said, 'Well, we'll take the Mobile to Paris.' I don't know why," Kimsey laughed. "He chose to put it in a . . . it was awful, really, on the outskirts and periphery of the city, in a train warehouse area. It was so bizarre. It was freezing cold. And we spent a couple of months there. And it was frustrating, because Mick was doing his society things and he would never turn up, and it became a hassle to get things done."

Mick did most of the vocal parts on *Tattoo You* in the Paris warehouse. But Bob Clearmountain recalls Mick singing "Start Me Up," including the backing vocals and harmonies, at the Power Station in New York with him recording. "I remember he came in the control room and said, 'What do you think of this?' and he sang it right in my ear," Clearmountain told *Mix* magazine with a laugh. "Up to that point, I never realized how loud he could sing. He was shouting over the track, and I was leaning backward, saying, 'Yeah, yeah. That's great! Why don't you try doing it out in the studio, on the mike?!'"

Aside from an overcooked automotive-sex metaphor mildly spiced up with a line lifted from an old blues song about making a dead man come, there is not much there lyrically. The sexy-car thing was done better by T. Rex. But it sounded so fun, so shiny and new, that few listeners seemed bothered by the increasingly vapid lyric writing Mick tossed off. The sound was explosive coming out of the speakers in 1981. It still sounded like the Stones, but almost radically updated sonically. As Kimsey noted, ". . . it's quite an incredible record actually, because you'd never know [the *Tattoo You* recordings are] from four different periods . . . Bobby mixed most of that. I think the mix is really good. But it was still, as I said earlier, if it's in the grooves, you'd be a fool to mess it up."

Clearmountain—who had also mixed the single version of "Miss You"—told *Mix* magazine that "Start Me Up" was the track on which he employed a trick he called "bathroom reverb," using an actual tiled studio bathroom downstairs as a live echo chamber, with a speaker piping out the dry signal and a microphone picking up the reverberated version. That sort of rich, clear reverb (listen to the first beat of Charlie's snare at the top of the track), along with an overall balanced and lively mix is what Clearmountain became known for. Here, the drums and guitars are right up front. But the Stones left the space and Clearmountain knew how to accent the pauses between the riffs. They added handclaps and cowbell on the bridges, bringing it a bit more snap.

The savvy Stones had managed to cobble together another great album in order to fulfill their contractual obligation, but just as important, it gave them something new to tour on, another number one album with a smash single. I asked Kimsey just how much extra material was there to warrant serious consideration? It didn't sound at all like scraping the bottom of the barrel. "I think there was a short list of twenty and we'd gotten it down to the final lot," he answered. "We ended up with a fast side and a slow side. I actually think that was Mick's idea. . . . That was a stroke of genius, actually. . . . It was an incredible, satisfying job for me, to discover all that and kind of say, 'Look what I've found.'"

"I was shocked," said Keith about Kimsey and Mick cobbling together a hit out of an outtake. "That was a throwaway track that had been in the can for a couple of years." "Start Me Up" is a fine upbeat but ultimately benign pop-rocker. It is a bit on the generic side, with just a bit more life to it than most of the songs on *Emotional Rescue,* but it was obvious why they did not feel the need to finish it during the sessions for *Some Girls,* when they had so much better material. It is dumbed-down and monolithic enough for the stadium tour that would take up most of 1981–82 and points the way for even dumber and more generic songs to come.

It didn't take as much to stand out as a rock band in 1981 as it did in 1972. While John Lennon and Yoko Ono's *Double Fantasy,* and AC/DC's *For Those About to Rock We Salute You* were on the US album charts, the Stones were mostly competing with bland acts like Kim Carnes, REO Speedwagon, and Styx. It was the start of a new era for the Stones and it sounded fresh and generally up to date within the context of the times. I asked Kimsey if he thought that a lot of that comes down to the Stones' continued role in defining their time.

"Culturally, they were still quite relevant at that point. They were just fortunate that the stuff left behind was some of the best stuff [laughs]." Material wise, they were on borrowed time. Borrowed from their own tape vaults.

43
Waiting on a Friend

RECORDED:

November–December 1972, Dynamic Sound Studios,
Kingston, Jamaica
April–May 1980, Rolling Stones Mobile Unit
at a warehouse on the outskirts
of the Paris Peripherique (ring road)

RELEASES:

LP: *Tattoo You*, August 1981
Single, November 1981, charting at number 13 in the US
and number 50 in the UK

A Game for Youth

This is really one of the most beautiful songs in the Stones' library. While the recording dates back to the 1972 sessions for *Goats Head Soup,* the lyric was mostly written later, around 1980, as a tender appreciation of an old friendship. "The lyric I added is very gentle and loving, about friendships in the band," Mick wrote in 1993. Genuine and deep emotion was in decreasing supply in their material as the band struggled throughout the 1980s, so the affection heard in this song and seen in the accompanying video was warmly received by fans of the band.

The ups and downs of Mick and Keith's relationship, friends since boyhood, and the challenges in maintaining a creative collaboration over the course of decades, had manifested itself in their songs. But they and the band as a whole had triumphed over much adversity together. They were the guys the other one would want in a foxhole. They were a gang. The tensions that started to threaten the existence of the band around 1980 and *Emotional Rescue* would last through most of the 1980s, as the Stones struggled to keep it together. Ultimately they would discover that time away from each other and solo projects provided needed outlets to relieve the pressure of keeping a twenty-year collaboration healthy. But as the 1980s would wear on, the time off between Stones albums and tours extended into years at a time and there would be moments where it seemed that the Stones had, for all intents and purposes, broken up. But they never did. And here they are on their fiftieth anniversary.

But sticking it out might not have been impressive enough for everyone. "You know, they're congratulating the Stones on being together 112 years. Whoooopee!" said John Lennon in *Playboy* in 1980, caustic to the end. "At least Charlie and Bill still got their families.* In the eighties, they'll be asking, 'Why are those guys still together? Can't they hack it on their own? Why do they have to be surrounded by a gang? Is the little leader scared somebody's gonna knife him in the back?' That's gonna be the question. That's-a-gonna be the question! . . . They will be showing pictures of the guy with lipstick wriggling his ass and the four guys with the evil black makeup on their eyes trying to look raunchy. That's gonna be the joke in the future."

---

* Bill was actually embarking on his second serious relationship since his 1960s divorce, breaking up with Astrid Lundstrom when he met Suzanne Accosta.

Of all people, Lennon, who was killed on December 9 of that same year, should have understood the value of a long-term collaborative relationship, and he did, with Yoko Ono. But no one could blame the Beatles for leaving that all behind after burning with historic intensity during the sixties. "We spent more time together in the early days than John and Yoko," Lennon explained in the same interview. "The four of us sleeping in the same room, practically in the same bed, in the same truck, living together night and day, eating, shitting and pissing together! All right? Doing everything together! . . . When Rodgers worked with Hart and then worked with Hammerstein, do you think he should have stayed with one instead of working with the other? Should Dean Martin and Jerry Lewis have stayed together because I used to like them together? What is this game of doing things because other people want it?" While it may be true that most artistic partnerships have an arc, and that the Beatles had run its unmatched and highly productive course, the fact remained that the strength and fruits of the Stones' partnership continued to grow, via peaks and valleys, over those decades.

Lennon's murder shook the world. And it certainly affected his friends in the Stones deeply. "He thought he had found a place to be on his own, have this life, and he was quite taken with the idea that he was no longer in the Beatles, that he didn't have to have a lot of protection, bodyguards. . . ." said Mick. "He wanted freedom to walk the block and get in the cab, and he felt in these big cities you can be anonymous. I just felt very sad for the loss of someone that I loved very much."

"He had a load of front—as they say in England, more front than Harrods," Keith said years later. "And if there was one way that guy shouldn't have gone, it was like that. But, at the same time, knowing John, I can imagine that he probably cracked a joke to himself as it happened. John was that human, you know . . . look what that guy gave and look what he got in return."

Lennon was loved in part for his blunt manner of calling them like he saw them. But taking the Stones to task for a sustained collaborative success reeked of unattractive professional jealousy unfitting an artist of Lennon's stature. Most bands have a shorter shelf life than the Stones and that's just natural. How the Rolling Stones managed to weather the storms and the creative struggles, the deaths, and the personnel challenges, this is what makes the rich history of the band almost as much an achievement as the music itself. Far from bearing the brunt of cynicism, that longevity should be lauded as exemplary of how to work well with others, subsuming egos to benefit an arrangement that undoubtedly has produced creative output greater than would the sum of its parts.

So while sometimes a love song is just a love song, other times it is about a bandmate. In case there was any doubt that "Waiting on a Friend" was one such instance, it was packaged for the then-new MTV cable channel that would go on to exponentially change the face of popular music over the ensuing decade. MTV proved seminal in giving new artists a boost, to be certain. However, it also cemented the legacy of older bands, prolonging or resuscitating the careers of some classic rockers like the Stones and The Who as they continued to release new material of varying quality.

The Stones had long exploited film and video for promotional clips dating back to "Jumpin' Jack Flash." And it was again Michael Lindsay-Hogg who directed the utterly charming video for "Waiting on a Friend." Unlike the hyper overcutting that later became ubiquitous on music video channels, Lindsay-Hogg luxuriates in long shots, often from across the street, of Mick "standing in a doorway," as he mimes the same line, on the stoop of 98 St. Mark's Place in the East Village of New York, the same building that appears on the cover of Led Zeppelin's *Physical Graffiti* album.* Mick

---

* Peter Corriston designed the covers for the Zeppelin album, as well as *Some Girls* and *Tattoo You.*

waits, along with his friend Peter Tosh and some token Rastas, as Keith ambles his way though a crowded street to reach him. In a scene that puts a lump in the throat of longtime fans, Keith stumbles to the stoop as the song hits the chorus and he embraces a seeming genuinely surprised Mick, who is now seated on the stoop next to Tosh, and he starts to mime the backing harmonies, which Mick had overdubbed by himself on the record, with no input from Keith.

Mick is dressed gaily, in a madras-like long-sleeve shirt, tight white jeans and shoes, and a straw Panama hat. He looks like he just helicoptered in from the Hamptons. Keith strides up in black and gray, in a cloud of cigarette smoke. Later they shuffle over to meet Ronnie, Charlie, and Bill up at the bar at St. Mark's Bar and Grill, all having a laugh as they sidle into middle age, probably tickled that they managed to pull out another record at this point in their career, a period during which Mick and Keith had not even been speaking. "There's always been [bad] periods like that with Mick and I," said Keith, who interestingly only makes one side reference to *Tattoo You* in his autobiography. "But there's always the opposite periods of total cooperation and good will, almost religious fervor as regards one another."

All seems to be momentarily forgotten, in the video, though. "It is a game for youth," sings Mick. Charlie's gray hair, growing back out from his severe crop during the late-1970s, cannot disguise the expanding bald spot on the crown of his head. Bill's naturally droopy face is drooping even lower. Keith and Ronnie had started to dye their hair and, yes, they are still wearing the Lennon-scorned eye makeup.

While Mick and Keith had at least put grudges aside in order to make the video, Ron was also becoming a problem, deep into a freebase cocaine habit that cost him a fortune and nearly cost him his life. Charlie was drinking more as the mixes started coming in for

Tattoo You,* and had insisted to Mick, Bill, and Ronnie that he was quitting and would not be touring to support the album. By the time they talked Charlie back in off the ledge, the issues of Ronnie had to be dealt with. Everyone but Keith wanted him off the 1981 US tour due to his drug-addled state. All agreed it was to be a new era of professionalism with the Stones, everyone agreeing to turn up to gigs on time, and it was only Keith's personal guarantee that assured Ronnie's inclusion on the tour. Nevertheless Keith believed Ronnie betrayed this trust by continuing to freebase on the road, leading Keith to go to his hotel room one night, where Keith punched Ronnie out, "socked him . . . he fell backwards over the couch and the rest of my punch carried me over the top of him," writes Keith, "the couch fell over and we both nearly fell out the window. We scared ourselves to death." Ronnie maintains that it was all a misunderstanding and he had merely stalked off to a friend's room after a fight with his "old lady," not on the prowl for drugs.

But Ronnie still got along with everyone, and the band needed him to serve a middleman role, especially between Mick and Keith's internecine arguments. Did he remain good at that aspect of the job? I asked Kimsey. "Yeah," he replied with a tone of warmth in his voice. "He's such a sweet guy. I think for Ronnie, later on— what was it, ten years or more before he became an official member of the Stones?—I think he found it very difficult because you have to choose: Are you in Keith's camp, or are you in Mick's camp? For the longest time, he was in Keith's camp. Then he went over to Mick's camp. It's difficult."

Ronnie does not play guitar on "Waiting on a Friend," though he is here on backing vocals. The cha-cha guitar parts were played

---

* Another source of conflict between Mick and Keith was that they had agreed the record was to be titled simply *Tattoo*. Mick, the only one on the cover, a la *Goats Head Soup*, insisted he had no idea how the "*You*" got added to the title.

by Keith and Mick Taylor back in 1972. The slow-swirling chorus effect on the guitar would have been added during the mix, as that was an effect more identified with the late 1970s/early 1980s, and it added a then-contemporary sound to the production. Keith strummed away on an acoustic guitar, joining the scratching, tapping, clip-clopping percussion ensemble that includes Jimmy Miller and Kasper Winding, layered over the cross-stick snare pattern that Charlie laid down as the foundation.

That "Waiting On a Friend" had been started during the *Goats Head Soup* sessions is unsurprising given the easygoing island feel of the song and the immediately identifiable, singular piano work of Nicky Hopkins. Listening to Stones records chronologically, the vacuum left by Hopkins's absence on the previous records is put in sharp relief with the resurrection of this older track. Hopkins can be heard on only a handful of tracks after *It's Only Rock 'n' Roll*. He is on only one *Black and Blue* track, and none of *Some Girls* or *Emotional Rescue*. But his playing here is as welcome as a cool gin & tonic on a hot island day. Once again, Hopkins manages the task of adding something essential to the track without grandstanding or making his part intrusive. In between the open-tuned jangling strums of Keith's main chordal theme, Hopkins plays some breathtaking runs in the intro, before Mick enters with the falsetto hook.

But most astonishing is how Hopkins would continue linearly through songs like this. As he did on "Time Waits For No One," he does not circle back and repeat himself, instead continuing an inventive trajectory all its own. As with any song that includes Hopkins, half the fun is listening while concentrating on just the piano parts, certainly a worthwhile endeavor here. The individual resourcefulness of the man was dazzling; he was continuously reaching into a seemingly endless trick bag of licks and riffs. Hopkins had a lot more sonic real estate to work with on "Waiting on a Friend."

Unlike the earlier song, though, "Waiting on a Friend" returns back to the vocal sections before the final vamp out of the song, when *Saxophone Colossus*'s Sonny Rollins graces the recording, classing up the song even more, restoring a level of pure musicality to the Stones that had last been heard when Mick Taylor was in the band. His sublimely lyrical melodic runs and effortless phrasing, with just a touch of guttural grit, take Mick's melody to a dizzying altitude. The solo is at once triumphant and melancholy, with a tinge of echo in the mix, which Rollins seemingly plays off of, with some repeated staccato riffs.

On paper, Sonny Rollins on a Rolling Stones song seems incongruous. After all, this is not the brassy King Curtis–informed Texas style of Bobby Keys, or other rock 'n' roll saxophonists like Clarence Clemmons. Rollins had long been a highly lauded, supremely influential, true jazz master decades before he was invited to play on this song. "My love for Sonny goes back a long way. I would have been 15 or 16 when I first played his records, first with Max Roach and Clifford Brown, then his stuff with Miles, and then of course on his own," Charlie wrote in tribute for *The Guardian* in 2010. "I first saw him in 1964 in the original Birdland club on 52nd Street, playing with a trio. To sit there and watch Sonny Rollins, my God!"

"I had a lot of trepidation about working with Sonny Rollins," admitted Mick. "This guy's a giant of the saxophone." Mick was taken to see Rollins at the Bottom Line in New York in 1981 and was introduced by a mutual friend. "Charlie said, 'He's never going to want to play on a Rolling Stones record!' I said, 'Yes he is going to want to.' And he did and he was wonderful. I said, 'Would you like me to stay out there in the studio?' He said, 'Yeah, you tell me where you want me to play and dance the part out.' So I did that. And that's very important: communication in hand, dance, whatever. You don't have to do a whole ballet, but sometimes that movement of the shoulder tells the guy to kick in on the beat."

Charlie remembers the initial invitation to have Rollins play on the track a bit differently. "I've been fortunate enough to get to know him a bit," he wrote. "Mick asked me about a tenor player for the Stones' 'Waiting on a Friend' and I suggested Sonny . . . It was an overdub, unfortunately, so we never played together. Probably just as well. My goodness, I'd sit there and think, 'Bloody hell, what am I going to do here?' I'd feel like an impostor, because that's the highest company you can keep."

Rollins said of his appearance that it was "an experiment [that] worked out as far as I was concerned." As mismatched as it might have first seemed, Rollins had recorded a masterpiece LP, *Saxophone Colossus* in 1956, which included the calypso-flavored sounds of the lead-off track, "St. Thomas," complete with a cross-stick snare approach from another jazz titan, Max Roach. The whole LP showcases the accessible, full-throated fluidity for which Rollins is known. It was a great fit for the vaguely Caribbean feel of "Waiting on a Friend." Apparently, the Stones invited Rollins to tour with them, an offer he turned down.

Kimsey says the song was done except for vocals when they left Jamaica in 1972. "There were no guitar overdubs on [*Tattoo You*]," he recalled. "There was only vocal, the sax, maybe some percussion. . . . It was mainly vocals, because lyrically, [Mick] hadn't had them finished. But there wasn't much to be finished, to be honest." The combination of the lyric, Rollins's sax, and Hopkins's piano result in one of the Rolling Stones' most elegant numbers, a toe-tapping heart-warmer. A note-perfect passage into middle age for the group.

"There are people who burn bright and fade quickly, and there are those who burn bright and keep going. You have to admire that," Charlie observed about Rollins, but he might as well have been talking about the Stones.

44

She Was Hot

RECORDED:

June–August 1983, The Hit Factory Studios,
New York City

RELEASES:

LP: *Undercover*, November 1983

Single, January 1984, charting at number 44 in the US
and number 42 in the UK

Not a very special record.

—MICK JAGGER

on the *Undercover* LP

Coming off the impressively successful tours of the US and Europe in 1981–82, with an attendant live album, *Still Life*, and a well-received concert film, *Let's Spend the Night Together*, the Stones signed a new $28 million record contract with CBS for four albums. "You know, everybody thinks I'm obsessed with money, but I just want to see artists get paid fairly," populist Mick explained. "They never used to." But unbeknownst to the band, the deal came with a side agreement for a Mick solo album, which Keith characterized as backstabbing. "What I didn't know until a good while later was that . . . Mick had made his own deal with CBS," writes Keith, "without a word to anybody in the band." Mick looked around at his solo-act friends, like Bowie, Elton John, and the King of Pop, Michael Jackson, and thought, *why not me?* "CBS Record head, Walter Yetnikoff let it be known later that everyone at CBS was thinking Mick could be as big as Michael Jackson," writes Keith, "and they were actively promoting it, and Mick was going along with it." As if twenty years in the Rolling Stones had merely been a launching pad for a solo pop star act.

The Stones had just finished working on their newest album, *Undercover,* which would be the last one to be distributed by Warner Brothers, when they signed the CBS contract for the next three albums. *Undercover* is a weak album, betraying the dissension in the Rolling Stones and the divergence of the vision for the band between Mick and Keith. "It got difficult later because you had to take sides," said Chris Kimsey. "I would be working maybe eighteen hours a day because on one side you've got Mick coming in while doing the overdub parts, when we were in New York. Mick would come in from about one to about seven [P.M.] and Keith would come in from midnight to six A.M., so you could imagine. That was ridiculous. That really got crazy, trying to be in both camps. I think at the end of the day I definitely favored being with the musicians rather than the lead vocalist, the businessman."

Ronnie said Mick was "not a very good drinker and drugger," but he really straightened up whatever few bad habits he had and became ever more conscious of business in the early-1980s, and this extended to an obsession with staying current with musical and production trends. Keith was wary of any technology beyond a '57 Telecaster and a tattered tube amp and remained immune to flavors of the month. Mick's vision largely won out on the *Undercover* album, which is plastered with the instantly dated sounds of

1980s synths and sequencers. While '60s and '70s analog synths had brought new welcome textures to guitar bands, early digital technology was harsh and cold.

The drop-off in the quality of sounds was mirrored by the precipitous drop of in the quality of the Stones' actual songwriting. "As soon I see the list of songs on that record I think, "Whoops, this is not a balanced concept album, it's all over the shop," Ronnie recalled of *Undercover*. Mick and Keith said all the songs were new for *Undercover*; none were left over from previous sessions. It's easy to think that the Stones started mailing it in around this time. But in fact, the record is a product of overthinking. Case in point: the lead single and title track was actually labored over, built up over tympani drum and Mick on guitar, with outside musicians like master reggae rhythm section, Sly and Robbie, layered on, and the arrangement digitally sequenced and edited to a bloody pulp. There is very little of the Rolling Stones in there, an admirable experiment for a band looking to explore new sounds and textures, but one that left fans of the Stones cold and looking for some characteristics of the band they loved to grab a hold of.

Those fans could take heart in the album's second single, "She Was Hot." If you try to recall the song without listening to it, your memory of it might leap first to the weak chorus. Despite the humor of it, the chorus is the Achilles' heel of "She Was Hot." However, it begins as vintage Stones-Berry, a little muted-rockabilly guitar with a slap-back echo, a snappy variation on a 12-bar blues, with a laconic vocal from Mick. Stu is playing some great old boogie-woogie riffs on the second verse. In short, it sounds like something that could be at home on any record from *Goats Head Soup* to *Tattoo You*. But as soon as the song hits that chorus, it falls apart like the proverbial cheap 1980s Don Johnson pastel suit. And cheap it is, with mildly humorous lines from Mick, but combined in a call/response with an annoying, over the top, multilayered, vocal part, panting out the title ad nauseam.

At least, we hope he is joking. By this point, Mick was separated from his totally "hot" supermodel girlfriend, Jerry Hall, and dogging around with plenty of much younger women. Mirroring Keith's complaints, Hall said Mick was like a genteel Jekyll at home, and an egomaniacal Hyde on tour. Mick has called "She Was Hot" a "road song," about one of his young conquests "on a cold and rainy night." Mick as a lecherous egomaniac was not exactly breaking news. Keith, who had left Anita, was in the process of settling down with another model, Patti Hansen, marrying her in 1983, with Mick as his best man. She was twenty-seven and he was forty (the wedding was on his birthday). They're still together thirty years on, with two adult daughters.

While the bulk of 1980s Stones records seem to be divided up into songs that reflected Keith's vintage heart and Mick's modern calculations, "She Was Hot" combines both. After the retro-rocking sound of the verses, with boogie-woogie piano from Ian Stewart, a chintzy digital synth comes in on the chorus, played innocently enough by Chuck Leavell, who had played with the Allman Brothers, among others (yes, that's Chuck with a virtuoso part on "Jessica"). Leavell had started to tour with the Stones on the European *Tattoo You* tour. He had been a fan of the Stones and a big admirer of Nicky Hopkins since he was a kid growing up in Alabama. Stu was the one who recommended him to the Stones. "The fact is that Stu and I hit it off right away," said Leavell. "I think he and the rest of the band liked that I am from the South. They have a deep affinity for Southern music of all kinds. From my perspective, I felt very comfortable from the first note I played with them at my audition. My attitude was, 'Hey, I played all this stuff when I was a kid in my first bands back in Tuscaloosa, Alabama,' and that seemed to serve me well. I just came as myself, with no pretension and (pardon the pun) no expectations. In the end it all worked out, thank heaven."

But, Leavell fell prey like most did to playing "that damn machine," in Keith's words, the synthesizer. "I'm not a big fan of synth stuff," Leavell admitted. "Sometimes when I hear records—not just Stones records, but any record—that has big synth parts, I think, 'That would be so much better without that noise.' . . . I've done it sometimes and piddled around with it, but it's just not my thing."

As heard on subsequent live versions such as that on the soundtrack for *Shine a Light*, "She Was Hot" definitely sounds better "without that noise." There was some groundbreaking and truly rewarding music from the early 1980s that was based around synths and sequenced drum machines. But rather than something interesting like the 1983 synth-driven song "Blue Monday," from New Order, much of *Undercover* sounds like an even less interesting "Owner of a Lonely Heart," from the band Yes the same year. The harder they (or at least Mick) tried, the more the Stones were losing their musical relevance, even if they maintained their profile via music videos and other outlets. "'Undercover of the Night,' 'Emotional Rescue,' these are all Mick's calculations about the market," said Keith in the 1990s. "And they're not the best records we've made. See, Mick listens to too much bad shit."

One of the most salient observations that Keith makes in *Life* is that somehow, somewhere along the line, Mick, one of the twentieth century's most natural, at-ease performers became "unnatural," and "uncertain . . . forgot his natural rhythm." It's this second-guessing, losing that instinctual confidence that would partially explain how Mick went from the unabashed, uninhibited, loose-limbed lead singer who licked the face of his new bandmate, Ronnie, on national television in 1978, to a self-conscious, calculating trend-jumper. Clearly, Mick's unquenchable curiosity and interest in new music was one of, if not the main driving force, that kept the Stones from being a boring old blues band. Of course, all of the band members brought in their individual set of influences, finding a large area of common ground. But at some point a band has to trust their instincts and not lose sight of what makes them unique to begin with. It was disheartening to watch the Stones lose their way in pursuit of staying atop pop charts in the eighties.

A few of the *Undercover* songs—"Undercover of the Night," "Too Much Blood," "She Was Hot"—are classic eighties songs inasmuch as they were created during an era where pop music was obsessed with embracing novelty, discarding good old analog rock 'n' roll sounds, and tailored for play on a video-hungry MTV. Most of *Undercover* consists of pathetically weak Stones songs. The ones that are worth listening to (and even those, just barely worth it) are the ones that were least beholden to the unfortunate trends of the era—songs like "Wanna Hold You" and "She Was Hot." Many, like me, had given up hopes on the Stones ever putting together another good album. This one sounded like they were toast and had nothing left to say. It was a great time to listen to underground stuff from the UK and on college radio in the States, which is where bands like REM, U2, the Cure, and the Police got their start, all becoming huge commercial successes on their own.

The Stones' day had seemed to pass. For those teens and twenty-somethings like me looking for genuine rock 'n' roll played with the old urgent attitude that the Stones had once displayed, we looked to the small punk and post-punk rock clubs where we could see the Replacements, X, and the Gun Club raving out new renditions of old blues-and-country-based rock music.

45
One Hit (To the Body)

RECORDED:

January–February, April-June 1985, Pathé Marconi Studios,
Boulogne-Billancourt (suburban Paris)
July–August, September–October 1985, RPM Studios,
New York City
November-December 1985, Right Track Studios,
New York City

RELEASES:

LP: *Dirty Work*, March 1986
Single, April 1986, charting at number 80 in the UK and
number 23 in the US

The horrendous atmosphere in the studio
affected everybody.... In retrospect I see the
tracks were full of violence and menace.

—KEITH RICHARDS

As the Stones stayed off the road and wandered the waste-
land of the mid-1980s, things got awfully weird. *She's
the Boss,* a Mick Jagger first solo record, was released in

1985.* This marked the first time in their twenty-year career that Mick or Keith released a solo record. The fact that it's not the oddest Stones news from these years tells you something. That item had to compete with Bill Wyman secretly dating a thirteen-year-old, Mandy Smith, whom he later married, six years later. He was forty-seven when he met her. Not quite creepy enough? Well, how about Bill's son, Stephen, getting engaged to Smith's mother when Stephen was thirty and his fiancé was forty-six? Stephen's son-in-law-to-be/father, Bill, was fifty-six at the time, and Mandy twenty-two.†

While Bill Wyman was wading into Jerry Lee Lewis territory, Ronnie was still struggling with the freebase pipe. Even Charlie had begun to check out. But the biggest hurdle was that Keith and the others felt deeply betrayed by Mick's development of a solo career. "It's like *Mein Kampf*," Keith said of *She's the Boss*. "Everybody had a copy but nobody listened to it." And that's the least vitriolic thing Keith has to say about Mick's solo material. But it was wishful thinking. The single, "Just Another Night," while absolutely dreadful, reached number one in the US, on the wings of an excruciating video featuring Mick tarted up like Tammy Faye Bakker and traipsing around with actress Rae Dawn Chong.

It was just emblematic of a bad time for mainstream music. With consolidation of the record industry, radio, and television into a few corporations, major channels played it safe, going for lowest-common-denominator dreck that filled video channels, and continuing to blindly support proven "classic rock" (then a new term and radio format) and pop dinosaurs. The new CD format gave record companies a chance to repackage and resell back catalogs, amounting to almost pure profit. And such ossification be-

---

* Though not the first solo album from a Rolling Stone. Bill Wyman had released *Monkey Grip* in 1974.

† Bill and Mandy divorced in 1993.

came further encouraged and roped off in the La Brea Tar Pits of music, the Rock and Roll Hall of Fame. While this institution—established in 1983*—might have been well-intentioned, the immediate implication was that the music's past was weighted more heavily than that being created in the present and the future, the MTV vision of which seemed to exist in a gauzy haze with a soundtrack of sequenced drum samples, the aggravating high-pitched buzz of digital synths, and a dearth of ballsy guitars.

Mainstream roots music fans could find some solace as neo-roots acts picked up the torch dropped by the Stones as they followed Mick's quest for eternal youth. Los Lobos, Robert Cray, George Thorogood, Guns 'n' Roses, and the Black Crowes all eventually stepped into the void. And new underground strains and independent record labels started to sprout up in America to satisfy true music fans looking for something of substance: gangsta rap, and ultra-creative hip-hop sampling as alternatives to the light R&B and cartoon rap shown on MTV; thrash, speed metal, and other heavy metal offshoots in response to the nauseating "hair metal" bands; and so-called "post punk" and "college rock" (the latter term a nod to the only type of radio stations then playing the music) started to flourish, filling in a post-punk void for genuine rock 'n' roll. Hüsker Dü, Sonic Youth, Mission of Burma, the Pixies, and many others, started out as club draws in their hometowns, branching out into national and international touring circuits, and paving the way for an "alternative," "indie" music that exploded after the breakthrough of Nirvana in 1992.

That was my world. The Stones had simply become irrelevant to me during the mid-1980s. And, in full disclosure, after *Tattoo You,* I really only kept one wary eye on them, occasionally picking up whatever the current record might be, and never again compelled to rush out to buy the new release to find out what the Stones were

* Keith Richard inducted Chuck Berry in the first class of the Hall of Fame, 1986.

up to. This is not to say they did not continue to release good new songs; in fact, there was almost always at least something on a record worth listening to and that quotient increased on later records. I can't say I felt betrayed by them as much as a natural feeling of, *Oh well, that train has run its course.*

Curiously, though, the Stones' members individually started to collaborate on more interesting, less self-conscious music projects with others, or writing often better songs for later solo projects. Among the many projects he took part in during the mid-'80s, Keith added his stamp to the genius Tom Waits's seminal *Rain Dogs* LP and famously organized the musical portion of *Hail! Hail! Rock 'n' Roll,* the compelling documentary tribute to Chuck Berry from director Taylor Hackford. Meanwhile Bill formed and produced Willie and the Poor Boys*, with contributions from Charlie and Ronnie. Charlie had started his big band the Charlie Watts Orchestra. And Stu and Charlie had been playing with a trad boogie-woogie-based side project called Rocket 88.

The Stones as a unit, though, were bottoming out. Soon after the completion of *Dirty Work,* in December 1985, the day after one of those Rocket 88 gigs, Ian Stewart died at age forty-seven of a heart attack. He would no longer be around to help carry his "little three-chord wonders," as he affectionately referred to the Stones. Stu had in the past been the solid foundation, and organizing force, the rock who never changed, never bent toward trends, didn't take drugs, and kept the guys' egos in check. The Stones were devastated, taking them off guard, leaving them without his rudder, a lingering cloud over the group that lasted years. "His death was very sobering, especially since he led a real clean lifestyle, though what he ate was not always the choicest," writes Ronnie. "That

---

* Formed partially with the intent to raise money for Ronnie Lane and AIMS, a multiple sclerosis charity. Lane was diagnosed with MS in the late 1970s. He died in 1997.

was the irony, that he always warned us not to burn the candle at both ends."

The Stones gathered to play in tribute to Stu in February 1986, and it was the first time they had all been on a stage together in four years. Though *Dirty Work* was completed by the time of his passing, the Stones poignantly added a thirty-three-second rough solo recording of Stu playing an old Big Bill Broonzy boogie-woogie "Key to the Highway" to fade the record out.

So who to turn to for stability? Well, there was Charlie. But he had developed a strange midlife heroin habit, out of nowhere. "It was one of the worst periods in my life," he told *Esquire*. "It was a crisis for me and it was in my midlife. I nearly lost my marriage. . . . I tried these things I'd never done before, like heroin. You can take heroin and nothing happens, then all of a sudden you're hooked on it. I took speed all the time: I'd live three days and sleep two. . . . I looked like Dracula. It was a minor league thing and I stopped it all myself but it was awful for the family." Charlie's slide continued for roughly a three-year period from 1983–86. He says he sobered up completely after a fall down the steps to his basement to get a bottle of wine resulted in breaking his ankle. He stopped drinking, drugs, and even smoking at the time.

And this affected the *Dirty Work* sessions. Bill threatened to leave the band and session drummer Steve Jordan was brought in when Charlie did in fact leave the sessions.* "I went completely berserk," he says. "When we were recording the *Dirty Work* album, I was mad on drink and drugs. I became a completely different person, not a nice one. . . . I was trying to be somebody else—either Humphrey Bogart or Charlie Parker—but it didn't work. I'm not very good on drink."

Not a great atmosphere in which to make a record. And Mick

---

* Ron Wood plays drums on "Too Rude" and "Sleep Tonight."

barely showed any interest in doing so, instead promoting his weak solo album, released coincidentally with the commencement of the sessions for *Dirty Work,* for which he arrived weeks late. Ronnie and Keith, meanwhile, had deepened their friendship and musical collaboration over these years, meeting a couple of nights a week to jam, resulting in four cowrites on the album for Ronnie, including for "One Hit (To the Body)." The lyrics of most of the songs are a black comedy representation of the mood in the band. In fact, the titles alone are reflective of the dyspeptic rancor in the group: "Had it With You"; "Fight"; "Winning Ugly"; and, of course, "One Hit (To the Body)."

The Stones had assembled in Paris in January 1985 for writing sessions. Mick showed up with nothing, apparently. They reassembled in Paris in April 1985. "We hadn't played together since the 1982 tour and it took us a while to get our chops back together, and the 'mind contact,'" Bill told *Creem* in 1986. "We usually jam around for a week and then start seriously getting into tracks. But this time we messed around for three weeks [in April]. Mick was flying back to London to do 12-inch re-mixes and video edits on his solo stuff. That was a sore point." They finished the sessions at RPM in New York in August.

Mick made the choice to hire the big-name producer du jour, Steve Lillywhite, who was having hits at the time with exciting new albums from modern artsy acts like Talking Heads, Simple Minds, U2, Ultravox, Siouxsie and the Banshees, Psychedelic Furs, and Peter Gabriel. But while most of that list might conjure up images of chiming new wave, moussed hair, fog machines, and shirts buttoned up to bolo ties, Lillywhite had cut his teeth pushing faders on old guitar rock bands like Golden Earring, and produced Johnny Thunders's guitar-raunch, *So Alone.* Engineer Dave Jerden, who had spun the knobs on *She's the Boss,* was along for the ride. Jerden later became known for recording alternative guitar-heavy bands in the 1990s. Lillywhite had to overcome Keith's bias of him as Mick's choice of a producer. Ronnie recalled, "Keith turned up at the studio saying, 'All right, who's Mick picked this time? He'd better be good.'"

Lillywhite, Bill notes, "bumped up the drum sound a bit, because Charlie plays very lightly. But as far as the rest of the band is concerned, there's not that much difference. There's lots of good editing, because most of the songs were ten minutes long, and they've all been cut to four for the album. Steve was good at remembering tempos, and was a good guy to bounce ideas off." Well, at least he was good at remembering tempos.

Jerden told writer Steve Appleford of an instance where Lillywhite had processed one of the recorded songs at a higher speed to brighten the tempo during the mixing sessions. "Keith walked in and he just went ballistic," Jerden recalled. "He goes 'Nobody, fucking nobody fucks with the Rolling Stones! That tempo was cut at that speed and it stays at that speed!'" Lillywhite distanced himself from the record a bit later. "Yes, I produced the worst-ever Rolling Stones album," he cracked to an interviewer. "Until the one after, that is."

Is it the worst? I feel *Dirty Work* is a better record than *Undercover*. Does it matter? Let's concentrate on the positives. Lillywhite was known for midwifing new textures without trading the good old sounds in for some cheap synth/sequencer trickery. And on many songs, "One Hit (To the Body)" included, Keith and Ronnie's guitars are full front in the mix, nice and hairy, the way we want 'em. On "One Hit," Keith played a National Resnophonic acoustic, joining the other acoustic played by Ronnie, which begins the track with a droning, pulsing tension. They were joined by Jimmy Page, who overdubbed some torrid solos, similar to what he had pulled out on the final Led Zeppelin album, *In Through the Out Door* (1979). Page and others, such as Bob Dylan, had dropped by during the New York overdub and mixing sessions en route to the giant Live Aid festival in Philadelphia, where Dylan made a poorly received wobbly appearance with Keith and Ronnie. Keith had never been a fan of Zeppelin, but he was present at the session with Page. Jerden said that Page was deferential and respectful and acted more like his pre-Zep role as a session cat.

While the guitars are what they want them to be, the drums just sound appalling, in line with the era. If this is Charlie playing live and unedited, I will eat my hat. During the album sessions he had cut his hand trying to open a nips bottle, requiring stitches, and he couldn't hold the sticks during a significant portion of the session. What's there sounds like a bad drum machine, all clipped and placed tersely within a grid, absolutely devoid of personality and feel. Any life that might have once been there has been sucked out, all of the air and extraneous noise, the humanity that makes records like *Sticky Fingers* and *Exile* so pleasing. Bill is listed as playing bass, but the bass is mixed so quietly as to be an afterthought. Bill could be forgiven for hiding in half-hearted notes placed somewhere on the grid. Lillywhite keeps the low end penned-off somewhere off to the side of the mix, lest someone go looking forensically for a groove. Where have you gone, Jimmy Miller? Stones Nation turned its lonely ears to you.

And then there are the vocals. Mick had by this point cultivated a faux-angry growl, barking out melodies like he wanted to get the whole bothersome business over with, rather than reveling in the sensuality of his best work. And vocal talents have rarely been misused to such abusive purposes as the all-star chorus assembled here, made up of soul pioneers Don Covay and Bobby Womack, along with Patti Scialfa, and actress/singer Beverly D'Angelo.* This is not the potent gospel juice of the golden era.

---

* It is possible that Lillywhite's then-wife, Kirsty MacColl, is also singing. MacColl became well known for singing with Shane MacGowan on the Pogues' "Fairytale of New York" in 1987.

Instead, we have a bunch of people shouting at us from an overly fussy, choppy arrangement. It's like listening to a bunch of angry old drunks arguing in the street. But there is a catchy song under it all, if they had not overproduced it. Keith's riff is convincing and the chorus is memorable. It's not too difficult to imagine what the song might have sounded like if the rhythm section had been allowed to lay into one of their usual funky grooves, Mick had relaxed the vocal approach a bit (less rock and more roll, as Keith would say), and if the production techniques in general did not sound so dated.

The Stones did not even tour on the record. Keith was livid, as he, along with Bill and Ronnie, were eager to get back out there. The decision was made unilaterally by Mick. "It became impossible to run the band the state they were worked up into," Mick said. He was having big-time commercial success with things like the atrocious cover version and video of "Dancing in the Streets," with David Bowie, which was embarrassing in an "Oh, no! Dad and his weird friend are singing old Motown songs after too much wine again!" way.

Because of his success on his own, Mick was also eager to get back and start work on his next solo record. "I didn't really know why they were so worked up, but I think a lot of it was just having too much of a good thing," he said in an interview with Q magazine in 1987. "It was all a bit knackered and I was the one who had to hold it all together and I just lost patience with everybody, it's as simple as that. I just could not deal with them anymore. It was like: don't expect me to pick up the pieces again and put everyone together again and make it whole because I can't be bothered anymore. You have to read between the lines a bit, I'm afraid, but it does come down to two people flying off the handle."

The promo video for "One Hit (To the Body)" captures the tension between Mick and Keith. If looks could kill. . . . Here were the

Rolling Stones, the Greatest Rock 'n' Roll Band in the World playing the part of Duran Duran's* middle-aged uncles in a cast-off set
from some sci-fi B-movie. (By the way, just what *was* the fascination
with *Mad Max* in 1980s music videos?) Director Russell Mulcahy
capitalized on the friction between Mick and Keith. "I guess I was
a little tense," admits Keith. "The director thought it was great and
wanted to get that tension on camera. . . . So the video is kind of
accurate in a way."

Mick didn't start his first solo tour until 1988, but when Keith
learned that Mick was actually vetoing a Stones tour in lieu of hitting the road with his solo act, he told writer Bill Flanagan, "I'll slit
his fucking throat."

---

* In fact, some of Duran Duran came into the sessions to jam with the Stones in April
1985. Just typing that makes me queasy.

46
Slipping Away

RECORDED:

March–May 1989, Air Studios, Montserrat, Virgin Islands

June 1989, Olympic Studios, London

RELEASES:

LP: *Steel Wheels*, August 1989

The Stones Were Just Another Dream That's Slipping Away

For all intents and purposes, the Stones were unofficially broken up from 1986 to 1988 with no touring and Mick and Keith working on solo records. In 1987 Mick released his second album, *Primitive Cool*, containing "Shoot Off Your Mouth," which was only interesting for his kiss-off, seemingly aimed at Keith: "I was a rising star/You hitched your wagon next to mine, mine, mine . . . Right at the moment that you saw my hand first slip/Just like a dirty rat you jumped the sinking ship." The future did not look so bright, eh? In 1987 he stated bluntly about Keith, "I don't feel we can really work together anymore."

Keith felt that Mick had given up and was basically issuing an edict that there would be no touring. Frustrated, Keith had released his own solo debut, *Talk Is Cheap,* in October 1988, and while his songwriting was spotty, it at least had more soul than what Mick was bringing in his first two productions. Keith's material, however, mostly sounded like not-quite-finished song sketches, alley-oop passes that Mick was not there to slam dunk through the hoop.

But they had not broken up. And the fact was that they were getting tired at sniping at each other through the press. Bill and Ronnie acted as go-betweens, relaying phone calls. Both Mick and Keith wanted to start work on another Rolling Stones project. In January 1989, Mick and Keith met in Barbados to talk about the future and start writing for a new album. "The first thing we did was say this has got to stop," Keith writes. "I'm not using the *Daily Mirror* as my mouthpiece. They're loving this; they're eating us alive. There was a little sparring, but then we started laughing about the things we'd called each other in the press. That was probably the healing moment." As Keith rightly points out, the two are not like a married couple and "may not be friends." They were more like brothers. "Best friends are best friends. But brothers fight."

Asked in 1995 if there had been "any talk of putting your heads together and airing issues?" Mick replied, "No, and I'm glad we didn't do that, because it could have gone on for weeks. It was better that we just get on with the job. Of course, we had to revisit things afterward."

Mick and Keith were back in the studio less than two weeks later, an interim during which the Rolling Stones were inducted into the Rock and Roll Hall of Fame by their longtime friend and fan, Pete Townshend.* Townshend offered the perfect eloquent

---

* Mick had inducted the Beatles the previous year.

blend of biting sarcasm, honesty, nostalgia, and heartfelt praise. His closing statement spoke for Rolling Stones Nation:

> There are some giant artists here tonight. But the Stones will always be the greatest for me. They epitomize British rock for me, and even though they're all now my friends, I'm still a fan. Guys, whatever you do, don't try and grow old gracefully; it wouldn't suit you.

It was against this warm and fuzzy backdrop of rekindled relationships, nostalgia, and a genuine ambition to keep it all going that the band returned to the studio, with Chris Kimsey now back at the helm as coproducer with the Glimmer Twins. "I was given associate producer credit [on *Emotional Rescue*], and then further down, a coproducer credit [*Undercover* and *Steel Wheels*], which Mick *hated* giving me!" Kimsey explained. "And it was only a credit, mind you, nothing else!"

"I turned down *Dirty Work*," Kimsey said. "They were just at a point where you'd get one answer from Mick and Keith would completely go the other way. I really couldn't deal with it . . . I said to them, 'I can't do this. This is crazy, I mean you're killing me, 'cause I have eight hours of you [Mick], and eight hours or more with you [Keith] at different times, so I think the next album, you've got to sit down and write songs together before we get back in the studio.'

"And then when I was asked to do the next album, I was busy and Steve [Lillywhite] suffered it. But then the great thing was, after that, they did come back to me for *Steel Wheels* and we sat down . . . and said it would be good to have some songs written before we go into the studio this time. So Mick and Keith went off together to Barbados and spent about six weeks down there getting their relationship back together and writing."

The atmosphere in Barbados was fantastic, says Kimsey. "I

wasn't sure how it would go," he said. "Working with them for so long, they needed cities to get their social life going and they just loved that dynamic of being in a big city. Being on an island was quite different. But it was unbelievable, because Keith said, 'Right, we're going to work Monday through Friday, and weekends off.' It was like: *What?! This can't be!* But his relationship with Patti was just starting, and sure enough, we had weekends off and Keith cooked barbecues out on the beach. And we'd work from about three until nine, we'd have dinner, all together, and then we'd go back in for a few hours and that was it. It was a wonderful routine."

I asked him if he thought Mick and Keith had just gotten to a certain age where the piss and vinegar was gone, were they just worn down?

"Yeah," he replied, "and I think just being in that situation, being on the island, and living with each other, and having dinner with each other, the business, the tour was starting to come together and people were coming to the island to see them, which was really good, so it kept everyone on the same place rather than all of them disappearing and trying to get them all back together again."

Their various side projects sparked new energy within them while reminding them of the special qualities about the Stones that they missed, resulting in a renewed appreciation for each other. "I guess Mick in his own way found out that you can't hire the Rolling Stones, and it doesn't matter if you hire the best musicians in the world, they don't necessarily make a great band," said Keith. "At the same time Charlie found out that he could organize a band and discovered what it actually means to take a big jazz band [Charlie's side project, the Charlie Watts Orchestra] all over the damned world." As Keith went on tour as lead singer and front man, he in turn found out what Mick does in "his day job."

Kimsey had a strong vision going into the record. "I was always thinking of sound all the time, and I was actually interested in having *Steel Wheels* sound very different than anything they'd done before," he explained. "I wanted it to be a wider landscape, a bit more *lush*. A bit more, I don't know, Technicolor, a bit more going on in the production. That's when I stopped recording and became the producer. I'd hired [engineer] Chris Potter to record. We went down to Montserrat and recorded it all down there and came back and did all the overdubs at Olympic, because there were horns, there were backing vocals, there were more overdubs on that album than on the previous albums. And I was very happy with the way it came out. It was a bit more polished sounding, a bit more slick, and I thought it was what I'd intended sonically and production-wise."

"We were incapable of writing to order, to say, we need a rock-and-roll track," writes Keith, speaking about their ratio of ballads versus up-tempo songs on *Steel Wheels* and later records. "Mick tried it later with some drivel. It was not the most interesting thing about the Stones, just sheer rock and roll." More often than not, on later Stones records, Keith would provide a ballad or two, and mix in some reggae tunes.

Keith's voice had aged dramatically in the '80s. On "Slipping Away," the last song on the album, he embraces the bruised husk of his voice and plays up the sweet spot, the ragged emotional tug, the breaking point in his rasp, at opportune moments. The opening verse alone is a study of how to do much with little, his phrasing exquisite. His vocal was now no longer the high-lonesome reedy instrument it used to be. Now Keith had more sonorous depth to his timbre, akin to Tom Waits's more melodious moments, and you can hear more of his chest in his voice. Kimsey captures one of Keith's most emotive performances and does lend the otherwise sparse arrangement elegantly lush production.

Keith is backed up here by a selection of vocalists that have been mainstays with the Stones ever since. Bernard Fowler and Lisa Fischer had both sung with Mick on *She's the Boss* and the subsequent tours. (That was the first time Mick had toured with backing singers and this would henceforth be the arrangement on Stones records and live tours, with Fischer and Fowler usually present, later joined by Blondie Chapman.)

The album was the last project recorded at Sir George Martin's Air Studios in Montserrat, Virgin Islands, before it was destroyed in a volcano eruption. "The room was a difficult room," said Kimsey. "It was quite a small room, and there wasn't much of an ambient sound in it. I had to build a big tunnel for the bass drum to get any sort of bass resonance from the bass drum . . . [The room] was quite dead. It worked out fine, but it was a tight space."

The production of "Slipping Away," leaves plenty of space for Keith's intimate vocal. Some well-placed brass appears, the Kick Horns, particularly pronounced on the two bridges. Matt Clifford, brought in by Kimsey, plays electric piano and strings, while Chuck Leavell plays gentle piano, in the spirit of Nicky Hopkins in one of his quieter moments. "Nicky . . . influenced me heavily, way before I ever played with the band or met him," said Leavell.

Bill Wyman plays a pretty prominent part here, a somewhat more steady R&B sound more in the style of his replacement, Darryl Jones. Nineteen eighty-nine was a huge comeback "dream year," in Keith's words, for the Stones, with a well-publicized album and two massive tours. But *Steel Wheels* marked the last album with Bill.* Bill had been dealing with a progressively disruptive fear of flying. In 1991, Bill informed the band that he would be leaving. "I got really pissed with him," said Keith. "I threatened to do everything in the world to him, including death at dawn—as I always say, *Nobody leaves this band except in a coffin.*" In the end, when it came time for the Rolling Stones to sign a $41 million deal with Virgin, Bill refused to put pen to paper. The Stones would now be down to three original members: Mick, Keith, and Charlie.

---

* He recorded one more single with them, the 1991 Gulf War response, "Highwire" b/w "Sex Drive."

In 1995, Mick said that despite the rejuvenation that the band all felt in 1989, Bill never quite bought back in. "Bill was not enthusiastic to start with—there's a guy that doesn't really want to do much. He's quite happy, whatever he's told to do, but he's not suggesting anything, not helping . . . a bit morose and bored."

"The events of the last few years had convinced me there were other things I wanted and needed to do" writes Bill. "I had to get my personal life in order and then I wanted to explore other creative ideas. . . . It was my career and, as with many people, a job is not necessarily for life."

Bill was the oldest, at fifty-four. I was as guilty as anyone for underappreciating his legacy in the overall sound of the band. Jones, who is an undisputed virtuoso on bass and plays an important role in keeping the sound vital, is not the loose, boogie-woogie, swinging old-school rock 'n' roll cat Wyman is. Jones brings a lot to the table, a young player primarily raised on jazz and funk. Bill's style was that of a guy who was raised on the upright bass of early rock 'n' roll combos and the left hand of boogie-woogie pianists. His later style was informed by American soul and R&B electric bass players like Donald "Duck" Dunn and James Jamerson.

More than anything, though, Bill and Charlie formed the greatest rock 'n' roll rhythm section of their era. When Dunn lost Al Jackson Jr., the MGs never sounded quite the same. The Stones lost a certain groove, that bone juice that Bill slides between Charlie and Keith. Despite occasional variations—Mick Taylor or Keith on bass, Jimmy Miller sitting in on drums—it was one of music's most identifiable and singular sounds, an elusive *je ne sais quoi* that could not be replicated.

Before Bill left, though, he took a stand for Ronnie Wood, who was not made a full partner in the Rolling Stones until 1990. "Before we went to Japan, on the *Steel Wheels* tour, my pals Charlie and Bill stood up for me," Ronnie recalled. "They said, *Are you earning as much as we are?* and I said, *No.* So they said, *Unless you earn as much as us, we're not going to carry on*. They brought this up at a meeting and I thought, *Thank you very much!* Bill and Charlie were very supportive. . . . And the rest of the band said, *Right, okay, we'll finally end your apprenticeship, you're finally part of the band."*

While Bill's departure marked the end of an era, the quality of the music had fallen off dramatically. After a long and fruitful career, everything the Stones produced was now just bonus and many fans just received new albums like they were token gestures to save the band from becoming a pure nostalgia act (as opposed to a 99 percent nostalgia act) and promotional tools to announce big moneymaking tours. If they came up with a good song or two in the process, well, that was just gravy. But the band's decision to soldier on, challenging themselves to write and record new material was admirable. They were pioneers again, this time searching for some way to age gracefully—Townshend's admonition notwithstanding—in rock 'n' roll.

As their great career retrospective documentary, *25X5,* was released in 1993, the Stones were faced with an existential challenge. "The hardest bit from that period, from about 1989 onwards," said Keith, "was the fact that we, the Stones, were thinking, *We're putting it back together again, we're determined to do it and anyway why not?* And at the same time we had to deal with the sledgehammer of people talking about the *wrinkled old rockers* and all of that bullshit. It's a question of how to deal with the music business and the press conception of what you are supposed to do at a certain age. There is also a certain amount of being wished to death, a certain amount of jealousy."

The momentum that would carry the band from the studio, to touring, back to the studio in the old days was not there after *Steel Wheels* and the subsequent world tour. It would take another five years, a few more solo projects, a stint or two in rehab, and a new bass player to get them back in the studio for the next record. Call them semi-retired at this point, but they weren't dead yet.

47
Out of Tears

RECORDED:

September–December 1993,

Windmill Lane Recording Studio, Dublin

January–April 1994, Don Was's studio and

A&M Studios Los Angeles

RELEASES:

LP: *Voodoo Lounge*, July 1994

Single, November 1994, charting at number 36 in the UK

and number 60 in the US

Bringing in New Blood

The Stones continued to come up with some genuinely good songs, especially in the form of heartfelt ballads like this one from Mick. Don Was was coproducer here and Mick later expressed disappointment that Was pushed them to make a "too retro" record. "He tried to remake *Exile on Main Street* or something like that," Mick said. "Plus, the engineer [Don Smith, who had worked with Keith on *Main Offender*] was also trying to do the same thing." Fans of the band, engineers and producers inclusive, wanted the Stones to reclaim their gritty organic past, to find that core around which to form their new records.

"My interview for the job was listening to Keith tell me why he doesn't need a producer," said Was. But he clearly convinced Keith. After all, he brought an impressive CV to the project, having founded Was (Not Was), followed by stints producing Carly Simon, the B-52s, Dylan, and Iggy Pop, among others—in other words, artists who balanced contemporary relevance with weighty histories. "Without realizing it, [engineers/producers] can start trying to recreate albums they heard when they were young," Mick said of this transition, as the Stones grappled with their legacy while forging into the future. "It's a real danger, because once you've done it, I don't really want to do it again." While some producers of legendary artists claim that they can't and won't approach the job as fans, Was does not pretend to have let go of that eleven-year-old in him who waited all night for tickets to see the Stones in Detroit in 1964. He remains awestruck at his role in part as a representative of all fans. "To be sitting in the middle of that room when lightning strikes is the most exhilarating feeling I've ever experienced," he gushes, as most of us would in the same position.

Chuck Leavell, whose piano begins "Out of Tears," had by then worked with Kimsey, Lillywhite, and Was on Stones records. "Don is simply one of the very best," Leavell states. "He understands the music and the people making it. He has an incredible evenness about him and he listens well and earnestly. He does everything he can to accommodate the artist and get them to where they want to be. . . . He has a fabulous set of ears and a deep knowledge of music and music history and is a fine bass player as well."

Speaking of bass players, the Stones were now making a record with a new one, Darryl Jones. Leavell offered a valuable point of view in comparing the two Rolling Stones bassists, as he had played extensively with Wyman and had spent eighteen years (off and on, of course) playing with Jones. There is "a pretty significant difference in styles, but both are masters of what they do," he replied. "Bill is perhaps more melodic in his approach, and Darryl is this amazing well-rounded player with a groove that is always there. Much like I try to pay homage to the piano players that came before me when we do songs that they played on and still put my own style into the mix, Darryl keeps certain elements of Bill in the tunes he is known for and also manages to put his own touch on them. It's a balancing act for both of us."

"You know, I'll tell you what, I was with Keith at his house in Turks and Caicos . . . a couple of years ago," said Bobby Keys. "And he had been listening to a lot of the outtakes from that [*Exile*] period, and he said to me, 'Man, Bobby, I never realized that Bill was such a motherfucker of a bass player!' he said. 'That sonofabitch was really good!'"

Keys continued: "The band sounded one way with Mick Taylor, and with Bill on bass. To me that was the quintessential Rolling Stones sound. . . . And then when Mick Taylor left and Ronnie came, that brought another change but I thought it was a good change." Keys has played live with Jones on many tours. "When Bill left, I thought, *well, that's really gonna change things* and Darryl came and it is a difference but it just sounds a little different than what Bill did," he said. "I love playing with Darryl Jones, man, he's one of the nicest guys and best-rounded bass players I've had the opportunity to play with. . . . You know, the bass situation was left up to Charlie, primarily."

"When Bill left we had to get a new bass player, a totally different bass player from a new generation," Keith writes. "I saw Charlie's face when he started playing with Darryl. It's a jazz connection. . . ." It was indeed Charlie who had the final decision. The Stones auditioned an estimated 25–28 bassists. "I couldn't hear another bass at the end of the week," said Charlie. "Darryl was the best."

Charlie was attracted to Jones's pedigree, which included a tutelage and friendship with the exalted Miles Davis. Prior to working with the Stones, Jones had also worked with Sting, Eric Clapton, and Madonna—other iconic figures, but stylistically disparate. His varied discography speaks to the impressive versatility of Jones. "You know, I've always been interested in playing the best I could with the most talented musicians. Period," Jones said regarding the distinctions.

All of a sudden, this quintessentially "English band," in Keith's estimation, had two full-time Americans in its ranks; the Southern veteran, Leavell, and the young Chicago pro, Jones. "Chicago musicians have a strong influence from Southern blues but are also affected by the urban nature of Chicago," said Jones, while also pointing out that such geographic distinctions mean less in the post-Internet age than in the past. "I think my connection to the blues has helped me fit in with the Stones, and I think Motown, Stax, and Chicago soul have as well. Maybe soul music to a greater extent."

"Darryl is incredibly accomplished, and he can also get down there in a funk," Keith noted at the time. "He's more precise than Bill and there's more power under there now." And Charlie also contrasts Bill's lighter touch and, "almost . . . effeminate kind" of playing to Jones's more driving style. Ronnie points out some differences as well: "Watching from afar when I was working with Bill in the band, I could see the way that Charlie, Bill and Keith interacted: it was the result of this time lapse between Keith's riff, Charlie hitting the beat and Bill hitting it slightly later, which is what gave the original shuddering effect to the songs. Bill had some simple magic . . . Darryl, being such a complete virtuoso, still makes that work, but he also makes it work even more efficiently now."

I asked Jones if he thought that the Stones choosing him was in part an idea of updating their sound to something more contemporary. "That isn't what I've ever had in mind," Jones replied. "Before I joined them, I thought the way I naturally play could fit with them. I've just been trying to fuse into their thing. And I have to admit that I've done better in some instances than in others. Changing something that has worked so well for so long is not the objective. That would be shortsighted. The more difficult and nuanced challenge has been to blend into their sound while not trying to copy what was there before. In this way, the essence remains the same but anything that changes still has the original goal in mind. Not to play the best bass but to play what's best for the songs."

The two new guys—Was and Jones—and the *relatively* new guy, Leavell, all shine here on "Out of Tears." The song's genesis was in the writing and pre-production sessions at Ronnie's home studio, Sandymount, in St. Kildare, Ireland in July 1993. From start to finish, writing to final mixing, *Voodoo Lounge* was produced in seven different studios. Bob Clearmountain's mix of "Out of Tears" was finished at the Right Track in New York. While not as stark and dry as producer Rick Rubin's treatment of Mick's *Wandering Spirit* from the same year, Was presents the music within a completely natural and mercifully unfussy tableau.

Leavell picked up a piano line written by Mick, who wrote the whole song on his own. "'Out of Tears' was a little bit like that [spontaneous], where I'm sitting at the piano in Ronnie's studio going *Da da ding, da da ding,*" said Mick. "Then you go and listen to it, and it's got this really good mood because it's you on your own. No one else is there, and you're creating the mood. There's a very sad mood to that song. The Stones are mainly a guitar band, but I think with a ballad sometimes it's nice to move away from that. And when a song is written on a keyboard, you get a different sort of melodic structure." It echoes "Memory Motel" with its piano-driven verses.

An early demo exists on a bootleg, with just Mick on piano and Charlie on drums. Mick teases out a basic version of the part that is honed by Leavell on the record. "It was his little riff, and it reminded me of Nicky," said Leavell. "I embellished it a bit, thinking of Nicky the whole time. WWNHD (What Would Nicky Hopkins Do?). It's a lovely little piece and Mick had most of it done when we learned it."

Nicky had "desperately wanted to" tour with the Stones again, according to his sister, Dee, and he had contacted them to see if he might be able to join them for the *Steel Wheels* tour. But though Nicky was sober at the time, he had been through some well-known struggles with substance abuse and was in ill health. The Stones passed along their regrets that they could not have him along on the tour. "He was heartbroken," Dee Hopkins told Julian Dawson, author of Nicky's biography. In 1993, the Rolling Stones paid some of Nicky's hospital bills stemming from a "life-threatening medical crisis," according to Dawson.

On September 6, 1994, as the band was on the *Voodoo Lounge* tour, Nicky Hopkins passed away at age fifty from his lifelong health complications, Crohn's disease, exacerbated by substance abuse. Bobby Keys was the only one from the Stones' camp that was able to attend the funeral, where he read a letter from Leavell explaining how much Hopkins had meant to him musically and personally. The Rolling Stones sent flowers and a card to his widow, Moira, reading, "To Diamond Tiaras. A good friend, sadly missed.—The Rolling Stones, Mick, Keith, Charlie, Ronnie and Bill."

The influence of Nicky Hopkins is certainly evident on the song, which sounds like it could be from the Stones' classic era of the early-to-mid-seventies. The bittersweet melody of the song was already in place on the demo, with a few lines of lyrics, including the title refrain. The band recorded the album version there as well. It was further fleshed out with flutey organ by Benmont Tench, of Tom Petty and the Heartbreakers, in Los Angeles. Was treats the piano with what sounds like a genuine tape echo, with a slight bit of flutter and quivering decay to the delay, which is also used on Ronnie's memorable slide guitar solo.

Mick is in superb voice on the single version. The most satisfying aspect is that he sings within himself, stays within his wheelhouse, and gives an ungarnished, straight, and soulful reading of the ballad, avoiding any artifice and steering clear of the clipped bark he seemed to slip into in the later years. His emotion comes through in the last verse, where he brings it down to a whisper. It sounds as if Mick handles all the backing vocals, certainly a harmony on the choruses, but also the answer part on the choruses. Mick also plays a very bright, crisp acoustic guitar. By the end, the production gets a little more syrupy, something like "Angie," with a similar swelling string arrangement.

The best we could hope for was a mixed bag on these later albums. The Stones' dignified ballads took on even more gravitas with the patina of their age, wisdom, and all that maturity stuff. They treated these lyrics more seriously and they displayed more craft than the rockier numbers. From a songwriting standpoint, *Voodoo Lounge* was a pretty encouraging and more consistent record than anything since *Tattoo You*, meaning the best batch of *new* material since *Some Girls*. Still, Mick was ambivalent about looking too far into past references when recording new material. "I think both Charlie and I didn't really like [*Voodoo Lounge*'s similarities to the sounds on their vintage records], but we could see that that was the direction you could go, and it might be successful. I don't think it really was that successful, because I don't think there's any point in having these over-retro references. I think it was an opportunity missed to go in another direction, which would have been more unusual, a little more radical, although it's always going to sound like the Rolling Stones."

48
Saint of Me

RECORDED:

March–July 1997, Ocean Way Recording Studios,
Los Angeles
February–March 1997, PCP Labs
(The Dust Brothers' studio) Los Angeles

RELEASES:

LP: *Bridges to Babylon*, September 1997
Single, January 1998, charting at number 26 in the UK
and number 94 in the US

I Know That I'm a Sinner

Coming off the huge tours for *Voodoo Lounge,* Mick was seen making the rounds with young hotties like actress Uma Thurman and model Jana Rajlich, gracing the gossip rags and pissing off his somewhat older hottie, his on-off partner Jerry Hall. So here he was on "Saint of Me," poking fun at his image as an aging Don Juan. "Augustine knew temptation, he loved women, wine and song/And all the special pleasures of doing something wrong," points out biblical scholar and rock singer, Mick Jagger.

The man only seemed to double down on being Mick Jagger. Hall had tolerated much of his philandering, but fathering an illegitimate child with a Brazilian model half his age (Luciana Gimenez Morad) was pretty much the last straw for their twenty-year relationship. "I find it quite easy to detach myself from Mick's private life but then it's ludicrous because it's not private at all," said Keith. "I sometimes see what the old bugger wants in life, he's intent on being Casanova or Don Juan. He's always looking for it, which is a little cruel on his loved ones. But he's always been like that. I don't talk to Mick about his love life, because it's like *Whoops! You've skidded on another banana skin!*"

Throwing up his hands, Mick sings his reputation off on this track, from *Bridges to Babylon:* "I know that I'm a sinner, I'm going to die here in the cold . . . [but] . . . You'll never make a saint of me." The track begins spontaneously. It seems they decided to keep the warming-up noises—someone shifting in a chair, Ronnie trying out his guitar riff—and then Billy Preston's organ comes in playing gospel chords. So far, sounds like vintage Stones. (This was the first Stones studio recording with Preston since 1976, though he was on *Love You Live, Tattoo You,* and Mick's *Wandering Spirit.*)

Next, Mick's vocal comes in with that quivering half-whisper he uses sometimes to intimate an intense little story, testifying over Billy's churchy organ. Meshell Ndegeocello enters on bass here, just more or less pedaling on the root notes. For some reason, Mick and/ or the track's production team, the Dust Brothers and Don Was, decided they needed a second bass, this one a 6-string played by the band's guitar tech and side-musician, Pierre De Beauport. If you're keeping score, that's ten strings of bass to play about four notes.

But the track kicks. "Saint of Me" is an indication of the Stones rediscovering the magic mojo behind their great up-tempo songs. Along with *Bridges to Babylon*'s lead-off track, "Flip the Switch," "Rough Justice," which is the lead off track from their next album, *A Bigger Bang,* there were some convincing new rockers they could use to pepper their albums and live set lists. The lyrics of "Saint of Me" and these others at least had some substance to them aside from being rocking songs about rocking out. "Saint of Me," though, is not some study in nostalgia. It combines the gospel of classic tracks like "Shine a Light," a catchy sing-along chorus, and a descending three-chord progression reminiscent of "Sympathy For the Devil," with an updated, crisp, and percussive mix. It sounds at once modern and classic, new and timeless. This is not an easy thing to pull off and it is precisely what Mick was going for.

"I talked to Keith about it. I talked to everyone in the band about it," he said. "I didn't want to do a record same as the last record, *Voodoo Lounge*—I don't want to do that record again. . . . The other thing was, if I write a song, or Keith writes a song, or we write one together, if I see it one way, I want to try it. I don't want to be some committee where everyone has 10 cents' worth of it. That's the bad part of being in a band."

The game plan that Mick laid out resulted in what has been referred to as "the Rolling Stones' *White Album*," for the manner in which they produced *Bridges to Babylon*. They built it up in components, with Mick, Keith, and Ronnie all commanding individual rooms at Ocean Way Studios modularly, using different producers and engineers, and bringing their core ideas to the band to finish off. Mick noted that some songs, "that lend themselves to other treatments can be taken out of that live environment for a moment and brought back and rebuilt. . . . And so Charlie and I talked a lot about the different ways of creating this. Changing the grooves a little bit . . . because you get a slightly different feel than you would get than if you play live."

Mick and Keith started out in writing sessions at Dangerous

Music, a modest studio in Greenwich Village. Over the winter of 1996, there were trips back and forth between New York and London, using a place there called Westside Studios. But they ended up working at Ocean Way Recording Studios in Los Angeles over the spring of 1997, taking over four rooms at the facility. The band were rejuvenated in Los Angeles, recording a record there for the first time since the 1960s (aside from the overdubs and mixing they had done throughout their career). Many of their recent sessions had been in remote studios on tropical islands, or in rock 'n' roll-bereft Paris.

In LA, the band also had their friends coming down to contribute. One of the X-Pensive Winos, Waddy Wachtel, is here on "Saint of Me," likely on the solo, and Blondie Chaplin is singing a great low harmony, on the chorus. South African Chaplin had been a member of the Beach Boys during their very interesting early-mid-1970s *Carl and the Passions/Holland* period. That's him singing lead on "Sail On Sailor." Bernard Fowler is here as well.

Mick chose to work with the Dust Brothers—a team consisting of Mike Simpson and John King—here, known for their work with Beck and the Beastie Boys (read: the youths). "Initially, Mick expressed an interest in working with us. He knew the Beck record [*Odelay*] and [the Beastie's] *Paul's Boutique,* and he asked if we'd ever recorded a band before," said Simpson. "We sat down with him and talked for about twenty minutes, just philosophically, about music in general. Then Mick said, *Oh, this is all nonsense. Let me just play you some stuff.*"

In the pair's private studio in young-hipsterville, Silver Lake (LA), Mick started fooling around with a classic old drum machine, a Roland 808, and using a digital keyboard, much as he had done when making home demos. Mick recalls: "I'm going, *I wonder if this is really such a good idea I'm doing this. . . .* So I'm sitting there playing my keyboard and playing 'Saint of Me' and I'm thinking, *Sounds like shit, this is terrible, how is it ever going to work out? . . .*

And it was very, you know, it's quite slow. I was having fun with it, but it's very low tech in that studio and I just didn't know how it was gonna build up." But true to the innovative spirit of the album, Mick brought the kernel into the studio and built it up in there, with Charlie overdubbing live drums, the backing singers, Preston on organ, Ronnie and Wachtel on electric guitars, Mick on acoustic, and another keyboardist, Jamie Muhoberac. Mick is listed on keys as well. (It is not immediately clear why two basses and three keyboardists were needed here, as it is a very simple track.) That all of this does not overburden the song, and in fact results in a light and sharp sound, is likely due to the superb radio-friendly mix of Tom Lord-Alge, who was a very hot name at the time.*

With contributions from producers like Don Was, the Dust Brothers, Rob Fraboni (who had done some work on *Goats Head Soup* and produced some classic records from The Band and Bob Dylan), and Danny Saber (producer and member of the post-Happy Mondays band Black Grape), as well as twenty contributing side musicians, *Bridges to Babylon* was an ambitious record that produced some truly compelling music. Keith was not thrilled with the concept and ended up doing all of his work with Fraboni and Was.

"Actually, I had very little to do with [the Dust Brothers]. I'm like, *What do you want me to do?* And they're like, *Oh, just do what you always do.* I'm thinking, *That's producing?*" Charlie said, "Although I found it really interesting, I knew that I would hate to make records like that [building up records in pieces] on a permanent basis, because then it becomes a producer's game—it's got nothing to do with the musicians at all."

---

* Lord-Alge's brother, Chris, also is an in-demand mixer and worked on a track from my band, Buffalo Tom.

49
Biggest Mistake

RECORDED:

August 2004, June 2005, La Fourchette

(Mick Jagger's home studio), Pocé-sur-Cisse, France

RELEASES:

LP: *A Bigger Bang*, September 2005

UK Single, August 2006, charting at number 51

Kicking Cancer and Being Knighted

Most of the talk surrounding the Stones by the mid-2000s was about the very existence and survival of the band and its members more than the new music they produced. In 2005, though, the usual conversation starter, *Can you believe Keith is still alive?* was usurped by *Have you heard Charlie has throat cancer?* Charlie was diagnosed in 2004, just as the band was gearing up for another record and tour.

"I'd had a lump in my neck for two or three years," said Charlie. "It was diagnosed as benign but then the doctor took it out, found it was cancerous, and then they found it in my left tonsil, too. I lay there thinking, *Well, normally you die.* . . . When I first found out about the cancer, I literally went to bed and cried. I thought that was it, that I'd only have another three months."

As we know, Charlie successfully battled the disease, but in the meantime, Mick and Keith had started the process of writing new material from scratch, shelving most of the thirty or so songs that they had recorded before the *40 Licks* Greatest Hits LP. Four originals were salvaged for *40 Licks,* including the excellent "Don't Stop," a riff-heavy up-tempo single designed to reach the back rows of stadiums, in the spirit of "Start Me Up." The Stones seemed to have their footing again in their ability to write confident up-tempo rock songs.

They had so much new, fresh material from the new writing sessions for *A Bigger Bang,* however, that there was no need to go back and revisit what they had started back in Paris in 2002. As Charlie had said, "The magic of the band is when Mick and Keith are [writing] together. What would be wonderful is if they ever sat down together and started writing together from scratch." And this is what the two were doing at Mick's house in France in 2004 as Charlie recovered back home.

The remarkable creative energy that resulted from writing together continued to produce vital results. So positive was the flow at Mick's house that they decided to record the whole record, *A Bigger Bang,* there. "There was a point I'm sure where he wanted to kick us out," said Keith. "But as I said to Mick, 'Listen, once upon a time, we cut a record in the South of France in my house, and it's called *Exile on Main Street,* and now it's your turn.'" They certainly had some individual ideas that they brought in, such as Keith's blistering "Rough Justice," but Charlie's illness brought the pair closer together personally and creatively than they had been in decades, so they wrote mano a mano. Keith said, "It's probably the closest that Mick and I have worked together since *Exile on Main Street.* Which says it all."

The result is a stripped-down album devoid of all the post-modern self-consciousness of *Bridges to Babylon.* In a way, it took the live-club spirit of *Some Girls,* and the "Let's make a record at my house" feeling of the old *Exile*-era days at Stargroves and Nellcôte to a new level. The Rolling Stones Mobile Unit no longer needed to be parked outside, though. With the revolution in digital technology, the whole contents of the Mobile were made virtually archaic, reproducable on a laptop. Likewise there was no need for separate control rooms, and though it would make real-time monitoring a challenge, Don Was's M.O. was always to be in the live room with the band during their performances anyway. He was thrilled to see Mick and Keith collaborating, everyone back in the same room together. "[Don Was] is always worried the songs won't sound like the Rolling Stones," said Mick at the time. "I don't care if it sounds like them—us. It would be an achievement if it didn't."

"Only Mick still thinks you have to take things into 'real' recording studios to really make a real record," Keith writes. "He got proved totally wrong on our latest—at the time of writing—album, *A Bigger Bang,* especially, because we did it all in his little château in France. We had got the stuff worked up, and he said, *Now we'll take it into a real recording studio.* And Don Was and I looked at each other . . . Fuck this shit. We've already got it down right here. Why do you want to spring for all that bread? So you can say it was cut in so-and-so studio, the glass wall and the control room? We ain't going nowhere, pal. So finally he relented."

When Charlie arrived, healthy and rested, he played as if he had something to prove, jettisoning Mick from the drum stool, where he had often been perched before Charlie's arrival, laying down basic beats during the initial writing and recording sessions. Ronnie hadn't really played much on basic tracks since *Steel Wheels.* So it is the same here, where he overdubbed his parts. "In the studio, [Keith and I are] not in the same room together. I'm usually with Mick and Don Was. Keith will often do his bits first. But One-Take Ronnie—that's what they call me. I'm always better on the first take. They'll play me the song, then they'll play it again for me to play on, and I'll do my thing: a lick here, a lick there, and sometimes bring in the slide. . . . I did all my overdubs in four days."

"Biggest Mistake" captures that simplicity. The song has that tinge of Solomon Burke, Arthur Alexander, and Don Covay, soul singers who melded their R&B roots with pop and country influences. Also detectable is the influence of Bert Berns, who had been the songwriter on songs like "Cry to Me," and "A Little Bit of Soap," a pseudo-Latin influence that can be heard here. It fits the Stones canon, from their cover of "Under the Boardwalk," through "Waiting on a Friend."

With contributions and collaborations that Mick and Keith had over the past twenty years with other iconic artists, like Tom Waits, Dwight Yoakam, Willie Nelson, and Peter Wolf, they had served up great country, soul, and rock 'n' roll. When Mick in particular worried less about making new "Rolling Stones" albums, they often come up with less self-conscious organic-sounding material, resulting in just plain better songs. Mick seemed to come around to Keith's point of view that the band didn't need to worry about whatever trend was happening at the time. Of course, this is not to say that there was not tremendous value to Mick keeping his fingers on the pulse of the underground, the indie hits, modern dance music and so on. It is his drive that kept the band moving forward, while in Charlie's estimation, it was balanced by Keith's spirit. Surely over forty years, the scale had to be rebalanced from time to time. For the first ten years, they seemed to be in perfect synch.

The Stones had long moved past any notions of ending the band. What else can a poor boy do? "Either we'd stay home and become pillars of the community or we'd go out and tour," Mick said at the time. "We couldn't really find communities that still needed pillars. I sing in a rock and roll band so I go on the road. It's not much more complicated than that. That's what my life is."

Yet apparently there was at least one more community that

wanted another "pillar of society." On June 14, 2002, at Queen Elizabeth II's birthday honors list, it was announced that Mick Jagger was to be knighted. Keith was one of those who would not be referring to Mick as "Sir" any time soon. "What did I feel when I heard about the knighthood?" he said. "Cold, cold rage at his blind stupidity. It was enraging, I threatened to pull out of the tour—went berserk, bananas! But, quite honestly, Mick's fucked up so many times what's another fuck up?" Mick told Keith that it was Tony Blair's insistence that Mick accept the knighthood. "You can turn down anything you like, pal, was my reply." Keith's position is that Mick was duped into going from "us" to "them." "The Mick I grew up with, here's a guy who'd say shove your little honors up your arse."

Charlie mused. "Anybody else would have been lynched: eighteen wives and twenty children and he's knighted. Fantastic!"

Sir Mick or not, he brings a certain amount of sincere humility to "Biggest Mistake." Mick sings the song with conviction, a dead honest lyric about messing up a good thing. On this one, Mick came out of his shell. He admitted as much. "Of course, you are as vulnerable as anyone else. It's crazy to think someone can't be hurt just because he's famous or he struts across a stage. If you go back through Stones albums, I'm sure you'll find vulnerability along with the swagger," said Mick. "It may not have been as easy to see, though, because it's not my temperament to share that feeling. I've often hid my feelings with humor. This time the songs were written very quickly, and I was in a certain frame of mind. I thought about some of the words afterward to see whether they were too personal, but I decided to just let them stay. Keith was very encouraging. . . ." It's that sort of honesty that makes all the difference in such songs. It may not be as obvious as knowing the exact source, but discerning fans can often tell right off the bat when Mick is once again singing about something real.

The band is just down to the basic core here, with Darryl Jones on bass and Chuck Leavell on organ. Leavell meshes in with the falsetto melodic hook that Mick uses to open and close the song. It would seem a perfect song to have some piano as well. "I don't always get my way with the band," he told me. "Certainly I would have played a piano part on that song, and there have been many other songs where I spoke my mind in the early stages of working it up only to be shot down in the end. There have been many tunes that I recorded parts that are either buried in the mix or that were just left off. Unfortunately, I don't get the last word on those matters."

Keith's spontaneously sloppy harmonies, and a brief ad-libbed counter-melody coming out of the bridge, are refreshing bits of Stones soul. Keith's backing vocals were appearing less frequently on each record, and certainly in live performances. His backing harmonies were whittled to a precious few and far between as the band transitioned from touring with backing singers to having them record with the band. The absence of simple things like that and Bill's touch on the bass had outsized impact on the overall band sound. Changing a band's dynamic over decades is inevitable. There is no sense in moaning about it. However, it's also inarguable that when such elements are successfully restored—be it Mick's sincerity, Keith's vocals, a post-Stones Mick Taylor overdub on an old outtake, or Bill laying down his gentle thumping bass again in 2011 on the Stones' Dylan cover, "Watching the River Flow"—it pleases the ears and warms the hearts of old Stones fans.

50
Plundered My Soul

RECORDED:

July and October–November 1971, Villa Nellcôte,
Villefranche-sur-Mer, France
(Keith Richards' rented house)
Autumn 2009, Henson Recording Studios,
The Village, Mix This! (All in Los Angeles);
One East Studio, New York City;
Unidentified studio in London

RELEASES:

LP: *Exile on Main Street Deluxe Reissue,*
May 2010; Single, April 2010, charting
at number 200 in UK

I'm lucky to have been with [Mick and Keith].
There's a magic about them that people like.
They always argue, but they always love each
other. . . . I'm fortunate to be in there as part of
that.

—Charlie Watts

> People distill their stories over time and they
> polish them up. And after a while you don't
> know whether they're true or not.
>
> —Mick Jagger

Talk about pleasing the ears of an old Stones fan; I literally pulled over in my car when I heard this for the first time on the radio. It sounded so much like vintage Stones, with an unmistakably current-sounding sheen of production, that I assumed it had to be some other, contemporary band adroitly mimicking prime-era Stones. What does it say that my first impression was that it would be another band doing the Stones as opposed to the Stones themselves reclaiming their Holy Grail sound, their secret formula, thought to be lost forever, buried under the cellar floors in Nellcôte?

But in just a few bars, it became clear that it was Mick singing. It sounded like current Mick singing over vintage Stones. They had not achieved that groovy laconic shuffle since *Some Girls*, if not *Exile on Main Street*. I thought that the band must have a new song, and that they had again struck, finally and truly, on the elusive mojo of their peak years. Unlike the "boy who cried wolf" pronouncements of graying rock critics declaring that the "Stones are back, with their best since *Exile on Main Street*," this really sounded like they were back indeed. It's a truly stunning recording.

Well, of course I soon learned that the record was a *Tattoo You*–like resuscitation of an outtake from those vintage years, specifically the *Exile on Main Street* sessions, and it was released to promote the remastered and repackaged 2010 release of *Exile*. But to this day, I count it as one of my favorite songs from the band. As soon as those guitars bend up and down, and Charlie comes in that typically off-kilter way, only to all click in and have the band fall in behind him, those old emotions well up and my heart swells.

With Nicky Hopkins, Bobby Keys on a baritone sax, Bill Wyman, and Jimmy Miller coming through the speakers like old friends, all that glue is back, that singular early-'70s hash. It contains that same crispy-fried-sunsetting-summer-hangover melancholy as "Tumbling Dice." It has that same heartbreaking tempo, and is one more of those "sad poems" that Kerouac wrote about. While it lacks the same sort of addendum outro, it does have a similar stand-alone intro lick as the familiar "Tumbling Dice."

Where did it come from? Didn't all you Stones completists think you had heard pretty much all worthwhile outtakes? How did they not find this when they were looking for old material for *Tattoo You*? Well, the Stones have a warehouse that Don Was compares to the one seen at the end of *Raiders of the Lost Ark*, "a mini-Smithsonian," that "goes on for blocks," of all the tape they rolled over the decades. And they were notorious for rolling tape continuously during their marathon sessions. Was got the job of not only remastering and repackaging the official release of *Exile*, but also the pillaging and plundering of those vaults, and shining up recordings that had only been around as bootlegs.

When they dusted off the old tapes and found "Plundered My Soul," the whole basic track of the song was there—bass, drums, piano, and rhythm guitars, all arranged and ready for vocals. But Mick reckons that he and Mick Taylor had been absent from, or arrived late to, the session that day in France. Mick overdubbed the lead vocal against a backdrop of new backup parts from Lisa Fischer and Cindy Mizelle, as well as an acoustic guitar and Taylor's leads in 2010. Everyone else is there on the backing track, playing in the same impossibly relaxed cadence. Charlie comes back in from those chorus breaks so unbelievably slow that you think there is *no way* he is going to get back to the beat in time.

Taylor's 2010-overdubbed lead lines sound very much of the time and place as the original backing tracks. They could come pretty close to matching the sounds if they followed the old crinkled sepia map: used the same guitar, amp, microphone, and player and possibly even print it onto analog tape before mastering it digitally. However, it would be impossible for Was to somehow match Mick's twenty-eight-year-old voice with sixty-two-year-old Mick. As with all of us, the tonality of his voice had changed over the years. And though Mick brought a dynamic and assured performance, singing a compelling lyric with steadfast conviction, the lead vocal is the one element that takes you out of the song a bit. But you can get by it. And repeated plays bring the reward.

As a college kid, Was had bought *Exile* upon the first week of its release, just as he had with all records up to *Voodoo Lounge* (when he got a "free copy" as the producer), he told NPR. But he initially found *Exile* "alarming . . . there was a sense that the revolution had been lost [laughs]." He notes, "Something like 'I Just Wanna See His Face,' [sic] it's funky, but it's a weird thing for *anyone* to be making in 1972." It's interesting that he brought up that song as an example. I would have suggested that he give Mick's vocal on "Plundered My Soul" the same sort of off-mike, low-fi, semi-distorted sound to mask Mick's contemporary voice. But, not surprisingly, I did not get the call to be producer.

Was *did* get the call and the charge of making the tracks ready to be heard. In many cases, especially those tracks from Olympic in 1969, they were on eight tracks, which meant that EQ, compression, and mixing decisions had to be committed to and printed to the master tapes, as opposed to recording just the flat, unprocessed signal and fooling with it later. So in the case of the jaw-dropping, super-sloppy-but-funky "Loving Cup" outtake from the *Let It Bleed* sessions (or as Was says, "it's not sloppy; it has width and depth"), Mick's and Keith's vocals were recorded, compressed, and EQ'd, with added echo, and mixed to one track of the eight available.* So if you were to

---

* This version of "Loving Cup" was a well-known bootleg, unlike "Plundered My Soul."

listen back to the master tape (not the two-track stereo mixes) most of the finished sound is already there. Though they had more tracks with which to work on the multitrack machines in France for *Exile,* Andy Johns and Jimmy Miller would have recorded many of the actual treated sounds and sub-mixes to the master tapes, resulting in the magical sound of *Exile* heard here on "Plundered My Soul."

Mick has talked about having to get into character, into the frame of mind he was in 1971, and he does capture much of the spirit on "Plundered My Soul." "He did not try to write as if he were still twenty-eight years old," said Was. "To his credit, I must say that he wrote from the perspective of who he is today. In fact, it was a very emotional session for me. Because just hearing him, just *watching* him do it, the visual that came, I saw the video in my head, [laughs] and it was him walking through that house in Nellcôte, but today, and there were like sheets over the furniture. . . ." As Keith told the *Chicago Tribune* in 2010, "I enjoyed going back through [*Exile*]. Going back through the tracks, I could smell that basement and all the dust. It was very evocative."

Keith, never one for the phone or email, but a great lover of the fax, faxed a handwritten note to Was before the 2010 sessions that read, "You don't have to make it sound like *Exile*. It *IS Exile*." At another point, Keith had also said that messing around with the album could be "like drawing a mustache on the Mona Lisa." It's a thankless task stepping into the job of producing the Stones in general, but certainly repackaging something as sacred as *Exile*. Any producer is going to get a backlash from old curmudgeonly Stones fans. But at the very least, Was's work with the band—old and new stuff alike—adhered to the old physician's adage, *first, do no harm*. He was conscious of overstepping, but wanted to make sure the finished overdubs were things that people wanted to listen to repeatedly, not just once out of curiosity. His charge, as he saw it, was to make Jimmy Miller proud. "I thought of myself as his designated driver," he said.

This plundering of the archives continues through 2012 with *Some Girls*, the *Brussels Affair*, packages of old live concerts and films, live DVDs, and all the inevitable and welcome hoopla for their fiftieth anniversary. Old suckers like me shell out money for stuff like a Scorsese Imax concert movie and official releases of music we have had on various bootleg copies since we were kids. Even after all of the favorite new artists we've discovered over the ensuing decades, the Stones are our guys. We make pilgrimages and pay homage via the heart-stopping face value of tickets that would have shamed even the most unrepentant scalpers in the old days.

"Plundered My Soul" went a long way to scratch that itch of nostalgia. As much as Mick is loath to admit it, nostalgia itself, just like "Tumbling Dice" and all of *Exile on Main Street,* is somehow engrained within the very marrow of the Stones bones. That same yearning can still be heard in Mick's sixty-something voice as he ad-libs out of "Plundered My Soul," as if that old music did indeed bring him walking back through the ghostly dreamscape of Nellcôte that Don Was had envisioned.

They are mythological heroes who still—miraculously, in Keith's case—walk amongst us. The image that we carry with us—of their lives as demigods who have discovered the Holy Grail and the "Secret Sign/That's known to all the artists who have known true gods of sound and stone"*—fuels this legend, the lies and the half truths, the glamorous sheen that glosses over the often ugly reality.

Sure, many want to slurp up the slimy gossip rags' latest litany of Ronnie's rehab stints or tawdry altercations with some juvenile Soho cocktail waitress, or Mick's latest May–December conquest. And who among us didn't laugh when we heard about Keith falling out of a Fiji coconut tree as the reason for the suspension of the Bigger Bang tour—but only after we found out he was all right. (Could you imagine the irony if he died *that* way?) We marvel at

* Patrick Kavanaugh's song-poem, "On Raglan Road."

the Rolling Stones as truly great artists who have collaborated for fifty years on a phenomenon so much bigger than any of them individually. The body of work is monumental, without parallel, and it seems certain that no one will ever come close to an approximation.

As the Stones hit their fiftieth anniversary, we "Raise a glass for the hardworking people." As long as they keep going, partying in the face of it, they shine a light in the darkness and give funky form to life's splendor.

Acknowledgments

Thanks to my wife, Laura St. Clair. (I am lucky to be married to a professional editor.) And thanks to my children, Lucy and Will, for the space, time, and support.

I am grateful to Kevin Pocklington at Jenny Brown and Associates for the inspiration and for getting this stone rolling.

And thanks, especially, for the patience and guidance of Kathryn Huck at St. Martin's Press.

Peter Guralnick offered advice and also shared with me a short piece he had written for the *Times of London* about seeing the Stones in 1965. It had not yet been published at the time.

Graham Parker's quotes about Nicky Hopkins are repeated here from my previous book.

Joe Viglione worked with Jimmy Miller in the 1980s and shared some recollections with me in e-mail and on the phone. (This material copyright © 2012 Viglione Archives). Given a relative lack of written material about, and/or interviews with Miller, Joe helps keep his memory alive and fosters an appreciation for Miller's contributions to the golden years of the Stones.

And thanks to those who helped facilitate communication with others, lent or gave me books, or otherwise provided support:

Chris Ballman, Dan Beeson, Rudy Calvo, Peter Catucci, George Christin, Audrey Schwartz, Chris Colbourn, Bernard Corbett, Robert Greenfield, Tom Maginnis, Morgan Neville, Mike O'Malley, Tom Perrotta, Tom Polce, and Matt Spiegel.

Sources

Interviews

Tariq Ali, e-mail, August 2012

Merry Clayton, e-mail and phone, August and November 2012

Andy Johns, phone, August and September 2012

Darryl Jones, e-mail, July and September 2012

Bobby Keys, phone, July 2012

Chris Kimsey, phone, June 2012

Al Kooper, in person, May 2012

Chuck Leavell, e-mail, July 2012

Andrew Loog Oldham e-mail, May and October 2012

Dick Taylor, e-mail, August 2012

Steve Morse, e-mail, November 2012

Books

Appleford, Steve, *The Rolling Stones: Rip This Joint: The Stories Behind Every Song*, New York: Thunder's Mouth Press, 2000

Booth, Stanley, *The True Adventures of the Rolling Stones*, New York: Vintage Books, 1984

Buskin, Richard, *Inside Tracks: A First-Hand History of Popular Music from the World's Greatest Record Producers and Engineers*, New York: Avon Books, 1999

Charone, Barbara, *Keith Richards: Life as a Rolling Stone*, New York: Dolphin Books, 1982

Dawson, Julian, *And on Piano . . . Nicky Hopkins: The Extraordinary Life of Rock's Greatest Session Man*, San Francisco: Backstage Press, 2011

Dodd, Philip, *According to the Rolling Stones*, San Francisco: Chronicle Books, 2003

Egan, Sean, *The Rolling Stones and the Making of Let It Bleed*, London: Unanimous, Ltd., 2005

Elliott, Martin, *The Rolling Stones Complete Recording Sessions*, London: Blandford, 1990

Faithfull, Marianne with David Dalton, *Faithfull: An Autobiography*, New York: Little, Brown & Co., 1994

Flanagan, Bill, *Written in My Soul: Conversations with Rock's Great Songwriters*, New York: Contemporary Books, 1986

Greenfield, Robert, *Exile on Main St.: A Season in Hell with the Rolling Stones*, Cambridge: De Capo Press, 2006

Guralnick, Peter, *Sweet Soul Music: Rhythm and Blues and the Southern Dream of Freedom*, New York: Harper Perennial, 1986

Karnbach, James and Bernson, Carol, *It's Only Rock 'n' Roll: The Ultimate Guide to the Rolling Stones*, New York: Facts On File, Inc., 1997

Kent, Nick, *The Dark Stuff*, Cambridge: De Capo Press, 1994

Keys, Bobby with Bill Ditenhafer, *Every Night's a Saturday Night: The Rock 'n' Roll Life of Legendary Sax Man Bobby Keys*, Berkeley: Counterpoint, 2012

Kooper, Al, *Backstage Passes and Backstabbing Bastards*, New York: Backbeat Books, 2008

Lysaght, Alan, *The Rolling Stones: An Oral History*, Toronto: McArthur & Company, 2003

MacDonald, Ian, *Revolution in the Head: The Beatles Recordings and the Sixties*, New York: Henry Holt and Company, 1994

Oldham, Andrew Loog, *Rolling Stoned*, North Syracuse: Gegensatz Press, 2011

Richards, Keith with James Fox, *Life*, New York: Little, Brown and Company, 2011

Tarlé, Dominique, *Exile*, Oxford: Genesis Publications Limited, 2001

Wood, Ronnie, *Ronnie: The Autobiography*, New York: St. Martin's Griffin, 2007

Wyman, Bill, with Ray Coleman, *Stone Alone*, New York: Signet, 1990

Wyman, Bill, with Richard Havers, *Rolling with the Stones*, New York: DK Publishing, 2002

Web sites

abasses.com

An interview with Darryl Jones from *Bass Player* magazine from 1995.

Allmusic.com

Biographical information and record and song reviews.

articles.sun-sentinel.com

A 1986 interview with Keith Richards and Bill Flanagan.

BassPlayer.com

An interview with Bill Wyman.

ChicagoTribune.com

Interviews with Mick Jagger and Keith Richards from 2010.

EdSullivan.com

Regarding the appearances of the Rolling Stones on the television show of the same name.

Furious.com

An interview with Jimmy Miller.

GoldMineMag.com

The Web site for *Goldmine* magazine for articles about the Rolling Stones in Los Angeles in the early days.

Google News

An archival article from Lodi News-Sentinel, October 13, 1975 about Bianca Jagger visiting the Ford White House.

GuitarPlayer.com

The Web site for *Guitar Player* magazine. A number of interviews were helpful here.

JannWenner.com

1995 interview with Mick Jagger.

MickTaylor.net

An interview with Mick Taylor and a long biographical piece.

Mojo4music.com

Mojo magazine's Web site, for an interview with Andrew Loog Oldham.

NPR.org

Don Was interview about *Exile on Main Street*. Additionally, "All Things Considered" 2012 interviews with Ron Wood, Mick Jagger, Charlie Watts, and Keith Richards.

NYTimes.com

For an article about where the video for "Waiting on a Friend" was shot, and
  Nicky Hopkins' obituary.

NewLeftReview.org and Independent.co.uk

Discussions of "Street Fighting Man" and the events of 1968.

nzentgraf.de

"The Complete Works Database," by Nico Zentgraf—I referred to this for
  recording session dates and personnel.

Olivier.landemaine.free.fr

An interview with members of the Velvet Underground.

RocksBackPages.com

This was used for old magazine articles and reviews from publications including *Rolling Stone, Creem, NME, Sounds, Los Angeles Times, Melody Maker,*
  and *Esquire.*

RollingStones.com

Biographies of the Rolling Stones members.

RollingStonesNet.com

Information about the women the Rolling Stones dated in the 1960s.

TimeIsOnOurSide.com

I often referred to Ian MacPherson's database of quotes, lyrics, recording details and chronology.

ShadyOldLady.com

A piece about Regent Sound Studio.

SoundonSound.com

An interview with Chris Kimsey.

Wikipedia

For reference on discography and various biographies.

Youtube

Including "A Story of Our Time—Brian Jones the Rolling Stone," a BBC story
  from March 2, 1971, produced by Michael Wale.

Films

Charlie Is My Darling (1966), ABKO Films, directed by Peter Whitehead.
Gimme Shelter (1970), Maysles Films, directed by Albert and David Maysles.
Stripped (1995), Graying & Balding Inc., directed by Jim Gable.
Shine a Light (2008), Paramount Classics, directed by Martin Scorsese.
Stones in Exile (2010), Passion Pictures, directed by Stephen Kijak.

Ladies and Gentlemen, the Rolling Stones (1973), Butterfly, Chesscol Bingo, Musicfilm, directed by Rollin Binzer.

Crossfire Hurricane (2012), Tremolo Productions, directed by Brett Morgan.

In some instances, I drew from my own previous writing on the Rolling Stones, including song reviews for AllMusic.com and my previous book, *Exile on Main Street,* Continuum Books, 2005.

Index